CONTINGENCY AND THE LIMITS OF HISTORY

HOW TOUCH SHAPES EXPERIENCE AND MEANING

LIANE CARLSON

Columbia University Press   *New York*

Columbia University Press
Publishers Since 1893
New York   Chichester, West Sussex
cup.columbia.edu

Library of Congress Cataloging-in-Publication Data
Names: Carlson, Liane, author.
Title: Contingency and the limits of history : how touch shapes
experience and meaning / Liane Carlson.
Description: New York : Columbia University Press, 2019. |
Includes bibliographical references and index.
Identifiers: LCCN 2018060637 | ISBN 9780231190527 (cloth : alk. paper) |
ISBN 9780231548977 (ebook)
Subjects: LCSH: Contingency (Philosophy) | Senses and sensation.
Classification: LCC BD595 .C36 2019 | DDC 123—dc23
LC record available at https://lccn.loc.gov/2018060637

Columbia University Press books are printed on permanent
and durable acid-free paper.
Printed in the United States of America

Cover design: Milenda Nan Ok Lee
Cover art: John Bellany, *Shipwreck, 1982.*
Private collection/copyright © Bridgeman Images

To my three great teachers
To Mark, for his iconoclasm and loyalty
To Wayne, for his erudition and kindness
To Jeff, for starting it all

CONTENTS

ACKNOWLEDGMENTS

This book began as my dissertation at Columbia University, where it would not have been possible without my two advisers, Mark C. Taylor and Wayne Proudfoot. The combination of Mark's iconoclasm, Wayne's careful grounding in scholarly literature, and their shared commitment to broadly-educating their students in the Western canon have shaped my ideal of scholarship. Yet, there never would have been a dissertation or book, if it had not been for my undergraduate adviser, Jeff Kosky. Jeff has been a friend, mentor, and kindred spirit who has taught me to think as a whole human. It is to the three of them I dedicate this book.

While at Columbia, I have also benefited enormously from working with brilliant faculty and friends. I am indebted to my other committee members, Frederick Neuhouser, Courtney Bender, and Rachel Fell McDermott for their careful feedback to the book. It is in large part because of my fellow graduate students at Columbia University that I came to believe that true thinking is only really possible among friends. I am grateful to Abby Kluchin for conversations about philosophy, fashion, food and literature; to Drew Thomases and Jocelyn Kilmer for India and many pleasant hours spent at Toast; to Dan del Nido for moral support and help thinking through my project; to Sajida Jalalzai for her thoughtfulness, wisdom, kindness and silliness; to Katie McIntyre for comradeship in philosophy seminars; to Todd Berzon for pizza, company, and indestructible sweat pants; and to James Reich for thoughtful conversation and first class puppy sitting. Ben Fong and Yoni Brafman helped continue my education through the reading group we formed together in our first year of graduate school. I am particularly grateful to Yoni—not only for years of thinking, reading, scheming, gossiping, and post-gaming Star Trek episodes together—but also for being a good friend when I needed one most, who helped carry my books home when the weight of them threatened to overwhelm me.

Along the way, I have been aided by grants, fellowships, and the exceptionally helpful editorial staff at Columbia University Press. Throughout graduate school, I was funded a Jacob K. Javits Doctoral Fellowship, an American Association of University Women (AAUW) American Dissertation Fellowship, the Core Curriculum at Columbia University, and a Mellon Interdisciplinary Graduate Fellowship, at the Interdisciplinary Center for Innovative Theory and Empirics (INCITE). I want to thank in particular Bill McAllister for his intellectual generosity and warmth during my two years at INCITE. Additionally, I would like to thank Wendy Lochner and Lowell Frye at Columbia University Press, the three anonymous reviewers of the manuscript who offered such helpful feedback, Susan Pensak for her meticulous editing, and the whole staff at Columbia University Press who made this book possible. I am also grateful to *Method and Theory in the Study of Religion* for allowing me to reuse parts of an article originally published with them in the introduction and the *Journal of Religion* for allowing me to reuse portions of an article originally published with them in chapter 2.

I am also grateful to Princeton University for supporting me as I turned my dissertation into a book during my time as the Stewart Postdoctoral Research Associate in Religion from 2015–2018. During my time there, I was supported by a number of people, including Seth Perry, Moulie Vidas, Jonathan Gold, Andrew Walker-Cornetta, Eden Consenstein, Toni Alimi, Davey Henreckson, Alda Balthrop-Lewis, Mary Kay Bodnar, Kerry Smith, and Patty Bogdziewicz. I owe particular thanks to Lorraine Fuhrmann for her uncomplicated kindness; to Shaun Marmon for talking novels with me; to Judith Weisenfeld for her graciousness, advice, and warmth; and to Jessica Delgado for being an invaluable confidante in moments of professional and political upheaval. Raissa Von Doetinchem de Rande felt like my academic sister by the end of our time together. Daniel May was the single most incisive critic I have yet found for my thinking and I hope to keep thinking with him as friends. Above all, I am indebted to Leora Batnitzky, who offered support, a sense of philosophical kinship, and a trenchant take on academic politics that made me feel sane.

Angel Zito offered me a new home at the Center for Religion and Media at NYU, where I finished up the last stages of the book as the Henry Luce Postdoctoral Fellow from 2018–2019. I am endlessly grateful for her generosity and solidarity. I only hope I can one day pass on a similar favor to another young woman.

My parents and my sisters, Heather Lam and Jennifer Carlson, have been a constant source of support and love during the long years I spent writing, then revising this book. My brothers-in-law, Matthew Tebo and John Lam, have made me welcome in their homes. My nieces, Inara Tebo, Talia Tebo, and Amity Lam have reminded me to make room for play. My mother-in-law, Michelle McFee, and her sister, Vicki Basil, have made me feel like I have a second home on the West Coast.

Finally, I owe my greatest debts to two people.

To Kali Handelman, for reading every page multiple times. But, even more than that, for thinking through the world we live in with me.

And to Brian McFee, for everything, forever.

"I love you without knowing how, or when, or from where,

I love you simply, without problems or pride:

I love you this way because I know no other way to love."[1]

INTRODUCTION

In 2006, the British philosopher Havi Carel found herself shouldering past a receptionist at the medical center her father ran, into the office of the radiologist who had taken her chest scan earlier that morning. Her father had left her in the car, promising to be back in five minutes. As five minutes stretched into ten, then twenty, panic overcame her, and she knew the reason she had been short of breath for months was about to be made catastrophically clear. When she pushed open the radiologist's door, the lights were low, and her father sat silhouetted against an image of her lungs bright on the wall, his elbows on the table and his head cradled in his hands. The radiologist looked up "surprised and displeased" to see her in his office. "'So you are the patient,' he said. 'Do you know what is going on?' 'No,' I said. 'What *is* going on?' 'I'll let you read about it. Sit down.' I stumbled into a chair and he handed me a diagnostic manual. . . . I read the bottom line. Prognosis: ten years from the onset of symptoms."[1]

In the years since Carel received her diagnosis, two things happened that she never expected when she first began writing her book on the phenomenology of illness: an experimental drug was developed for her disease (Lymphangioleiomyomatosis), arresting the progressive decline of her lung capacity, and she became a mother. Revisiting her book in a second edition, she frankly acknowledged these two events as nothing short of miraculous before adding a caveat. "But I am also deeply conscious of the precariousness of life and the extraordinary luck that brought about the two events. I remain acutely aware that it could have been otherwise." This bodily drama that stretched over nearly a decade, beginning with a death sentence at thirty-five and including the shrinkage of her world to the distance she could walk with an oxygen tank, the disintegration of friendships, the restriction of dreams, the bitter realization of how little she could hope for, and finally, unexpectedly, a reprieve—all of this left her with a thankful, anxious, fearful, soul-felt awareness of her own contingency. The preface ends with this humbled admission of how different her life could have been, the only thing left to say after being betrayed by her body in her youth.

This is not a book about Carel or illness. It is not a book about the brutality of the medical establishment or the indifference of doctors in the face of women's pain (though another version of this book could have been). Nor is it even a work about illness and phenomenology, though it touches on both. Instead, it is a book about how the vulnerability of bodies conjures the kind of half-thankful, half-terrified acknowledgment Carel ends her preface with: *I remain acutely aware that it could have been otherwise.* It is about contingency felt through the body, rather than recounted through history.

It is a book, in short, about what contingency feels like. What does chance mean to those whose lives have been upended, forcing them to recognize that everything they thought was stable is in flux? In what circumstances do they experience the fragility and arbitrariness of their lives, and how do they orient themselves in the world after that flash of insight? Above all, what does Carel's wondering confession share with other, older expressions of contingency—not just those of philosophers or critical theorists who debated whether history is the collision of chance events but of Christian theologians who imagined contingency as the lot of creatures buffeted about by their passions, wounded by their flesh, and defined, always, in contrast to an impassive, necessary God? These questions and the afterlife of that passionate, bodily model of contingency among continental philosophers who sought to understand the contingent through its etymological Latin roots in *tangere*, "touch," will be my focus.

I will get to the stakes and substance of my claims in time, but history is not discarded easily. For the moment, then, I want to spend some time thinking about the role and limitations of contingency in my field of religious studies. To do that, I need to turn to its most obvious home in contemporary scholarship: genealogy.

CONTINGENCY AND CULTURAL CRITIQUE

When I speak of the role of contingency in contemporary theory, I am interested in one particular question: what are the limits to the critical and persuasive power of history?[2]

I ask this question from the field of religious studies at the end of a decades-long experiment in historicizing concepts. Tomoko Masuzawa and David Chidester have traced the concept of world religions back to the internal debates of Christian missionaries.[3] Maurice Olender has written a history of philology's roots in colonialism and antisemitism.[4] Daniel Boyarin has unearthed the invention of Jewish masculinity.[5] And Talal Asad has written a genealogy of secularism.[6] Collectively, they have composed an engaging, sophisticated, diverse body of work reframing our most basic natural concepts as born out of histories fraught with conflicting values, power struggles, and accidents. At the center of this work has been the assumption, sometimes baldly stated, sometimes assumed, that these concepts are contingent.

Trying to parse exactly what contingency means in a context where it is more often assumed than argued for leads straight into a morass. The *Oxford English Dictionary* cites at least eight different meanings of the term, with multiple subheadings. The definitions have slightly different meanings and relationships to causality, ranging from "possible or uncertain event on which other things depend or are conditional; a condition that may be present or absent," to "the quality or condition of being subject to chance and change, or of being at the mercy of accidents," to "the befalling or occurrence of anything without preordination; chance; fortuitousness," to "the condition of being free from predetermining necessity in regard to existence or action; hence, the being open to the play of chance, or of free will." A contingent event, could be wholly undetermined by any previous events, subject to chance, determined but dependent on a series of antecedent causes that are themselves conditional, or determined by an antecedent cause like God's will but without any logical necessity to its existence.[7] For the purposes of discussing contingency in history, I want to bracket the larger questions of causality and use the following definition: a contingent event or term is one that could have been otherwise, for whatever reason, and by whatever chain of causes or noncauses.[8]

While the exact meaning of contingency is often unclear in contemporary thought, the implications of calling an event or institution contingent can at times feel deceptively clear, largely because scholars in the humanities have shared a similar set of assumptions about the significance of contingency, drawn from the philosophical tradition of genealogy. Even though not all the thinkers mentioned explicitly self-identify as genealogists, it is not an exaggeration to say it is impossible to understand the last thirty years of scholarship devoted to historicizing concepts without a working grasp on the claims of genealogy. So what do I mean by genealogy?

Genealogy is a method with a technical meaning. When I talk about genealogy, I do not mean the increasingly popular use of genealogy in common parlance as synonymous with an intellectual lineage. Rather, I mean genealogy as Michel Foucault defined it in his 1971 essay, "Nietzsche, Genealogy, History." Before all else, a genealogy poses the question "What is the value of our values?" In pursuing this, genealogists reject timeless origin stories that would paint our present as a fall from an idealized past or teleological accounts that valorize our society as the culmination of a bloody but necessary history. Instead, as Foucault so influentially phrased it, the genealogist opposes these stories of a unitary origin with stories of descent that seek the roots of all we value in the missed opportunities, the reversals, the errors, and the absurdities of history.[9] When writing these stories, the genealogist attends to the singularity of events. She recognizes the impossibility of capturing the exact essence of institutions or identities. And so she focuses on the different roles each institution played at different times. The phenomena she chooses to study may vary, but they will be in "what we tend to feel is without history—in sentiments, love, conscience, instinct."[10] The genealogist chooses her topics fully aware that she writes with historically determined values and agendas, uncertain of the future the past will open up into.

Above all, genealogy is meant to upend neat stories about the present and to challenge the self-evidence of the status quo. A genealogy does not merely inform or offer an alternative sequence of events; it must move or destabilize or disenchant the reader in some way in order to be "effective history." This point is key, especially for a genealogy's reception. Foucault comes back to it again and again in different forms throughout his essay, insisting that the historical beginnings a genealogist uncovers "are lowly: not in the sense of modest or discreet like the steps of a dove, but derisive and ironic, capable of undoing every infatuation."[11] The genealogy disenchants its readers, "dispelling the chimeras of the origin,"[12] when it simultaneously "introduces discontinuity into our very being as it divides our emotions" and "uproot[s] its traditional foundations and relentlessly disrupt its pretended continuity."[13] "What convictions and, far more decisively, what knowledge can resist it?" Foucault asks rhetorically, before pithily summing up his characterization of genealogy a few pages later with the remark "This is because knowledge is not made for understanding; it is made for cutting."[14] Nietzsche had already made the point even more succinctly by giving the *Genealogy of Morals* the subtitle "A Polemic."[15]

The projects written in the shadow of Foucault have not been neutral projects, then, content simply to leave us a little less ignorant of the past than before. Rather, they have been political projects, written out of an intellectual tradition that believes every thinker works in a particular moment in history that guides her aims and shapes her horizon of imagined possibilities. They have been critical projects, meant to question the conditions for the possibility of knowledge by showing that our most basic categories come overburdened with unspoken biases, repressed voices, and plays of domination. They have been ethical projects, intent on reclaiming the memory of those lost to history. And they have been persuasive projects. For these scholars, contingency became more than merely a critical tool, meant to show the historical accidents that shaped our most fundamental concepts in the service of "getting the facts right"; it became a political tool used to shake loose old pieties. If these works fulfill their promises, readers will emerge skeptical of traditional accounts and forms of history and armed with new questions about whose voices get heard, what questions do not get asked, what comparisons are not drawn, and what sort of moral subjects a discursive tradition produces. They will leave, hopefully, a little more aware of colonialism, a little less racist, a little more open to a different world that may yet come.

And yet never have the political gains from this form of cultural critique looked more fragile.

My question is *why*. Why is it still possible in 2018 to make statements like "Islam hates us" after forty years of cultural critique aimed at showing that broad concepts like Islam never existed as unitary ahistorical wholes? In asking this, I am not interested in the sociological, economic, or institutional reasons behind why certain forms of critique gain traction at times. Rather, in asking about contingency's critical power forty years after Foucault, I am asking something more basic: What can contingency *do?* Does it really have the ability to disenchant us, to smash our plaster of Paris idols, to trouble our most basic categories, to move us into a different way of seeing the world? If so, when? For whom? Under what conditions? How? For how much longer? Most of all, is the claim that certain contingent models of history have political significance compatible with genealogy's commitment to the radical historicity of all concepts? If we find that genealogy's critical power is as subject to the vagaries of history as any other concept, what is its relevance for the discipline today? And what comes next?

GENEALOGY AND ITS CRITIQUE

There have been attempts to answer these questions, most notably by philosophers. There are whole stacks of books written by philosophers aimed at debunking the idea that genealogy is a political tool and, by extension, proving most other disciplines practice some bastardized form of genealogy. Philosophers like Colin Koopman and Raymond Geuss have argued that genealogies are critical in the Kantian sense of critique: they investigate the conditions for the possibility of human knowledge.[16] Whereas Kant sought those conditions in the structure of the human mind, Foucault and Nietzsche looked for it in the history of our concepts and values. Genealogists problematize concepts by showing that what we have taken to be ahistorical, in fact, has a past; they do not pronounce on the value of these concepts or make broad claims about how we ought to live or attempt to persuade readers to adopt a particular set of values. Any scholars who claim otherwise are either importing the type of normative commitments the method explicitly calls into question or, alternately, are confusing writing a critique with being critical, in the quotidian sense of skeptical or hostile. In short, according to Koopman and Geuss, genealogies seek to dismantle metaphysical ideas, not radically transform the social values or lifestyle of an individual.

I am not making one of those arguments. Not because I think that Nietzsche and Foucault were indifferent to metaphysics or because philosophers are wrong to question the political power of genealogical critique, but because I think such arguments are too dismissive of the work done in the last thirty years in other fields. There simply *are* lines in Nietzsche and Foucault that suggest genealogy is a form of social critique, meant to jostle people out of their comfortable preconceptions, to "dispel chimeras" and "uproot traditional foundations." When scholars across the humanities write genealogies of gender or race or religion, they are not somehow misappropriating a philosophical tool merely meant to debunk metaphysical assumptions for political ends; they are being faithful to Foucault's famous assertion that he is interested in what is dangerous. "Dangerous" is a changing category, defined by its particular social and historical context. A certain set of metaphysical ideas, like truth or nature or teleology, may happen to have been dangerous at the times when Nietzsche and Foucault wrote, but if these concepts were to be somehow neutralized they would no longer be a proper object of genealogical critique. In that scenario, essentialisms, for example, might one day cease to be a meaningful target of genealogy because their significance and social role have changed, rendering them no longer a threat or reflective of social values.

No, the real problem with genealogy is that, precisely because it is an intervention into a particular present, the success or failure of its critique is bound up with its ability to dismantle ideas held by particular, embodied people in a distinct moment in time. Those people are subject to history and change just as surely as concepts are, yet the genealogical method has no way of accounting for how those changes in the audience affect the power of its critique. Genealogies are meant to dissolve self-evident identities and static subjects, yet the reader always seems curiously the same: untouched by history, invested enough in the sanctity of Christianity or the stability of the self to be appalled by the alternate story proffered, but not so invested as to shut down altogether in the face of the genealogist's offerings. The myth of the inviolate, modern subject has to be displaced onto the audience in order to maintain the illusion that genealogies can, be in any sort of regular, meaningful way "effective history."

The problem begins with the commitments and affective lenses a reader brings to a genealogy. Affect theory is by now a thriving scholarly conversation and one that touches on many of the themes that concern me.[17] I will have more to say about the relationship between affect theory and contingency in the conclusion of the book, but will largely refrain from using it in my analysis past the introduction because it would be anachronistic to apply it to earlier thinkers. For the purposes of my discussion, however, I am drawing primarily on Eve Kosofsky Sedgwick's discussion of affect as feeling, or a type of emotional charge, that is not necessarily tethered to a particular object.[18]

The freedom of affects (as Kosofsky Sedgwick puts it) or their contingency (as other have labeled it) is key to understanding the difficulty of predicting a genealogy's effect on its audience.[19] There is no good reason why an individual might not read the most meticulous genealogy of gender ever written, fully grasp that both sex and gender are categories shaped by undetermined, arbitrary historical events and practices, close the last page of the book, and conclude, "That could have been so much worse! Better, far better, to adhere to traditional roles when history provides so many examples of our best intentions misfiring." She would not even have to feel pangs of conscience from the charge that she is abdicating social responsibility with her response. After all, she could easily draw on statistics about the economic benefits of a two-parent household or, depending on her politics, offer a criticism of capitalist expectations that women should abandon the satisfaction of raising children in pursuit of money. It is fully coherent for an individual or group to cheerfully concede that they stumbled across their values by happenstance and nonetheless commit to their social norms based on a belief that they provide the best possible life. There is nothing in genealogy that necessarily entails support of any *particular political* agenda as a consequence of its analysis. Indeed, we are not bound to *any* presumed or intended politics or conclusions at all.

Genealogical critiques, such as Nietzsche's dismantlement of "the will to truth," could also be deployed toward actively reactionary ends. (We need only to think here of Bruno Latour's famous struggle with the fact that climate change deniers co-opted the conclusions of critical science studies.)[20] Genealogical narratives militate against a very particular line of conservative thought—namely, a broadly Burkean sense of conservatism that sees value in preserving tradition. In that respect, genealogies do open up the possibility of radical politics that remake society by breaking with the past. It would be a mistake, however to assume that the radical politics such critiques open up have to be leftist. They could just as well be fascist, or conservative in the more general senses of resisting liberalization or reform. This is the point that Hannah Arendt made so well in the *Origins of Totalitarianism* when she wrote, "Until now the totalitarian belief that everything is possible seems to have proved only that everything can be destroyed."[21]

Alternately, the contingency of current social arrangements might even be a source of communal bonding. A group could relish the near misses of their own history, turning an account of the contingency of the past into an opportunity for collective bonding and self-mythologizing. Psychologically, mulling over and glamorizing contingency is an incredibly normal experience. Nothing, for example, is more common in the early stages of love than to marvel over the unlikely accidents that brought two people together. Lovers actively trace out the times they might have brushed past each other or misconstrued a tentative smile, glorying in the unlikeliness of meeting and meeting at a moment when they were receptive to each other. They often even confess the sordidness, the wounds, the unhappy events that played a role in their lives leading up to the moment they met, confident that their love will absolve and redeem everything unsavory in their past. For the people already committed to the value of the relationship or institution they participate in, an account of contingency can act as an expression of gratitude for the present in all of its unlikelihood. They are not wrong in welcoming contingency; they are just one more example of how preexisting commitments and affective lenses inescapably inform the meaning contingency has in the stories we tell.[22]

It is not just the reader's affective and intellectual commitments that are subject to history, however. The very authority of historical narratives is subject to flux. Piecing together a history of terms previously thought to be timeless or self-evident, such as "religion" or "race" or "gender," might very well invalidate a claim to authority grounded in nature or essence—but what happens if an institution has multiple claims to authority? Look at the United States government. It certainly has its own mythology, ripe for a good genealogical critique. American culture broadly fetishizes the Founding Fathers, the sanctity of the Constitution, and the sacrifice of soldiers for an ideal of freedom. These symbols have tremendous psychological power, and an effective attack on them would be a deep wound for faith in the government. Ultimately, though, these myths do not legitimate the government; the process of democratic election does. Of course, from the perspective of elected officials, it would be *easier* if the populace still revered the Founding Fathers as paragons of virtues, but the Senate still meets, even with the story of Sally Hemings.

I want to stress this point because even Foucault slips into vastly overestimating the critical power of history when he speaks about its "curative power."[23] The grounds of authority cannot be reduced to the stories institutions tell about themselves. Some demand our assent in exchange for goods and services in the present; some ground their authority in democratic consensus; and, yes, some impose their authority through brute physical force. None of these justifications for authority depend on history or origin stories. They might coexist with the sort of origin stories Foucault and Nietzsche worried about, but, presumably, the persuasive power of such narratives is itself subject to the vagaries of history and waxes and wanes accordingly. To assume that a genealogy, even one that carefully justified the values guiding its claims, might be sufficient to undermine an institution or identity would be to ignore these complexities. At best, a genealogy might manage some symptoms, but the cure for any long-standing social ill would have to involve other tools of critique.[24] To imagine otherwise would risk committing a version of genetic fallacy. If the genetic fallacy is the belief that a thing can be explained and evaluated wholly in terms of its past, then the thoughtless genealogist tacitly subscribes to the idea that the present is so totally determined by its past that a critique of its history is sufficient to shatter faith in the present.

Most of all, genealogy faces the challenge of its own success. Nietzsche wrote *A Genealogy of Morals* in 1886 to an audience that had never seen anything quite like it. His readers lived in a predominantly white, Christian culture. When Foucault died there was still a Soviet Union. We, however, live in a twenty-first century culture that is not nearly as religiously or intellectually homogenous as the one Nietzsche attacked. Moreover, it is a culture so saturated with genealogies that Colin Koopman, the disgruntled philosopher mentioned earlier, actually made a parlor game out of trying to name a different genealogy for every letter of the alphabet.[25]

To anyone trained in the humanities in the last twenty years, genealogy is part of the canon. Within religious studies, the figures who introduced genealogy into the field, like Masuzawa and Asad, are now tenured, well-established, feted authority figures. In a final irony, even genealogy is being cannibalized by the traditional philosophical canon. Recent articles have attributed the beginnings of genealogy as we now understand it to Rousseau's *Second Discourse,*[26] Foucault's reading of Nietzsche, Foucault's misreading of Nietzsche by way of Deleuze,[27] the historicization of Kant's efforts to find the conditions for the possibility of knowledge,[28] and, more generally, to the Enlightenment ethos of constant questioning unmoored from the desire to find a transcendental basis of knowledge.[29] However fine these articles may be individually, basting them together creates a history for genealogy that runs roughly as follows: Rousseau begat Kant, Kant begat Nietzsche, Nietzsche begat Deleuze, and Deleuze begat Foucault. But if Nietzsche and Foucault have taught us anything, it ought to be that we should immediately suspect this sort of narrative of unbroken influence running from one canonical author to the next in a sexless procreation of minds. What, after all, does that narrative do except confirm the power of the established male European canon to arbitrate what counts as critique? What is its overall effect, if not to absorb Foucault into the canon and domesticate genealogy as more of the same critical project we have been engaged in for three hundred years?

None of this is meant to condemn those of us who genealogy seduced or even to claim that Foucault and Nietzsche expected the method to last indefinitely.[30] Genealogy dazzled. It taught us to be deeply wary of figures who lay claim to essential definitions or timeless truths and to question the sorts of histories that we write about our past. It reshaped the field of religious studies and the humanities more broadly. And, for a time, it really did disenchant readers and shatter convictions. Genealogy *mattered.* The mistake was not in allowing ourselves to be swept up in the reflected brilliance of Nietzsche and Foucault; the mistake was in imagining genealogy's ability to disenchant as inherent to the method rather than as a product of the moment it irrupted into the academy. Yet that moment is no longer our own. "Problematizing" a term or era means nothing if the sort of reader who would be shocked into recognizing the problem lived and read forty years before a text was written. Genealogy might very well be committed to the idea that history's contingencies *ought* to be able to shake us to our core, but that set of claims is at odds with the method's central precept that everything has a history and nothing is stable, reader included.

THE LIMITS OF CONTINGENCY'S CRITICAL POWER

A historically situated reader is not *necessarily* a dead or indifferent reader, however. It is still theoretically possible for genealogies to move people, given the right circumstances. It is just not guaranteed that even the savviest critique will move readers to action. A scholar might be able to dismantle the claim that the categories of "religion" or "gender" or "race" have always existed with the same meaning by attending to the contingencies of their histories. What she cannot do, bluntly speaking, is force her reader to care. But even if her critique were to strike home, the genealogist cannot prevent her readers from immediately appealing to any of the other benefits that institution or term offers to ground its authority. History cannot necessarily disenchant or move its readers to action because disenchantment depends as much on the reader's receptiveness as the writer's tactics, and the reader's receptiveness is itself a product of historical contingencies.

Even if genealogies were utterly moribund, though, that still would not mean historians would have to abandon history's drowned in favor of triumphalist stories of the saved. There are plenty of other approaches to history that focus on the voices of the dispossessed. Nor would the collapse of genealogy make those, like Judith Butler, who understand the broader project of cultural critique as exposing "the contingent acts that create the appearance of a naturalistic necessity" into frauds with no good reasons or justifications for their political commitments.[31]

What historicizing the readers and writers of genealogies would entail, however, is a reevaluation of contingency's own history. Anyone truly committed to the idea that different concepts mean different things, and that they can mobilize people in different ways at various points in history, needs to take seriously the idea that contingency cannot be a static concept. And if contingency is contingent on context to give it significance, its critical power becomes much more equivocal. To the person truly invested in the idea that all concepts have a history, the correct questions are not why we think contingency and critique relate, or how we fit the two together; the correct questions are about *when* contingency has had critical power, under what circumstances it has moved people, how people have understood it differently, and what conclusions people have drawn from their experiences of contingency about how to order their lives.

The best place to look for that history, as I noted at the beginning of the book, is in Christian theology. Returning to Christian theology allows us to see that what we mean when we talk about contingency in history is only a fragment of a broader theological anthropology. This understanding of how the human relates to God casts contingency as the lot of mortal creatures who change in time, yes, but are also buffeted about by their passions, wounded through their flesh, and denied any comprehensive understanding of their mortal lives by the finitude of their gazes.

I would be remiss, after my discussion of genealogy's audience, if I did not acknowledge that this project can mean vastly different things, depending on the reader. Some may take it as a condemnation of critical theory's reliance on contingency, as proof that even seemingly radical history is cryptotheology. Others may see it as part of a rehabilitative project that proves Christian thought has its own radical potential. Still others may read it primarily as a continuation of conversations within continental philosophy about finitude, vulnerability, and embodiment. Martin Heidegger, Maurice Merleau-Ponty, Jacques Derrida, Jean-Luc Nancy, and Luce Irigaray have all touched on these themes and on the relation between philosophy and theology more broadly. For my part, I take Christianity to be the inescapable backdrop to all Western philosophy. Accordingly, I am looking primarily for a sense of history and clarity as I sketch that alternative theological understanding of contingency in the next section before offering a few thoughts on why it is we came to forget it in favor of a different theological conversation about suffering, necessity, and meaning in history.

TWO MODELS OF CONTINGENCY IN THEOLOGY

The two models of contingency I am interested in can be crudely summarized as contingency experienced through time and contingency experienced through the body and the passions. The memory of theology's influence on these models of contingency has not completely vanished, it has only become truncated and confined to the first, temporal model. Accordingly, most people interested in such questions, I think, could give a reasonable thumbnail sketch of the relationship between theology and contingency in history that went roughly like this. Early on, Christian theologians found themselves faced with the question of suffering once posed by Epicurus: "Is God willing to prevent evil, but not able? Then he is not omnipotent. Is he able, but not willing? Then he is malevolent. Is he both able and willing? Then whence cometh evil? Is he neither able nor willing? Then why call him God?"[32] Theodicies attempting to answer the question and vindicate God emerged and reemerged in a number of iterations, such as the free will defense,[33] the vale of soul-making theodicy,[34] metaphysical redefinitions of evil,[35] and the best of all possible worlds defense,[36] to name a few. The key point is that such explanations often subsumed earthly suffering under some greater, necessary plan of God's. From God's perspective, then, the misery on earth is necessary, whereas from the human perspective, suffering presents itself as a series of purposeless contingencies—the hailstorms that come from nowhere and ruin crops, the plague that devastates one village and leaves another unscathed, the illness that strikes dead the virtuous young mother but leaves the criminal untouched. A successful theodicy is one that allows the reader to trust that one day she will understand every miserable stroke of bad luck she ever experienced as contingent, as, in fact, necessary, orderly, and congruent with a higher good when viewed from the proper perspective. Contingency would become an illusion of perspective.

Theodicy, this narrative goes, did not die out as philosophy began to pull away from explicitly theological concerns. Any number of canonical philosophical figures in the Enlightenment adopted the tradition for (nominally) secular political ends. Gotthold Ephraim Lessing (1729–1781) suggested that religion had been a stage human history needed to pass through in order to

reach the rationality of the Enlightenment;[37] Jean-Jacques Rousseau (1712–1778) pieced together a narrative attributing the origin of human suffering to inflamed *amour propre* in his *Discourse
Concerning the Origins of Inequality*;[38] Immanuel Kant (1724–1804)
wrote an essay suggesting that the suffering brought about by
the violent conflict and innate "unsocial sociability" of human
groups might be understood as a necessary means for producing
the sort of moral, autonomous species capable of administering
a maximally just society;[39] Marx thought class struggle in history would end with a communist state; above all, Hegel infa-
mously compared history to a slaughter bench upon which the
best desires and souls of humanity had been sacrificed in order
to make way for the unfolding of freedom in history, primarily
through the actions of a few select "world historical" agents like
Napoleon.[40]

Most of the thinkers I began by mentioning—Asad, Masuzawa, and Chidester—are in more or less conscious rebellion
against this model of history as theodicy. There are very many
thinkers that could be cited on the subject of rebellion against
this particular mode of theological history, most notably Walter
Benjamin, but within religious studies the most trenchant criticisms come from postcolonial scholars. Following Edward Said's
classic *Orientalism*, thinkers have pushed against historical narratives, Christian and crypto-Christian alike, that have been
used to justify colonialism and violence against the non-Christian
world.

But, as I alluded to before, theodicy is not the only model
for thinking about contingency in theology. There is another
tradition rooted in the passions and flesh. One of the clearest
articulations of this models comes in the work of Baruch Spinoza. Spinoza famously and vehemently denied the existence
of contingency, if contingency is understood to be a causally

undetermined event or state of being.[41] And yet, he thought we are most prone to thinking of ourselves as exempt from the chain of preceding causes determining our behavior when we reflect on our emotions. Whenever philosophers write about the emotions, Spinoza claims, they seem to immediately jettison any attempt at a scientific, causal explanation, as if they were suddenly dealing with a phenomenon exempt from the usual laws of nature. Instead, they treat humans as subject to their own laws and deride them for inherent defects whenever they are assailed by weakness or frailty. He, by contrast, wants to subject the emotions to the same rigorous laws as all other scientific phenomena. For Spinoza, affect is mediated through the body. "Human infirmity in moderating and checking the emotions I name bondage: for, when a man is a prey to his emotions, he is not his own master, but lies at the mercy of fortune: so much so, that he is often compelled, while seeing that which is better for him, to follow that which is worse." Spinoza certainly believes that his contemporaries are wrong for treating the passions as outside of the laws of nature, but he crucially recognizes that *something* about the tumult of our passions routinely persuades people that they are prey to chance influences, flung about haphazardly in a stormy world—that is, contingent in the sense of being causally undetermined, not slotted into an orderly chain of events and causes. He acknowledges the peculiar power of the passions to convince the unenlightened of their contingency, even if only as a starting point for teaching them how to master their passions.

Throughout the last few pages, I have been talking about these models of contingency as if they are opposed. In reality, the distinction between the two is a heuristic one. These two ways of thinking about contingency—one temporal, one bodily and affective—often peaceably coexist in a single thinker's work. Augustine wrote as movingly as anyone in the history of Western thought about the way our desires pull us into the world and our bodies remind us of our changeability and mortality. He also devoted hundreds of pages to understanding the sack of Rome and the manifestations of God's will in history. To cut out either aspect of his work would leave a maimed corpus. Even Georg Wilhelm Friedrich Hegel (1770–1831), the thinker most singularly associated with an account of history that erases every contingency in pursuit of a teleological history, argues for the need to assume an attitude of philosophical detachment toward the shipwreck of history because viewing it as contingent, meaningless, and unnecessary arouses "feelings of the deepest and most helpless sadness."[42] The perspective of contingency has to be disavowed with the thought, "so it was at one time; it is fate; there is nothing to be done about it now," precisely because dwelling on contingency sweeps us out of our own lives through morbid feelings of helpless distress. He is not ignorant of the way we experience contingency through passions that upset our equanimity; he is opposed to it.

These examples point toward a deeper affinity between the two accounts of contingency, one that can be explained by their mutual debt to a third, more capacious model rooted in the vision of humanity defined in contrast to an absolutely necessary God. The touchstone for debates about God's necessity has historically been Anselm's ontological proof in the *Proslogion* (1077–1078). Famously, Anselm claimed that "God is that than which nothing greater can be conceived." The argument runs roughly as follows. If I understand a proposition, that proposition exists in my understanding, if not necessarily in actuality. Even if I am a fool who thinks in my heart that God does not exist, I can still hear and understand the phrase "that than which nothing greater can be conceived." Therefore, at minimum, "that than which nothing greater can be conceived" exists in my understanding.

However, it is greater to exist in reality than to exist merely in thought. Thus, if "that than which nothing greater can be conceived" existed merely in my understanding, it would not truly be "that than which something greater could be conceived" because I could imagine something greater—the same Being existing in reality, rather than merely in the mind. Therefore, "that than which nothing greater can be conceived" must exist in reality as well as the understanding. God is that than which nothing greater can be thought.

If that were the end of the debate—another proof of God, destined to be knocked down by the all-crushing Kant in another seven hundred years—this argument would not provide much help for thinking about contingency. Anselm, however, goes on to do two more things with his proof. First, he explains that his proof is not just a proof for God's existence; it is a proof that God is a *necessarily* existing being. Second, he ties God's necessity and status as "that than which nothing greater can be conceived" to a series of attributes that stand in contrast to the condition of contingent creatures.

For my purposes, there are four attributes that Anselm derives from the formulation "that than which nothing greater can be thought" that matter. The first is independence. A God that depended on some other substance or being for his existence and creative power would be less great than a wholly independent God who created *ex nihilo*. The second is incorporeality. Anselm asserts it is better to be incorporeal than corporeal. He is telegraphic on his reasons for this assertion, but it is reasonable to assume, given broader arguments current during the era, that he believed corporeality referred to finite bodies bounded in space. A being unlimited by a finite form would have to be greater than a limited, bodily being that depends on its senses for perception. The third is impassibility. A being that could be affected by an external force and moved to feel passions would be subject to change and thus not completely independent or eternally unchanging. Finally, Anselm attributes eternality to God. Unlike mortal creatures, whose lives have a beginning and an end in time, God's eternality exists outside time and is not subject to the same decay as mortals.

As he enumerates the traits that flow from the necessary self-standing God, Anselm relentlessly marks his differences from humanity. God's cognition is "not like" an animal's cognition,[43] "he alone" exists without beginning or end, and he "alone" is what he is.[44] And so by highlighting the uniqueness of God, a vision of human nature begins to emerge by secondary contrast. God is necessary and independent; humans are contingent, depending on an impenetrable God and capable of ceasing to be without any logical contradiction. God is incorporeal, free to cognize through disembodied understanding alone; humans are bound to finite bodies. God is impassible, immune to change and the passions; humans are roiled by desires, fears, and hatreds. God is eternal, existing unchanged outside time; humans are born in sin and destined to death.

To be contingent in this model still means that there is no logical reason why a person, or even humanity, could not have been otherwise. More than that, though, contingency is associated with a profound dependence on God. Focusing on merely the temporal, or the sense of vertigo every child has at the realization she might never have been born, misses the depth and pathos of contingency in this strand of Christian thought. A solely temporal account of contingency glosses over or, at best, takes for granted, the bodily and emotional vulnerability that comes with depending on something that exists before us and without us. With dependence comes the vulnerability of knowing that, unlike God, humans will never be safe from the influence of outside forces that mislead them, move them, wound them, and ultimately bring about their deaths.

But if contingency is so much more multifaceted than the emphasis on history and theodicy suggests, why has the discussion surrounding contingency gradually drifted away from this broader discussion of theological anthropology? This question is not meant as an accusation or a reproach. On the contrary, those writers thinking about chance, necessity, and history have often written from a genuine engagement with some of the most existentially and ethically important questions posed in the centuries since the Enlightenment. In the interest of doing justice to the dominant temporal conversations around contingency, I want to spend a few pages thinking about why contingency in history came to be so much more important for contemporary theory, what conversations and concerns influenced it, and what we should salvage from discussions of history and theodicy.

CONTINGENCY IN THE MODERN AGE: BETWEEN LISBON AND AUSCHWITZ

According to Susan Neiman's *Evil in Modern Thought*, contingency became a problem for modern philosophy at 9:30 A.M. on All Saints Day 1755. Or perhaps it was 9:27 or 9:32; watches were uncommon and idiosyncratically set in the eighteenth century. Sailors sensed the problem first. Aboard the *Jean*, 120 miles west of the Cape St. Vincent in Portugal, the crew received their first warning something was wrong when a wave flung them "eighteen inches from the deck." More than three hundred miles west of Lisbon, another ship "'had her Cabin Windows shattered to Pieces' by a 'Shock.'" A third ship was struck with such force that its "artillery leapt of their carriages."[45]

Hundreds of miles away in Lisbon, the churches were crowded with worshippers and the streets with beggars as ships rocked in the stormy sea. Thousands had made the trek into the city from local villages to attend mass the day before, eager to celebrate one of the most popular holidays of the Catholic liturgical calendar in the great cathedrals of the capital. Still more were pushing through the streets on that fine, clear morning to make a 10 A.M. mass when the tremor that had rocked the sea hit land. One witness, an English vicar staying with his younger brother to improve his health, described witnessing the earthquake from the safety of a hill where he happened to be taking a walk. At first he heard a rumbling he took to be the noise of several carriages rattling down the road. Then the ground began to rock, at first gradually and then so violently that he had to clutch a nearby flagpole to stay upright. In the city below him, the Castle São Jorge crumpled into a pile of rubble, and the morning erupted with terrified screams of *Misericórdia*, "Mercy," to God.[46] Lisbon had just been struck by an earthquake estimated to rank between 8.5 and 9.1 on the Richter scale—larger than the San Francisco earthquake of 1906 (7.9), the Haitian earthquake of 2010 (7.0), and possibly on par with the Sumatra-Andaman earthquake of 2004 (9.1), which killed more than 230,000 people in Sri Lanka, Indonesia, Thailand, and India.[47] And the Portuguese, who had not experienced an earthquake of any size since 1722, "could neither give a name to what was occurring nor decide to flee it," according to one priest who witnessed the devastation.[48]

Flood followed the earthquake. Thirty-five minutes after the third and final tremor ended, three waves, speeding along at 500–600 miles per hour, crashed against the narrowing angle of the coastline and arced upward in a wall of water. Many of the survivors, who had sprinted toward the coastline, begging the ships moored there to take them away to safety, ran directly into it. The waves were a teletsunami, or ocean-wide tsunami, stretching a hundred and fifty miles wide. Estimates suggest that anywhere between 900 and 3,000 people were swept away by the wave.[49]

After the earthquake and flood came the most devastating part of the disaster: the firestorm. If not inevitable, the inferno that followed was at least the understandable result of human causes. Many of the victims had left their stoves burning in anticipation of preparing a meal for the feast day. When the open flames tumbled to the ground, they met a staggering supply of fuel left in the earthquake's wake. The individual fires that ensued soon joined together and reached such a high temperature that it began sucking in the surrounding air. The air began to spiral into a fiery whirlpool that created a vacuum effect, pulling even more oxygen in to feed it. Many who had been merely trapped under the rubble suffocated from smoke inhalation or burned alive. Some of the skeletons found suggest that skulls exploded from the heat. In the days that followed, accidental fires were augmented by arson as looters tried to drive out the disoriented survivors. All told, accounts claim the fires raged between five to fifteen days and for as long as six weeks in certain parts of the city.

There is always something arbitrary in an attempt to single out one event as inaugurating a new way of thinking about the world (as Foucault taught us in his discussion of origin stories). Nevertheless, the contemporary focus on contingency as a question of history, rather than creaturely life more broadly, is best understood as a development born out of the twin catastrophes of Lisbon and the concentration camps of the twentieth century, both Nazi and Soviet. Given how completely Auschwitz has overshadowed Lisbon, it may sound surprising or even incongruous to pair the two. After all, as Neiman so trenchantly put it, "Modern readers may feel wistful: lucky the age to which an earthquake can do so much damage."[50] Nevertheless, I want to suggest that Lisbon posed the problem of contingency in history with particular forcefulness in at least two different ways.

The first way is obvious, reading through historical records: Lisbon caused contemporary thinkers to ask whether or not there was any necessity or order in history. Intellectuals across Europe met news of the disaster with disbelief and deep, existential doubt about the goodness of the ordered universe. Voltaire is the obvious example, most famously in *Candide* but also in his 1756 "Poem on the Lisbon Disaster." Scathingly, the narrator of the poem mocks those who claimed to see a purpose behind the death of children in the pious city of Lisbon, asking: "Yet in this direful chaos you'd compose / A general bliss from individuals' woes? / Oh worthless bliss! in injured reason's sight, / With faltering voice you cry, 'What is, is right'?"[51] Voltaire's indictment of disingenuous philosophers who claim to understand the reasons for suffering leaves him with an image of the world consisting entirely of contingencies.

Voltaire's doubts about whether there is meaning or necessity to suffering in history would be followed in later years by similarly minded thinkers, like David Hume (1711–1776), Fyodor Dostoyevsky (1821–1881), Friedrich Nietzsche (1844–1900), Theodor Adorno (1903–1969), and Emmanuel Levinas (1906–1995). Not everyone took to Voltaire's skepticism, though. Rousseau responded to "Poem on the Lisbon Disaster" with a histrionic letter to Voltaire, summing up the message of the piece with a rhetorical question. "Now what does your poem tell me? 'Suffer forever, unhappy man. If a God created you, no doubt he is omnipotent; he could have prevented all your evils: hence, do not hope that they will ever end; for there is no understanding why you exist, if not to suffer and die.'"[52] Voltaire's mistake, Rousseau argued, was in attributing any cosmic significance to the earthquake. Earthquakes happened all the time, but no one cared when they struck a desert.[53] True, thousands had died in this particular one, but that was merely because they lived unnaturally clustered together in cities. If they had lived the pastoral life Rousseau advocated in his *First Discourse* as the most conducive to human happiness, there never would have been a city to destroy. Rousseau's answer is at once self-aggrandizing and callous, but it signified a true intellectual development. It decoupled natural evil (earthquakes, plagues, floods, and droughts) from moral evil (murder, theft, rape, and war). The earthquake had no theological significance and was not punishment for anything. It just happened, and humans, due to their own bad choices, happened to get crushed beneath it. Practically, this distinction meant that scientists and philosophers, including a young Immanuel Kant, could focus their energy on scientific explanations for earthquakes. Natural disasters were stripped of their moral significance, and God's beneficence was preserved. All that needed to happen now was for some Newton of the mind to uncover similar laws of human nature that would allow social reformers to work around human weakness, educate the populace to be better, less violent citizens, and possibly even rebuild society on better, more humane grounds.

The distinction between natural and moral evils was an effort to limit the significance of Lisbon and the questions it posed about God's beneficence. Ironically—and this brings me to my second point about the significance of Lisbon—that division also gave contingency unprecedented power to undermine moral judgments and the sovereign power of reason. Nowhere is this clearer than in Kant, the single thinker most concerned with separating the world into nature on one side and the realm of human freedom on the other. For Neiman, the clearest articulation of this point comes in Kant's last essay, "On the Supposed Right to Lie for Philanthropy" (1797). More often cited than read, the essay is variously mocked or puzzled over as a possible sign of the aging Kant's dementia. The argument is simple enough, set up and dispensed with in a few short pages. A friend of mine pounds on my door, begging for a place to hide from a murderer. A little while later, the murderer comes to my door, asking if I have seen my friend. At the point at which I am asked directly, am I authorized to lie in order to protect my friend's life? Kant says "no."[54]

His explanation has two parts, though people usually only remember the second. The first takes aim at the idea that a lie is only a problem if it harms another. *Every lie* harms someone, Kant argues, if not a specific individual, then humanity in general. By lying, no matter how noble my motives, I am making a world where no contract or oath can be believed. The second explanation is the one people tend to remember. I am not authorized to lie because in doing so I may become accidentally culpable for the death of my friend. I have no way of knowing if my friend has slipped out the back door while I was speaking. If he did, and the murderer runs into him as he leaves my house, I am responsible for his death, even though I lied with the best of intentions. If I spoke the truth, however, and the murderer finds my friend, I am not responsible for anything that transpires. Kant frames this odd defense as a question of legal culpability, but Neiman argues, persuasively, that Kant is worried about the much deeper problem of how little control we have over our actions. Her reading is worth quoting in full.

At first glance, the essay does appear ridiculous: its central argument looks less appropriate to philosophy than slapstick. The vision of the murderer and the victim crashing into each other is enough to raise guffaws or eyebrows—if it weren't also a vision of the tragic. For just as surely as comedy, tragedy lives on wrong identifications, opportunities missed and grabbed in the split of a second, paths crossed at the least expected moments, intentions that hit marks their agents never aimed at. It is, in short, about the power of the contingent, and the importance of the fact that we don't control the natural world. Kant's discussion of the murderer underlined all of that. His point was not that it's *better* to betray your friend than lie about his whereabouts, still less that telling lies is far worse than death. . . . His point was, rather, one that we have no wish to hear: our power over the consequences of our actions is really very small. What lies in our hands is good intention itself.[55]

More recent thinkers, like Thomas Nagel (1937–) and Bernard Williams (1929–2003), would question if even that much remains in our power. In his 1979 essay "Moral Luck," Nagel points out that nearly every action we take seems to be influenced by factors outside our control.[56] I have no say over the most basic facts of my existence. I did not choose to be born a woman, or American, or with certain temperamental quirks that make me more or less courageous or likely to fold under pressure. I have no say in the nature of the decisions that I face, and whether lives will hinge on them, or if I will lead a quietly inconsequential life. I can be as punctilious as I please and act with every intention of fulfilling the moral law, but ultimately it is not up to me whether a child runs in front of my car as I am driving. I am hemmed in by circumstances outside my choice. It is all very well to think, as Kant does, that I should ground morality in my good intentions because my intentions are the only things under my power, but on closer inspection even my capacity to form good intentions hinges on factors outside my control. Contingency does not just limit the scope of our moral judgment; it destroys our capacity to judge at all.

Perhaps the debate about whether to domesticate contingency in teleological narratives of progress or to embrace its disruptive power as an opportunity for social critique would have remained relatively evenly matched within academic circles if not for the second catastrophe of the modern age: Auschwitz and the Gulag. After Auschwitz, the great philosophical question about evil was no longer how or if evil could be justified as part of a necessary plan for history but, rather, whether or not we *ought* to justify evil on such a scale. For some thinkers, the answer was "yes." Marilyn McCord Adams, John Hick, Alvin Plantinga, and Richard Swinburne, to name the most prominent figures, have all attempted to write postwar theodicies with greater or lesser degrees of sensitivity. For a far greater number of thinkers, though, the attitude toward theodicy after the Holocaust is better summed up by Rabbi Irving Greenberg's statement: "No statement, theological or otherwise, should be made that would not be credible in the presence of burning children."[57] For Greenberg, for Levinas, for Adorno, for most of the major Jewish figures of postwar thought, we simply do not have the right to stand back on the shore and watch the calamities of history. We cannot and ought not claim that the death of twelve million is understandable and, in the final analysis excusable, by some grand necessary plan. To erase contingency is to erase the suffering of the silent dead.

Erasing contingency would also silence the voices of the living. Anyone who has spent time reading memoirs from the major atrocities of the twentieth century, particularly those about the Holocaust and the Gulag, cannot help but notice how prominently chance figures in nearly every work. Lives often hinged on the most arbitrary of events and mistakes. A misheard word, a misread number, an indoor work assignment was enough to save a struggling prisoner or condemn a healthy one. As one woman wrote on Stalin's purges: "My mother worked in a bread factory, and one day, during an inspection, they found bread-crumbs on her gloves. That was enough to constitute sabotage. They sentenced her to ten years in prison."[58]

Or Primo Levi, on the selection process in Auschwitz:

Even before the selection is over, everybody knows that the left was effectively the "*schlechte Seite*," the bad side. There have natu-rally been some irregularities: René, for example, passed commis-sion immediately in front of me and there could have been a mistake with our cards. I think about it, discuss it with Alberto, and we agree that the hypothesis is probable; I do not know what I will think tomorrow and later; today I feel no distinct emotion.

It must have equally been a mistake about Sattler, a huge Tran-sylvanian peasant who was still at home only twenty days ago; Sattler does not understand German, he has understood nothing of what has taken place, and stands in a corner mending his shirt. Must I go and tell him that his shirt will be of no more use?[59]

On work assignments upon arrival at the Gulag:

The major walked along the line, quickly examining the bodies. He was choosing goods—to production, to the sewing factory! To the collective farm! To the zone! To the hospital! The produc-tion manager wrote down the surnames.

But when he heard her surname, the Major looked at her and asked,

—"What relation are you to Professor Gagen-Torn?"

—"Daughter."

—"Put her in the hospital, she has scabies, she has red marks on her stomach."

As she did not have red marks on her stomach, Gagen-Torn assumed, correctly as it turned out, that the man had once known and admired her father, and was saving her, at least temporarily, from hard work.[60]

And not only lives depended on luck. Faced with the sheer arbitrariness of individual circumstances and constitutions, the most thoughtful conceded that self-knowledge became impossible.

> I never in my life betrayed anyone or sold anyone down the river. But I don't know how I would have held out if they had beaten me. I passed through all of the stages of the investigation, by the greatest good luck, without beatings—"method number three." My interrogators never laid a finger on me. This was chance, nothing more. It was simply that I was interrogated early, in 1943—before they resorted to torture.[61]

There are more, tens of millions more, examples that could be quoted on the arbitrariness of life and death in the mass murders from the last century. My point is a simple one, though one that bears making: it may very well be that philosophers in the last few decades have gravitated toward thinking about history as contingent because it seems a factual description of the world we live in.

Ultimately, this is the insights I want to retain from the long debate about necessity and contingency in history: even at its most abstract and abstruse, contingency is a question of suffering.

CONTINGENCY AND TOUCH IN
CONTINENTAL PHILOSOPHY

Contingency intrudes on bodies. The earthquake crushes the pious in Lisbon's cathedrals, which happened to have been built on a landfill centuries prior. Kant's murderer skids into his victim through the freshly tilled earth of a garden. Even Judith Butler's claim that contingency is a central moment in critique is ultimately in service of allowing bodies to dress how they want, love how they want, live how they want without capitulating to claims about the timeless essence of gender. What I have offered so far is an argument for why we need to ask "whose bodies suffer from contingency, and how?" And while the question "whose bodies, whose suffering" needs to be asked, again and again and again, it is not yet an argument for why contingency needs to be understood *through* bodies, rather than as something that merely affects bodies.

So what, exactly, do the body and touch allow us to see about contingency that thinking about history misses? This book is the long answer, but in the short term my response can be broken down into two different claims, one about the body's role in forcing us, through old habits, to confront how abruptly life can change, and one about how touch raises a problem for subjectivity. To sketch out the first case, I want to return to my opening story about Havi Carel and look at what happened in the weeks after she sat with the diagnostic manual resting heavy in her hands.

Perhaps Carel would not have been so starkly aware of the problem of contingency if her disease had manifested when she was older, or if the onset of symptoms had been more gradual, or if there had been less of a disjunction between her life before and after diagnosis. Her disease might have still terrified and disoriented her, but memories of being able to run and hike and kickbox would not have intruded so insistently if they had not been so recent and if her lung capacity had not declined by 50 percent over a single year. But that abrupt decline was Carel's reality, and it meant that every day she was forced to confront—on the most visceral bodily level—how different her life had been only months prior and how different her life could have been had her illness never happened.

In the earliest days after her diagnosis, that disconnect between the life she had been living and her newly circumscribed reality dogged her constantly. When she woke, she would enjoy just for a moment complete forgetfulness of her new life. Inevitably, though, "the realization that something had gone horribly wrong would crash down on my sleepy head."[62] That sense of unreality upon waking lasted about a week. The habits of her previously healthy body lingered longer. At first, when she walked, her body would set out at its old brisk pace, only to be stopped short by the diminished capacity of her lungs. When she climbed stairs, she would be surprised into stopping to gasp for breath. She would set out for a walk to a pub 200 feet away without her oxygen tank, only to discover that what had been easy the week before was now an impossibility. The skills and memories of her old body strained constantly, maddeningly against the new reality of her life until she formed new habits. When, after a year, she finally forgot what it felt like to run freely, she experienced her blunted memory as a relief, not a loss.

Carel writes as a phenomenologist and consequently found in Merleau-Ponty and Heidegger the concepts to express the warring experiences of her body. Drawing on Merleau-Ponty, Carel writes of the essential ambiguity of the body, which is at once biological, an object made of matter like every other object, and a subject, lived in the first person. Most of the time, we never stop to consider the two dimensions of the body. The biological thrums as the backdrop of our thoughts in the lived body, unnoticed so long as it functions properly. Illness, however, thrusts awareness of our biological body upon us. As she writes, "Our attention is drawn to the malfunctioning body part and suddenly it becomes the focus of our attention, rather than the invisible background for our activities."[63] I take Carel's point to be roughly that of Heidegger's tool analytic in *Being and Time*. So long as a hammer works, I never notice it. The instant it breaks in my hand, however, it becomes an object to me and the focus of my attention.

Hammers can be thrown out or replaced, but the broken body remains there, me but not me, the home of my subjectivity become an object to me. Worse, in illness the relationship between the lived and biological body inverts. The malfunctioning biological body, which had seemed at first an aberrant intrusion on the healthy lived body, becomes primary. It forces a subjectivity to view the world through its limitations, even overwriting the most basic experiences of space and time. The world itself appears different to the sick body. "Distances increase, hills become mountains and stairs become obstacles rather than passageways."[64] New features of the landscape are thrown abruptly into relief. What had previously failed to register as anything other than the slightest incline becomes insurmountably steep. Places that had seemed seamless extensions of home—the street where Carel walked her dog—stretch to unimaginable lengths in a brutal mimicry of the camerawork in *Citizen Kane* as the table between Orson Welles and his wife expands to push the two ever further apart. The sick body may still register as an object or a burden, but it also has the power to co-opt the lived body, to refract subjectivity through its limitations and its struggles.

These transformations allowed the extreme arbitrariness of life to show up to Carel as a problem for the first time. Desires that had seemed mediocre and modest in her previous life, such as the wish for a child, suddenly seemed exorbitant and unreasonably dependent on good fortune. "Did I really think that this list of infinitely complex, luck-dependent elements would just come true as a matter of chance?" she marveled.[65] The whole unlikely machinery of the universe that had allowed her to inhabit her life comfortably was thrown into relief, as was the feebleness of the stories she had told herself about why her life would turn out well. In illness, she was forced to see that it didn't matter that she worked out regularly or ate the correct food while others smoked three packs a day. No matter how often she asked what she called the "beginner's question of suffering"—why me?—she was thrown back on the brute, meaningless fact of her disease. The question "had no answer, or at least no answer we know of with current medical knowledge. It was an arbitrary stroke of very bad luck."[66]

Yet the virtue and pathos of Carel is that she does not allow the experience of contingency to remain solely an unanswerable question of meaning. Instead, she shows how totally the experience of contingency can engulf a life. She teaches us to feel how the lag between what she thought her life was and the new reality of her present can be encoded in her body. She cannot help but marvel that her life could have been otherwise when every thoughtless breath drawn by the muscle memory of her old, healthy body throws back at her the sharp gasping reminder of her new limitations. To be struck, truly struck, by contingency as a problem can mean the total transformation of spatial and emotional geography. These experiences are not incidental to Carel's sense of contingency; they are its content.

I began with her work because she captures better than any thinker I have read why the vulnerability of the body triggers an awareness of contingency and how that awareness often comes alongside a deeper transformation in a sufferer's experience navigating space and existing as a body in the world. Focused as she is on the experience of illness, she does not and cannot provide the sort of detailed explanation of the relationship between contingency and touch that interests me in this book, but she does offer a starting point for understanding why the body is so very well suited to triggering these thoughts about the precariousness and changeability of life.

While Carel writes as a phenomenologist, working with figures like Merleau-Ponty and Heidegger who will concern me in this book, contingency only shows up for her through catastrophe. Illness can make visible the ways in which the aspirations and identities we hold are, in fact, contingent and dependent on luck, but, for her, the revelation of contingency comes from the body and remakes her experience of the world. I do not mean to trivialize this contribution; illness comes for us all, often alongside the depredations of aging. But my thinkers are interested in an experience even more basic still: touch. The revelation of contingency coming from the world through the touch, not from the breakdown of the body as it navigates the world. That is why the thinkers I will discuss, in different ways, play with the link between the contingent and touch, *tangere*.

This is more than an etymological pun. Rather, it is a claim about the nature of subjectivity born from the intuition that to be contingent is to be dependent on the collisions of events, bodies, and circumstances outside one's control, a change in any one of which would produce a different reality. For continental philosophers, increasingly convinced in the wake of Descartes that there is no way to divide mind from body, touch is a way of thinking through the dependency and interconnectedness at the heart of contingency. If it is true that we are radically embodied—that we *are* our bodies, not incidentally, not in the way a turtle inhabits its shell—then the boundaries of my body are the boundaries of my self. More to the point, the skin is the boundary between the body and world and, like any boundary, it can keep others out or let others in. Under the right circumstances, the sensibility of my skin can fade to the backdrop of my thoughts as I imagine I am a disembodied mind hammering at my keyboard. In other moments, when I feel violated or vulnerable, it can feel as if the membrane of my skin has been peeled away, leaving me terrifyingly open to the world. Touch is the sense that makes possible the constantly shifting relationship between body and world.

Touch gives the world to me as alternately hostile, abrasive, resistant, caressing, wounding, and wondrous. *I* am different, depending on how the world touches me. My past, my life possibilities, my horizon of hope can change radically when I am forcibly touched against my will or when I am enfolded in the comforting arms of a lover or even when I brush unnoticed through a crowd. Thus the body is the site of contingency, not just because the moments in which my body is wounded force me to confront how very vulnerable my plans are to derailment but because my sense of self, my subjectivity, is dependent upon the way the world touches me.

This is the basic phenomenological intuition behind this book. In the next section I will more fully contextualize my methodology, conversation partners within the field, choice of texts, and structure of the book. From this point on, I will not be explicitly addressing genealogy or its significance to contemporary readers until the conclusion, but that does not mean I have abandoned it. This whole book, in its way, is a response to my earlier call to think of contingency and its critical power as subject to the same historical processes genealogy taught us to attend to.

METHODOLOGY, THEORETICAL ASSUMPTIONS, AND SCOPE

In the chapters that follow, I pursue three different lines of inquiry. First, I explore the phenomenological experience of contingency. Second, I place each author's articulation of contingency in the context of the historical, intellectual, philosophical, and religious debates of the day. Third, I draw out the ethical conclusions each thinker reaches based on the combined phenomenological and historical experience of contingency.[67] In these lines of inquiry, I am indebted to major trends in scholarship within religious studies and philosophy. As a result, this book is interdisciplinary in its method.

Regarding the first thread, phenomenology, my argument borrows its structure from Heidegger's analysis of "mood" (*Stimmung*) in *Being and Time*.[68] Briefly put, Heidegger argues that the basic condition of human subjectivity is "thrownness" (*Geworfenheit*)—the state of finding oneself born into a life one did not choose and forced to relate to surroundings as either mattering or not mattering on a personal level. In the abstract, such a life offers limitless possibility; in concrete experience, however, only some of those possibilities present themselves as live and significant. His question, much like my own, is not the metaphysical one about the origin of the choices, but, rather, is about the conditions under which some of those possibilities present themselves as meaningful. One of the key features of experience in such a world is moods. According to Heidegger, I always find myself in a mood, whatever that mood may be, and that mood shapes my entire perception of the world. When I am in a depressed mood, the whole world shows up to me as gloomy, hopeless, and filled with shuttered possibilities. When I am in a buoyant mood, the world shows up to me as full of possibility and brightness, and so on.

The phenomenological thread of my inquiry follows Heidegger's lead by eschewing metaphysical questions in favor of an account of how a certain phenomenon—in this case, contingency—shows up as a problem for a given thinker, with the key difference that I am interested in touch. Thus *in theory* every moment of our lives is contingent and *in theory* every moment our skin meets the world is an occasion to recognize that even the seemingly stable boundaries of our selves are open to change. In practice, though, contingency—both the historical and embodied sense of it—is largely invisible in our lives. Only on rare occasions are we shocked into recognizing that our lives, our bodies, our identities could be otherwise. I am interested in the role of touch in these moments when contingency shows up as a problem. Much as Heidegger suggests in his analysis of how moods shape our reception of the world, I hold that phenomenologically there is no pure, objective experience of contingency. There are only particular perspectives, realized by particular bodies, in particular physical, tactile encounters with the world. Each encounter with contingency emphasizes certain possibilities and dangers, while deemphasizing others.

In exploring how contingency shows up as a problem, I am also interested in scholarship within religious studies that emphasizes the role of history in shaping experience. This brings me to my second line of inquiry. I hold as a basic philosophical principle that there is no experience outside history. Even the most seemingly pure and transcendental experience of the numinous is mediated through the values, intellectual concepts, biases, and religious practices of a given writer. My greatest influence on this point is Wayne Proudfoot's *Religious Experience*,[69] but I have profited from a number of other thinkers who have questioned the link between experience and culture, including late Heidegger,[70] Anne Taves,[71] and Joan Wallach Scott.[72] Accordingly, a substantial portion of each chapter is interested in tracing the intellectual influences, historical events, shifts in technology, and theological debates that shape each thinker's framing of the problem of contingency.

As a scholar of religious studies, I am particularly interested in drawing out the centrality of religion in shaping the analyses of contingency I discuss. My interest is partially motivated by a pragmatic concern with the contexts and the concerns of the texts I discuss. The thinkers I discuss—Novalis, Friedrich Wilhelm Joseph von Schelling, Maurice Merleau-Ponty, Jean Améry, and Michel Serres—are writing in response to long-standing Christian theological debates, whether about the nature of God and pantheism, in Novalis's case, a version of theodicy that attempts to define evil as the absence of the good, in Schelling's, tropes about flesh, in Merleau-Ponty and Améry's cases, or debates about the nature of human stewardship over the earth, in Serres's.

More broadly, though, my interest in the religious dimension of these discussions of contingency stems from my belief, mentioned earlier, that there is no Western philosophy as we know it without Christianity.[73] I mean this claim on multiple levels. Many of the interlocutors of the canonical texts in the West are theologians. Descartes dedicated *Meditations* to the Jesuit faculty at the Sorbonne; Spinoza argued against contemporary Calvinist theologians in *The Theological-Political Treatise*, just as much as he engaged the philosopher and scholar of Torah Moses Maimonides (1135–1204); Kant only rose to fame because Karl

Leonhard Reinhold wrote a series of letters arguing that Kant's work provided a middle way between blind faith and rationalism; Hannah Arendt wrote her dissertation on Augustine. Moreover, key thinkers in the Western canon, like Anselm, Aquinas, Spinoza, Hegel, Schelling, Kierkegaard, and Heidegger, were trained in theology and actively invoked Christian terms like flesh (*la chair*),[74] spirit (*Geist*),[75] or "freedom of the will" to develop their systems. Nor did Western philosophy's debts to Christian, and increasingly Jewish, theology end once philosophy began to differentiate itself as a distinct discipline, with its own training. Heidegger, Derrida, Benjamin, Arendt, and Levinas were all deeply concerned with theological questions about flesh, finitude, messianism, and the end of history. Not all these thinkers are Christian in practice or in background—indeed, some of the thinkers I will discuss, such as Spinoza, Jean Améry, and Vladimir Jankélévitch, are Jewish—but as philosophers, they are participating in an intellectual tradition inescapably influenced by Christian thinking, terms, and concerns. The influence of Christianity is, of course, not the whole story but it is my story because my training is in Christian thought. I have no doubt there is more to be said about how Jewish sources shaped the discussion of contingency, history, and flesh in some of my thinkers. I lack the background to make those connections, however, and can only leave an open invitation for others to tell the parts of the story I cannot.

Thus, when I argue that contingency is a concept shaped by Christian debates about the nature of God, evil, and the theology of history, I am not claiming that contingency once had a theological valence that it shed as philosophy entered a new, more secular stage. Rather, I mean that Christian theological debates about the nature of God and human subjectivity set the stage for understanding contingency as bound up in human finitude, temporality, and embodiment. The thinkers that interest me picked up this notion of contingency, suffused with a theological past, and reimagined it in conversation with the theological, scientific, and philosophical debates of their own days. The nature and stakes of those theological debates vary from figure to figure and across time, but each of the thinkers I discuss blur the lies between philosophy and theology in fruitful, heterodox ways. It would be a disservice and historical anachronism to these figures to excise their theological concerns from their work.[76]

Likewise, I believe it would be a disservice to ignore the ethical conclusions each thinker draws out of his experience of contingency. This brings me back to the third thread of the book, My attention to these projects and conclusions is an extension of my earlier argument about genealogy that contingency entails no necessary political or ethical conclusions. Equally, though, it is born from my conviction that the types of bodily experiences a person has shape the types of problem contingency poses for the thinker. Recognizing my contingency in a moment of violation means something very different—and entails a different ethical relationship to the world—from recognizing my contingency in a moment of tenderness. As with my other lines of inquiry, this turn to the ethical is also informed by recent works arguing for renewed attention to the values and constructive projects within philosophy coming from figures as different as Eve Kosofsky Sedgwick,[77] Rita Felski,[78] and Thomas A. Lewis.[79]

Combined, these interests in phenomenology, history, and ethics have led me to structure each chapter on a different thinker and tactile, affective situation where contingency shows up as a problem for them, with particular attention to the different literary and philosophical genres each experimented with in their efforts to articulate the radically destabilizing experience of contingency, and the conclusions each drew about how to live in the world following that revelation of contingency. The thinkers I have chosen are not meant to provide a comprehensive history of contingency in the modern era or to offer a systematic account of contingency. That would be a different project, better carried out by an intellectual historian, not a philosopher of religion. Instead, I have sought out figures who discussed contingency from markedly different perspectives and reached substantively different conclusions about how to live in a radically destabilized world. These thinkers may echo each other on themes, worries, and even terminology, but they are not meant to come together in agreement on a single conclusion. My choice to have discordant voices was deliberate. For different reasons, the writers covered think of philosophy as rooted in individual, particular intuitions, which are only later expanded into a system. I share their general view of philosophy and have accordingly refrained from trying to synthesize their writings on philosophy into a grand theory. Such a unified account of how contingency is experienced, or what projects ought to be built in response, would be contrary to the deep commitments these thinkers share to the idea of philosophy as a personal, antisystematic, antifoundationalist project.

I have ordered these chapters chronologically, starting with early German Romanticism. Others might have chosen to start earlier, with Leibniz or Spinoza, or the sentimentalists, such as the third Earl of Shaftesbury and Adam Smith. For my part, I have been guided by my focus on continental philosophy and the overwhelming importance of Hegel's thoughts on contingency and the philosophy of history within that tradition.[80] As a result, I have opted to begin with figures who run parallel with Hegel but chose to emphasize the bodily experience of contingency, rather than the historical one.

In choosing particular figures within that time frame to focus on, I have deliberately sought out relatively understudied figures in continental philosophy of religion in hopes of expanding the range of thinkers discussed in the field. Although the early German Romantics, and Schelling in particular, are undergoing a revival in the discipline of philosophy with exciting new work by Manfred Frank,[81] Frederick Beiser,[82] Dalia Nassar,[83] and Bruce Matthews,[84] among others, much of continental philosophy of religion focuses on figures such as Derrida, Nancy, Irigaray, Jean-Luc Marion, Hegel, Levinas, Julia Kristeva, and Heidegger. While I am indebted to many of these thinkers, and freely acknowledge that they touch on many of the themes of finitude, embodiment, theology, and flesh that interests me, I take broadening the conversation to be its own good, given how constricted the canon of continental philosophy of religion can at times be.

Accordingly, there are four chapters. Chapter 1, "Illness," begins with a strange, fragmentary encyclopedia written by Friedrich von Hardenberg, better known as Novalis, shortly before his death. In it I explore the confluence of political debates, philosophical wars about the possibility of a universal system of thought, anxieties about the unmasterable proliferation of texts in the age of the printing press, and new theories of illness rooted in a tactile theory of the nervous system. This complicated play of influences, I suggest, at once led Novalis to laud the tactile experience of holding a book as a check on the hubristic dream of creating a universal system of knowledge unbound by bodies and to fear it as a source of illness. That ambivalence leads Novalis to writing literature, in hopes that it will allow him to regain balance with the world.

Chapter 2, "Loneliness," turns to a philosophical myth written and abandoned by Friedrich Wilhelm Joseph von Schelling in 1813 about a primal will, driven to create an other to relieve its suffering. In later works, Schelling very explicitly equates the caprice of this desire with contingency, seeing creation as a wholly free undetermined event. I argue that, far from being random, contingency shows up as loneliness in Schelling's text, as the lack of binding ties and relationships to an other afflict it with the type of suffering that cannot be comprehended by a third-person account of theodicy but only relieved through creation of an other to give the primal will roots. I then suggest that, in his argument that contingency presents itself in loneliness and lack of ties, Schelling anticipates more recent work on the phenomenology of solitary confinement where the lack of touch often leads prisoners to hallucinate the presence of others. I end by questioning whether Schelling's psychological model, where passions can neither be controlled nor directed, contributed to the reactionary politics of his later life.

Chapter 3, "Violation," takes up the question raised by Novalis about the relation among place, wonder, and the recognition of contingency, but seeks its darker implications. In it, I read Jean Améry's autobiographical essay describing his torture during the Third Reich with Merleau-Ponty's description in *The Phenomenology of Perception* of a type of "dark space," described by people suffering from schizophrenia, where distance dissolves between a person and the external world, creating the experience of contingency as the touch of objects violates boundaries. For Améry, the confrontation with his fragility and contingency is figured as a type of exile, with his body as the home he can never feel fully at ease in after its boundaries were breached by another's blow. Améry takes from this experience a moral obligation to refuse to forgive those who violated him.

Chapter 4, "Love," asks whether or not the experience of contingency is solely disruptive, or if it can be incorporated into lasting social structures. I open with Michel Serres's discussion of contingency and eroticism in *The Five Senses,* which offers an account of contingency, dependency, and coimplication with the world experienced through the shifting boundaries of bodies as they caress each other. I argue that this model of contingency, as "common tangency," underlies his environmentalism, leading him to urge the creation of a "natural contract" where humans combat global warming based on a recognition that they are in constant, coimplicated contact with nature in much the same way as two lovers during sex.

1

ILLNESS

BOOK MADNESS, BODIES, AND THE ABSOLUTE IN NOVALIS'S ROMANTIC ENCYCLOPEDIA

For a hundred years before Novalis was born in 1772 in a secluded Saxon manor, intellectuals across Germany had been making grim prognostications about a new disease troubling the land: *Lesesucht,* sometimes called *Büchersucht* or *Bücherwut,* the reading sickness, or book madness.[1] Something was wrong with the new, too-easy circulation of pamphlets, monographs, and journals in the age of the printing press, but the symptoms and the consequences of contracting this illness were an open question. For Johann Gottfried von Herder, the problem lay in the grand delusion that a reading public could exist unbound from time and space.[2] His teacher, Johann Georg Hamann, echoing that thought, mockingly dedicated his *Socratic Memorabilia* to "the Public, or Nobody, the Well-Known."[3] In Leipzig a bookseller published a pamphlet called "A Plea to My Nation: On the Plague of German Literature," begging the literate public to *please* stop contributing to the flood of texts too numerous for any one person to master.[4] Wolfgang von Goethe, whose overwrought novella *The Passion of Young Werther* inspired a rash of young lovelorn men to button their yellow waistcoats and empty bullets into their skulls, muttered darkly that the real issue was Romanticism, symbol of everything sick about the age.[5]

To this world of morose ruminations, Novalis abandoned a stack of handwritten, fragmentary pages written between 1797 and 1799. At first, owners and collectors did not know what to make of them, filled as they were with short, often cryptic, observations, organized under repeating headings ranging from "fashion" to "medicine" to "physiology" to "encyclopedistics." In the years since, scholars have generally come to agree that Novalis wrote the fragments as entries in an experimental encyclopedia, organized by analogies in order to deny the reader the sort of schematic overview of facts and figures typically associated with the genre. They have even grudgingly agreed on *Das Allgemeine Brouillon,* or "Universal Notebook," as a name. Its early collectors had none of that, though—neither the name nor the genre nor knowledge of the background philosophical debates on the contingent material basis of human knowledge that gave the manuscript meaning. They had just a scattering of telegraphic observations written by a man famous for his poetry and philosophical fragments. So they did what made sense; they took a blade to the papers.[6]

To Novalis's admirers, he was the slender young man with light flowing locks, brilliant brown eyes, and large, expressive hands, as fine and pale as his nearly transparent forehead, who died tragically young after a life marked by loss. When his beloved child-fiancée, Sophie von Kühn, passed away at the age of fourteen, Novalis wrote the melancholy, lyrical *Hymns to the Night*, which would establish him as one of the greatest writers in German literature. He composed fragments, poetry, and even an incomplete novel; he was the poet of pain and pining. And when, in 1805, a scant four years after his death, a friend wrote a memorial essay unglamorously titled "Friedrich von Hardenberg Assessor of Salt Mines in Saxony and Designated Department Director in Thuringia," Novalis's admirers were scandalized, as only wealthy young artists can be, at the reminder that their favorite poet was a scientist who worked for a living and sometimes went by Fritz. Novalis wrote delicate fragments, not cumbersome encyclopedias, and if some assessor of salt mines named Fritz thought he was doing otherwise, well, so much the worse for Fritz.

The textual surgery performed on *Das Allgemeine Brouillon* was as great an archival abomination as any since Pascal's heirs picked apart his stitches and pasted his reordered fragments on clean parchment, but it was an understandable one. From the very beginning, Novalis's book was untimely: 1798 was an untimely moment to begin an encyclopedia. The conversation among the Prussian intelligentsia about how to keep up with new discoveries in the age of the printing press had escalated from an irritable chunter to hysterical proclamations about the "book madness" sweeping Europe; 1799 was an even more untimely moment to be interested in the problem of contingency but not the philosophy of history. The revolution in France that had sent Louis XVI's head tumbling from a guillotine seven years prior was ending with Napoleon's coup d'état. If Novalis had been the unworldly poet he has so often been made out to be, his choice to write about the contingency of bodies rather than that of history or institutions might have been understandable. But Novalis had followed the revolution avidly as part of a young, radical social circle, and so his choices are a puzzle. Most of all, it was an untimely moment in his own life to sink two years into a project and abandon it because by 1801 he would be dead.

All these puzzles, for my purposes, might be reframed like this. This is a book about a neglected understanding of contingency that claims we feel the flux, instability, and intuition that things could be otherwise most acutely through the vulnerability of the body to change through touch and the upheaval of the emotions. This tradition is neglected largely because it was overshadowed by a certain reading of philosophy of history that sees contingency as a problem of history, most fully realized in Hegel.[7] Contingency is found in events that could have been otherwise, the reading goes, and the job of the philosopher of history is to find the narrative that reveals that contingency to be merely apparent, a part of a larger, necessary plan. Centuries of readers have argued about whether Hegel has an ethical reading of history, and they have argued about whether this is a good reading of Hegel on contingency, but what they have largely not done is argue about whether Hegel was right to see history as a philosophical problem. *That* particular set of insights—that the conditions of human knowledge develop through time and what we say about history matters deeply for how we view present institutions—has been taken as foundational for the last two hundred years of philosophy.

Novalis was a contemporary of Hegel. He had many of the same friends, was steeped in the same texts, and witnessed the same political events, at least until his early death. Yet Novalis never made the leap (that seems so obvious now) from talking about contingency to talking about contingency as a problem for the philosophy of history. My question is not, "Why wasn't Novalis doing what Hegel did?," but rather, "what material, philosophical, and psychological conditions made this bodily, affective experience of contingency so compelling for Novalis?" What was the world like for Novalis and for his contemporaries on the eve of Hegel's ascendance, before their understanding of

contingency was gradually overshadowed by debates about necessity and meaning in history?

Answering that question requires looking at philosophical
debates reconstructed from documents seized during an
eighteenth-century police raid of young Kantians, theories of
sickness born out of the dissection of live animals by an opiate-
addled Scotsman, and a detailed analysis of Novalis's text for
both form and content. The vision of contingency that emerges
is fractal, repeating at different scales in different sites the same
configuration of concerns about epistemology, finitude, and—
above all—illness.

Underlying these manifestations of contingency is the puzzle
that Novalis's unfinished encyclopedia posed for its bemused
future owners. Why would Novalis, a poet famous for fragments,
choose to write an encyclopedia at all, especially during a moment
when the technological innovation of the printing press seemed
about to render the whole genre defunct?

CONTINGENCY AS
EPISTEMIC HUMILITY

The decision to write an encyclopedia might have been the
strangest of the creative choices Novalis made—fully as strange,
in its own way, as writing a traditional encyclopedia would be
today, after thirty years of public access to the Internet. Scholars across Europe had spent the three centuries since Gutenberg's
1440 invention of the printing press experimenting with new
forms of reference books to manage the influx of new texts. They
compiled quotations in the old medieval genre of florilegia, built
elaborate curio cabinets where scholars could pool their notes
on a subject and check out the passages of their friends, wrote

provisos in their will about the inheritance of their notes; shredded old books and medieval manuscripts to paste into new compendia, wrote the first dictionaries, and reinvented the encyclopedia. At stake, they thought, was nothing less than the preservation of civilization in Europe. They were acutely aware of how many ancient works had been lost after the fall of the Roman Empire and were determined to prevent another catastrophe by consolidating and compiling as many texts as possible. At the same time, certain quarters began to fear that the proliferation of new texts *was* the catastrophe. How could they possibly preserve everything published? And even if they did manage to save everything printed, how would future generations ever manage to find the truly valuable books amid the accumulated chaff? If they slipped up, if they failed to get a handle on the inrush of texts new and old, Europe might slip back into the barbarism of the medieval era.[8]

Even if these worries were not new, they were particularly acute in Prussia at the moment Novalis began his encyclopedia. After nearly a century of warfare, which devastated the population, the German printing industry began to thrive in Novalis's lifetime. From 1740 to 1800 the number of books listed in the catalogue for Leipzig's book fair, the center of the German printing industry, climbed from 755 to 2,569, more than tripling the number of texts in circulation.[9] The pandemic of printing brought two of the ideals of the Enlightenment into conflict: the expansion of knowledge and the ethical duty to educate the public. Knowledge thrived through the specialization made possible by clusters of conversations in journals, but that very depth of detail undermined the imperative to make knowledge useful and broadly accessible. There was simply too much being created too fast to ever begin to properly survey it.

The encyclopedia was not collateral damage that Novalis might have plausibly pulled out from the flood of books and resuscitated; it was the center of these worries. In Novalis's day, the encyclopedia was primarily a bloated, Sisyphean attempt to gather together scientific discoveries scattered across languages and continents into one orderly hierarchical book. The most famous French encyclopedists, Denis Diderot and Jean le Rond D'Alembert, invited this top-down approach to knowledge when they described their endeavors primarily as mapping the branches of the sciences. As D'Alembert writes:

> It [the Encyclopédie] is a kind of world map, which is to show the principal countries, their position and their mutual dependence, the road that leads directly from one to the other. This road is often cut by a thousand obstacles, which are known in each country only to the inhabitants or to travelers, and which cannot be represented except in individual, highly detailed maps. These individual maps will be the different articles of the Encyclopedia and the Tree or Systematic Chart will be its world map.[10]

While Chad Wellmon insists that Diderot and D'Alembert had a relatively nuanced awareness of the arbitrariness of encyclopedic entries and understood themselves as providing one out of many possible maps of knowledge, their eighteenth-century successors largely lacked the same self-reflexivity. Instead, writers such as Christian Heinrich Schmid sought to compose an encyclopedia that would be an universal map.[11] For Schmid and the tradition he represents, to know is to abstract oneself from the tumult of life and survey it from above; thus the encyclopedia should act as a handbook that saves the reader from ever confronting the wholly unknown. It was this position that the sheer proliferation of books made unsustainable.

Novalis, in short, arrived right at the moment when the material conditions that made encyclopedias possible and necessary—the proliferation of knowledge and scientific material in the wake of the invention of the printing press, which seemed to demand some sort of organization—had decisively undermined the possibility of that very endeavor. Novalis understood that the printing press had killed the dream of compiling a systemic overview of all human knowledge, but, unlike the previous generation, its death suited him perfectly. These material conditions allowed him to extend a series of arguments he had begun making in the years prior when he was studying philosophy. Namely, there is no universally valid first principle that leads all thinkers to the same truth. All knowing is particular, embodied, local, and contingent.

These connections between contingency and the printing press could remain mere speculation on my part, if Novalis had not composed a short, unpublished dialogue making the relationship between the two explicit at the same time he was working on *Das Allgemeine Brouillon*. The dialogue opens with two friends quarreling over the latest book catalogue from the Leipzig fair. Both agree that the contemporary age suffers from an overabundance of books, but they differ on the importance of that fact. Interlocutor A, the figure of Enlightenment rationality, begins by lamenting the black letters crawling over the page. "What a burden are these letters!" he exclaims, before noting that the contemporary human "is characterized 'by his fatal habituation to the printed nature.'"[12] Interlocutor B, representative of Novalis's own position, counters by praising the intellectual vibrancy of the culture that circulates more "honest and worthy ideas" than all of the competing cultures combined. He goes on to compare books to mines. "Everywhere we are bringing together the crude ore or the beautiful molds—we are melting down the ore, and have the skills to imitate and surpass the molds."[13] Books are material, earthy, and—as the metaphor of mines suggests—raw materials to be refined and reshaped for use.

Embedded in Enlightenment logic, Interlocutor A dismisses this idea as absurd, a reduction of books to fragmentary physical object. He insists instead that each book belongs to an educational chain that exists as part of a timeless, necessary systematic order.[14] The ideal book would be an encyclopedia that placed each individual book in its appropriate position. Mockingly, Interlocutor B rejoins, "It goes with you and with many like the Jews. They hope eternally for the Messiah, and he is long since here. Do you believe, then, that human destiny or, if you will, the nature of humanity first needed to frequent our lecture hall in order to experience what a system is? . . . Contingencies [*Die Zufälle*] are the sole certainty—the configuration of contingencies—your encounter is not chance, but rather law."[15] He then states that every book has fertilized some ground, even if only that of the author who composed it. There *is* no system of books filling holes in our knowledge in the inexorable movement of progress; there are only contingencies, only chance encounters with books that can never be entirely sterile. The natural metaphors of "fruit," "trees," and "fertilization" are more than poetic license for Interlocutor B; they signal a very real belief in the physical continuity between books and the material world of Nature.

In the next moment, Interlocutor B makes the central suggestion of the dialogue: what if there were no abstract realm of ideas, only books in their materiality, in their tactility, in their heft? What if, in his words, "Es gibt nur noch Bücher"?[16] There are only books. Yet even as the quantity of books grows, we are becoming alienated from their materiality. "Why else do we cling so strangely," he muses, half-wistfully, half-wryly, "like thin and meager moss to the printer's vignette?"[17] We grow even thinner as time progresses, clinging desperately to the materiality of the wooden blocks even as our own senses grow more abstract, as we learn to focus on ideas, not things. Soon, Interlocutor B says sadly, "We will see books, but not things . . . We will no longer have even our five bodily [*leibliche*] senses."[18]

The dialogue ends on an explicitly theological note. Interlocutor A, the representative of Enlightenment thought, declares himself to be so hemmed in by bad books that he wonders if it might not be better to restrict his intellectual company rather than fritter his life away without having thereby won anything eternal for his efforts. Interlocutor B, suddenly jovial, rebukes him: "You speak like a religious man—Unfortunately, you meet a pantheist in me—to whom the immeasurable world already is quite wide enough."[19] With this abrupt confession, Novalis's text declares its loyalty to the realm of contingency. He renounces the Enlightenment thinker's pure-minded quest for the necessary, immutable, and eternal in favor of the material world filled with people, books, and things that pass in and out of being.

Novalis packs a tremendous amount into a few pages. For the moment, I want to bracket his references to theology and the dwindling of the senses for later sections. Instead, I want to focus on one line: "Contingencies [*Die Zufälle*] are the sole certainty—the configuration of contingencies [*die Zusammenstellung der Zufälle*]—your encounter is not chance, but rather law." Before going any further, I want to make my case for translating *Zufall* as contingency, since it can be translated as either contingency or chance. In English, of course, contingency has its roots in the

Latin infinitive *tangere*, "to touch." Those roots in touch get at the sense in which the unpredictability of contingency stems from a contingent event's imbrication in the world. Whether or not a rock sets off an avalanche is dependent upon—contingent upon—whether it collides into another rock with enough force to dislodge it and send more rocks cascading down the mountain. It might not happen. The landslide always could have been otherwise, if the initial pebble had caught a draft and listed slightly to the left or right. The other way to hear *Zufall* is as a chance event that falls from the heavens. Unlike the cascading connections of contingency, it is an isolated, wholly other disruption of the status quo. It is not necessarily related to connection, touch, materiality or any of the other concepts that interest me. I think Novalis is getting at the former meaning. Linguistically, he builds the sense of connection between *Zufälle* into his language when he speaks of *Zusammenstellung*," since *zusammen* means "together." *Zufälle* come together, bounce off each other and influence each other, much like the pebble in my example. The context of the dialogue also clearly roots contingencies in the material world, since the *Zufälle* he worries about are how a physical book arrives in a city, when an individual stumbles upon it, or whether the reader receives a book in a mood that makes her receptive to it.

Putting these arguments together, the first claim about contingency in Novalis's work could be roughly formulated like this. Novalis attributes contingency to human knowledge by arguing that reading, our best chance to build a universal body of knowledge, depends on the unpredictable circulation of particular material objects. There is nothing necessary in what we know or how we came to know it. Insisting on the contingency of our encounter with physical books is a way of undermining the hubristic dream of mastering science. Contingency resides both in the conditions for knowledge (material books) and the limitation of the knower (the reader who holds the books).

For all the seeming clarity of the dialogue's main point, the conversation between the two characters sounds like nothing so much as a Chekhov play filled with characters talking past each other. There are some commonalities, of course. Both speakers agree that Interlocutor A dreams of a disembodied, orderly chain of knowledge where one book links neatly onto the previous. Likewise, they both agree that the proliferation of printed material is sweeping away any reasonable hope of getting a handle on knowledge. Based on that shared recognition of the printing industry, Interlocutor B asserts that the Enlightenment ideal of an abstract, orderly system of knowledge is practically impossible to attain; nowhere, however, does he say that it is wrong. Put otherwise, Interlocutor B never offers a reason why the Enlightenment ideal of education could not be a regulative ideal in the Kantian sense. The two figures could easily decide that a system of knowledge, however incomplete and impractical, was nonetheless a worthy aim to guide their actions. Yet both characters skip past that possibility. Why?

To answer that question, I want to turn to recent literature on Novalis's criticisms of foundationalism, particularly in the work of Manfred Frank.

CONTINGENCY AS PHILOSOPHICAL REBELLION

It may very well be that Novalis saw the proliferation of books as a way to push back against the hubristic and practically untenable vision of humanity building an evermore expansive, disembodied, and total system of the human sciences. It might also be true that reframing the acquisition of knowledge as a fundamentally contingent encounter between physical books and specific individuals provides a better phenomenology of reading. It might even be the case that Novalis saw something valuable in the way reading throws us up against the realization of our contingency, both in the way it forces us to recognize the sheer unlikeliness of *this* book, weathered and dog-eared as it is, landing in our hands at this moment, and the way we recognize how easily our experience of a given book might have been otherwise in another mood or another moment in our lives. All that may be true, but it does nothing to explain why Novalis welcomed rather than recoiled from that contingency.

Thirty years ago that question might not have been answerable, based on the state of scholarship. When the early German Romantics were credited at all with a philosophical outlook, it was generally shunned as an irrational, reactionary one. Georg Lukács even went so far as to construct a history directly linking Romanticism to the rise of the Nazis in *From Schelling to Hitler: The Destruction of Reason*.[20] However, today, thanks to recent scholarship by Dieter Henrich and Manfred Frank, it is possible to see Novalis's emphasis on contingency as part of his larger philosophical reaction to foundationalism. In the 1980s Dieter Henrich began "constellation-research," focused on reconstructing conversations that took place among Karl Leonhard Reinhold's students between 1792 and 1795. Foremost of those students, at least for the leading scholar of German Romanticism Manfred Frank, was Novalis.

As Frank and others have recounted, from 1790–1791 Novalis was the student of Karl Leonhard Reinhold (1758–1823). Reinhold along with Johann Gottlieb Fichte (1762–1814) were the dominant interpreters of Kant during the 1790s and were particularly famous for criticizing Kant as insufficiently systematic.

Kant, Reinhold's critique ran, had failed to justify the necessity of the categories or to ground his system in the idea of a whole and then deduce the (necessary) relation of the parts to each other.[21] Thus Reinhold, and later Fichte, decided that to save Kant from the charge of arbitrariness he had to reground the Kantian system in a first principle from which all subsequent propositions could then be derived. The first principle was meant to be self-explanatory, the maximally general term under which all other concepts existed as subspecies, both the sufficient and necessary source of all propositions and a self-evident truth. They chose as their first principle, in different forms, Kant's transcendental unity of apperception, the idea that I am aware of myself thinking.

For decades, Novalis was taken to be a follower of Fichte, when scholars paid attention to his philosophical notes at all.[22] Then Dieter Henrich made a peculiar find that helped recontextualize Novalis's thought as part of a wider criticism of Fichte and Reinhold's foundationalism. Under the pretext of responding to the Vienna Jacobin conspiracy of July 1794, the reactionary Austrian police conducted a raid on suspected subversives who had been radicalized by studying Kant. Among the suspects was Baron Franz Paul von Herbert, owner of a lead factory and patron to both Reinhold and Friedrich Immanuel Niethammer, a philosopher of Jena and friend to Novalis. In a letter from June 2, Niethammer confided in von Herbert his skepticism about Reinhold's search for a single principle that would serve as the foundation for all knowledge.[23]

For Niethammer, the true problem with Reinhold's effort to make representation a first principle of philosophy was that self-awareness is a contingent empirical proposition. Reinhold grounds his philosophy in a phenomenological account of consciousness, and it is "impossible to get from a contingent empirical proposition to an apodictically a priori valid proposition."[24] In later years, Novalis's friend Friedrich Schlegel would expand Niethammer's skepticism of Reinhold's foundationalism to a much broader point. As he wrote in *Athenaeum*, "Philosophy, like epic poetry, always begins in the middle and it is impossible to present philosophy and to add to it piece by piece, so that the first piece would be by itself completely grounded and explained."[25]

Novalis's own objections to Fichte's and Reinhold's search for a foundation came from a few different sources. The first was his understanding of philosophy as an individual, personal project. He writes,

> The representation of the philosophy of philosophy will always have something of an individual philosophy in it. Equally the poet represents only individual philosophy, and moreover anyone, no matter how vigorously he may acknowledge the philosophy of philosophy, will in practical terms be only more or less an individual philosopher, and despite all his striving he will never be entirely able to step out of the magic circle of his individual philosophy.[26]

All philosophy, all thought, can never be anything but particular, shaded by individual experience, location, and—as Novalis suggests in the passage cited earlier about recognizing one's truest self—moods. As with reading books, there is no knowledge that can be separated from a person's position in space and time.

His second objection is a bit more complicated. In one of his most famous remarks, he muses:

> What do I do by philosophizing? I am searching for a foundation. At the basis of philosophizing there lies a striving toward

the thought of a foundation. But foundation is not cause in the actual sense—but rather inner nature—connection with the whole [coherence]. All philosophy must terminate in an absolute foundation. If this were not given, if this concept contained an impossibility—then the urge to philosophize would be an infinite activity. It would be without end, because an eternal need for an absolute foundation would be at hand— and thus it would never stop. Through the voluntary renunciation of the Absolute, infinite free activity arises in us—the only possible Absolute which can be given to us, and which we find only through our incapacity to arrive at and recognize the absolute. This Absolute which is given to us may only be recognized negatively, in that we act and find that through no act do we arrive at what we seek.[27]

In this point, Novalis is a good Kantian. In Kantian terminology, the unconditioned or the idea of totality is an idea, or a concept, for which no concrete intuition is appropriate. We, however, base our judgments on a finite number of intuitions of the material world. There is no way to bridge that gap between our limited intuitions and the idea of something limitless. As Manfred Frank puts it, "We finite beings, for obvious reasons, strive toward a completeness of knowledge, but can never arrive at it, since we have a finite number of intuitions upon which to base our judgments."[28] We know what we know in the way that we know it. We know through the senses; we know as finite creatures; we know things, not the unconditioned.

These criticisms fit nicely together with my previous analysis of print culture. Novalis's insistence on the contingency of our encounter with books as central to knowledge should be read as expanding his critique of foundationalism to include a material dimension. It is not simply that thinking begins in a certain time or place and seeks to expand outward until it discovers the limits of its knowledge. Rather, the philosopher is embodied in a very real sense. Thinking depends on the physical books; *this* book, in *this* time and place, is the condition for the possibility of knowledge.

In part, this emphasis on the material book as a means to knowledge is a reflection of Novalis's dismissal of Cartesian mind-body dualism.[29] At points, he even marveled that such a bizarre and unnatural idea had ever come into being. Thus the creation of knowledge had to be as much a bodily physiological process as a mental one. He solved this problem by creating a model of epistemology where knowledge needed to be stimulated by some external object. Books were uniquely suited to bridge the chasm between self and world, inner and outer, as he noted when he remarked that "the essence of a letter is to excite a certain train of thought."[30] As physical objects, books stimulate the body, arousing it to action. As partly spiritual media, however, they also stimulate the mind by triggering memory.[31]

One way of understanding this point is to turn to Bernard Stiegler's much more contemporary account of technology as a form of prosthetics. The human, Stiegler asserts early on in *Technics and Time*, "exceeds the biological."[32] His powers are at every turn extended, created, and amplified by, "the evolution of the 'prosthesis,' not itself living, by which the human is nonetheless defined as a living being, [the prosthesis] constitutes the reality of the human's evolution, as if, with it, the history of life were to continue by means other than life."[33] The prosthesis is much, much more than the false leg that straps on to an amputated stump. Rather, it is every tool that blurs the boundaries between "natural" human powers and their surroundings, from the knives that act as our claws because our unadorned hands are soft and ill-suited for hunting, to our clothing that serve as the pelts to clothe our naked skin, and, finally, to our computers that become our memory as we click, save, and forget. These are not externalities we can shed, in Stiegler's theory. Technology has altered the course of our evolution in a completely literal biological fashion, by accelerating the development of our increasingly complex brains.

Under this reading of Novalis, the effort to write a new, peculiar encyclopedia that emphasizes contingencies is nothing less than a challenge to the foundationalism of Fichte and the disembodied ideal of knowledge. He chooses to reinvent the encyclopedia, not some other genre, precisely because it is the form most freighted with ideals of systematicity and universality. If he can transform the encyclopedia, he can show the inconsistencies inherent within the ideal of knowledge it represents.

Yet reading Novalis's encyclopedia as a solely critical or polemical project is still not enough. Doing so misses the religious dimension hinted at by Interlocutor B when he rebukes his friend for seeking lawlike order in knowledgewith the remark, "You speak like a religious man—Unfortunately, you meet a pantheist in me—to whom the immeasurable world already is quite wide enough."

CONTINGENCY AS REVELATION

Pantheism was not a neutral term when Novalis wrote his dialogue at the close of the eighteenth century. By identifying as a pantheist, he was intervening in a controversy about the compatibility of faith and reason that had peaked a decade prior on New Year's Eve 1785. That night, the famed philosopher of the Jewish Enlightenment Moses Mendelssohn hurried to the printer, his coat forgotten in his haste to publish his latest defense of his friend Gotthold Lessing against the charges of Spinozism raised against him by Friedrich Heinrich Jacobi (1743–1819). Less than a week later, Mendelssohn, old and overtaxed by his recent public altercations, died of a cold. The stakes of the argument were clear to everyone involved: if Jacobi were right that the recently deceased Lessing, the most widely respected Enlightenment figure in Prussia, had admitted that reason led him ineluctably to Spinozism—which is to say, to atheism and fatalism, according to the dominant understanding of the time—then the entire Enlightenment emphasis on reason could be called into question as antithetical to faith. Just as clear are the outcomes of that debate. In response to the scandal, Reinhold published his *Briefe an die kantische Philosophie*, catapulting Kant to fame by arguing that his philosophy alone provided a way to mediate between the demands of faith and reason. And ironically enough, rather than discrediting Spinoza or leaving him to lie as a "dead dog," Jacobi's attack introduced Spinoza to a new generation of enthusiastic readers among the young intellectual left of the early German Romantics.

Novalis was one of these enthusiastic young readers of Spinoza, introduced to his scandalous equation of God with nature at the exact moment when both the French Revolution and Pietism, with its emphasis on the personal, affective experience of God, was pushing young, radical intellectuals to look for a democratic form of religiosity accessible to all. As Frederick Beiser has glossed the situation, the far left-wing of the German Enlightenment felt that the Reformation had ended by betraying its initial insights into the priesthood of all believers, freedom of conscience, and the necessity of a personal relationship with God. While Luther had achieved his direct connection to God through the Bible, after Spinoza published his *Tractatus Theologico-Politicus* arguing for a historical interpretation of Scripture, the literal authority of the Bible came into question.

Unable to trust the authority of the Bible, and alienated from the formal structure of the Church, many of these thinkers looked inward for an immediate experience of the divine. The God of pantheism, they reasoned, was internal and accessible to anyone who reflected on herself, whereas the God of theism only selectively revealed himself to the external world. Thus, in Heinrich Heine's words, pantheism became "the religion of the radicals" who saw it as able to fulfill a political and religious promise for equality and direct access to God.[34]

Contingency, for Novalis, was the pantheist's central form of religious experience. In *Das Allgemeine Brouillon*, he even goes so far as to call contingency "contact with a higher being—a problem, and the *data* of the active religious *sense*."[35] That is to say, it is a *positive* source of religious knowledge. How that comes to pass and what this religion looks like will be the subject of this section, first in a consideration of the theological roots of the encyclopedia's structure and then in an analysis of how chance encounters with books feed into a much broader set of philosophical and theological beliefs about the human relation to the infinite or absolute.

Any discussion of religion in *Das Allgemeine Brouillon* inevitably centers on the meaning of entry 557, "My book shall be a scientific bible—a real, and ideal model—and the seed of all books." Earlier scholars, such as Hans Blumenberg, speculated that Novalis meant to write a Romantic gospel of sorts. Such a work would be a response to Lessing's call at the end of *The Education of the Human Race* for "a new, eternal gospel, which is itself promised in the elementary books of the new covenant."[36] In 1799 Novalis *did* in fact consider collaborating with Ludwig Tieck, Friedrich Schlegel, and Friedrich Schleiermacher to compose something along those lines, though it ultimately never came to fruition. In contrast, most contemporary scholars tend to interpret the term *bible* as a catchall, or a *Gattungsbegriff* for any book meant to organize a discipline as a whole. Under this reading, we should understand Novalis's project as more akin to popular guidebooks, such as the "Bartender's Bible," than to the Christian Bible.[37]

Ultimately, though, this debate seems misguided. While I agree with contemporary thinkers that *Das Allgemeine Brouillon* cannot be feasibly understood as a gospel in any straightforward sense, buzzwords do not define the presence of religion. Even if the word *bible* were dropped altogether from Novalis's encyclopedia, his work would still be implicated in theology, both through his reliance on analogy throughout the work and by his consistent coupling of chance with revelation.

Novalis's reliance on analogy structures *Das Allgemeine Brouillon* and explains some of the idiosyncrasies of the text, particularly when compared to more traditional encyclopedias. The sheer strangeness of its structure does not immediately present itself to the new reader of *Das Allgemeine Brouillon*. Like other encyclopedias, it has entries with different headings. Those entries are relatively short, sometimes a few lines, sometimes a page or two, but never much longer than that. Yet, the headings are not alphabetized, or even put in *any* discernible order, though they are idiosyncratically numbered. Rather than weaving together individual entries on countries or birds or continents, *Das Allgemeine Brouillon* speaks of sciences, disciplines, and genres. Some typical entry headings include "physiology," "mathematics," "philosophy," "medicine," and "encyclopedistics," by far the most common category. And the headings are strange, not least because they repeat throughout the text at apparently random intervals, but never cross-reference other topics. Instead, the categories are organized around analogies of the relationships between sciences.[38] As he notes in his clearest discussion of encyclopedistics, he devotes one hour each day to studying, "encyclopedistics in general. This includes scientific algebra—equations. Relationships—similarities—equalities—effects of the sciences on each other."[39] Instead of relating vertically to a species or genus of a particular concept, each entry connects laterally to different sciences and to different readings of itself. Novalis denies the reader a stable perspective on the sciences she studies, shuffling her instead from question to question.

This reliance on analogy feeds into the broader epistemic humility evidenced in Novalis's antifoundationalist commitments. At the time when Novalis wrote, there was a debate raging about the use of analogy in scientific work. Was it unscientific and sloppy or a mark of a thinker's willingness to accept his own limitations? Analogy was one of the greatest points of contention between Kant and the generation that followed him. For example, Kant famously rebuked the work of Herder, his former student, for using analogy as a form of philosophical reasoning, despite the fact that Herder cribbed the method from Kant's early work, *Allgemeine Naturgeschichte und Theorie des Himmels*. Analogy was insufficiently rigorous, the argument ran, incapable of proving scientific truths and substituting instead illegitimate speculation as fact. In a magnificently haughty moment, Herder retorted,

> Just as our whole psychology consists of figurative terms, for the most part it was a single new image, a single analogy, a single striking metaphor that gave birth to the greatest and boldest theories. The philosophers who declaim against figurative language and themselves serve nothing but old, often uncomprehended, figurative idols are at least in great contradiction with themselves. . . . But how so? Is there in this "analogy

to the human being" also truth? Human truth, certainly, and
as long as I am a human being I have no information about any
higher.[40]

In the previous section I read Novalis as consistently referring
back to his implication in a much wider natural, spiritual, and
intellectual world. He used analogy and unorthodox arrangement of his encyclopedia entries to do that work methodologi-
cally; he made reference to the material dimension of the book
he wrote and the contingency of his reader to do the same
philosophically.

In so doing, Novalis was participating in a theological tradition as much as a mathematical one. While analogy first arose
among Greek mathematicians such as Achytas and Euclid to
denote proportions or equal ratios between two sets of numbers,
theologians in the intervening centuries had transformed it into
one of the primary ways of speaking about an ungraspable God
or, alternately, extrapolating legal rulings for new social situations based on rules or verdicts found in Scriptures. The Neoplatonists used analogy in two senses: first, to speak about God
and, second, to "provide a principle of unity between various levels of reality."[41] As the scholar Battista Mondin explains, for the
Neoplatonists, "reality is proportionately distributed in different
degrees. This proportionate distribution is called analogy. The
degree of reality of something is designated by its definite 'pro-
portion' to things of higher and lower grades."[42] Similarly, Thomas
Aquinas offered the most famous Christian example of this trend
when he asserted that humans were so far beneath God that they
could not properly be understood as sharing the same qualities
any more than human love could be equated to the relation
between a drone bee and its queen in a hive; yet, given that

humans were created in the image of God, their goodness could at least point toward God's transcendent version of the same quality. Thus, human qualities, like goodness, could only be analogous to God's version of goodness.[43]

Novalis was hardly a traditional theist in Aquinas's line, but, like a good Thomist, he was sensitive to the limits of human knowledge. And that, I think, was why locating revelation in contingency was so appealing to him. It stripped away the pretensions of controlling revelation or gaining full knowledge of transcendence. Even more important, whatever insight we gain from "chance contact" returns us to the material world.

To fully explain why I think Novalis ties the chance contact with religious datum to the world, I want to explore his most significant passage on contingency in his first volume of philosophical fragments called *Pollen*. The passage opens with Novalis dismissing the idea that humans can never rise above their senses as tantamount to equating human with animals. He does admit that doing so is extraordinarily difficult for man, writing:

> It is true that under these circumstances reflection, the discovery of himself—is very difficult, since he is so ceaselessly, so necessarily connected with the change in our other circumstances. But the more conscious of these circumstances we can be, the more lively, powerful and ample is the conviction which derives from them—the belief in true revelations of the spirit. It is not seeing—hearing—feeling—it is a combination of all three—more than all three—a sensation of immediate certainty—a view of my truest, most actual life—thoughts change into laws—wishes are fulfilled . . . The phenomenon becomes especially striking at the sight of many human forms and faces—particularly so on catching sight of many eyes, expressions, movements—on hearing certain words, reading certain passages—at certain views of life,

world, and fate. Very many chance incidents, many natural events, particular times of day and year bring us such experiences. Certain moods are especially favorable to such revelations. Most last only an instant—few linger—fewest of all remain.[44]

The crux of the difficulty Novalis locates is embodied in the grammatical shift in person in the first sentence. In German it runs, "Freylich ist die Besonnenheit in diesem Zustande, die Sich Selbst Findung -sehr schwer, da *er* so unaufhörlich, so nothwendig mit dem Wechsel *unsrer* übrigen Zustände verbunden ist." *Er*, "he," refers clearly enough to *der Mensch*, introduced in the previous sentence, who seeks to find "himself" (*Sich Selbst*), but in the latter half of the sentence the subject switches abruptly to "*our* circumstances." I take this shift to be signaling just how difficult that man's goal is to attain. In a certain sense, if it were his own circumstances that were hopelessly bound up in his circumstances of reflection, he would be halfway to a solution. To be able to delineate "my" circumstances, a sphere proper to my own life and action, would be to have at least a start on the question of what constitutes my self and my concerns. Novalis's grammar, however, undermines that pretension of (relative) autonomy by reminding us that circumstances are never solely one's own; they are always tied to other people. *Nothing* is really ever solely mine, not so long as I covet things other people can see, admire landscapes where others walk, and own objects that brush up against other objects.

We have no choice, then, but to rise to the glimpse of our truest self by going through our embodied, embedded senses, because the content of revelation, for Novalis, is not some self isolated from the world, it is a glimpse into a whole where everything is connected. The link he draws between chance moods and events that momentarily allow us to see that fact is not accidental. Rather, the very essence of contingency—of the fact that events and moods and objects can come from other quarters of the world to disrupt our lives—is that it clues us into a reality where everything is connected, everything touches.

But what sort of touch does Novalis envision between the human and divine? Mystical union? Endless longing? The answer, I think, comes from the line I cited a few pages ago: "All chance is wondrous—contact [*Berührung*] with a higher being—a problem, and the *data* of the active religious *sense*."[45] Put simply, contact always has a double meaning of distance and closeness. He states that fact baldly in certain passages, but the very structure of his sentence mirrors the relation it describes. Here dashes set contact apart as a fragment that both breaks and sutures together two halves of a sentence that would never make a symmetrical whole. Does the interjection "—contact with a higher being—" make the transition from the wondrous to a problem, from affect to intellect, from an adjective to a noun, more or less jarring? I am never sure, even after the hours I have spent reading this line.

I do know that Novalis riffs on that disruptive, connective ambiguity with other structures throughout the text. In other places contact comes in a parenthetical remark, as in entry 295 on "cosmology," where he writes, "(No connection without separation. Contact is both separation and connection)."[46] Still in others contact (or touch) functions less as an interruption than as one in a series of words, sentences, and clauses telegraphed to the reader, as when Novalis jots down the following: "904. Instinct, as the feeling of need and incompleteness—is also the feeling of cohesion, of constancy—the conductive—orientating sense of touch itself—(Thus it is instinct that causes the bolt of lightning to strike down into the metal chain.) The raw, synthetic completing impulse—is a transitory—pointlike ego."[47] The entirety of *Das Allgemeine Brouillon,* taken as an aesthetic, visual object, hangs together by dashes that at once push their way between words and lasso them back together to form new cadences and new meanings. I believe this is not an accident; rather, the text, taken as an aesthetic object, serves as a synecdoche for Novalis's theology, a vision of a whole at once connected at every part and riddled with empty spaces of disjunction.

As such, *Das Allgemeine Brouillon* provides clues on how its reader should approach both itself, qua text, and the whole or the infinite it stands in for. Or, perhaps given Novalis's love of analogy, a better way to formulate this proposition would be to say that the reader's relation to the text in front of her is analogous to the subject's relation to the whole. What do I mean? Return, for a moment to the passage I just cited. At its base, Novalis suggests, instinct—the most primal, unreasoning, prerational facet of any creature—is a feeling of wanting. Yet in its sense of incompletion and need, instinct creates a coherent identity of sorts, albeit of a creature reaching out in every direction, fumbling to feel out the contours of its surroundings. Lightning strikes the links of a metal chain because it is incomplete within itself; the eye of the reader runs from letter to letter, word to word, dash to dash in order discover in their connection the meaning of the passage that she wants; and the subject blindly gropes for the totality that surrounds her, knowing herself best in the moments when she is most sensitive to the circumstances that surround her.

Novalis's emphasis on incompletion, contingency, and particularity feeds into an broader understanding of revelation. All philosophy, all thought, can never be anything but particular, shaded by individual experience, location, and moods, as Novalis suggests in the passage cited earlier about recognizing one's truest selfs. And that means that the experience of thumbing through a book, of feeling myself thrown against my contingency in my contact with a world that eludes and the horizon of my thoughts cramped and confined by the position of my body, is not merely incidental. It is exactly the point; it is exactly what Novalis takes to be the central insight of philosophy. Contingency always has a double movement for Novalis. It at once lets us touch an immeasurable reality while throwing us back on our particularity. Chance is never empty; it is always an opening into a broader reality. Still, there is nothing outside chance, at least not for me. There is nothing other than that moment of contingency realized in my reading, my contact with new knowledge; there are only books.

CONTINGENCY AS SICKNESS

And yet this very sensitivity to the thingness of books, to the heft and depth of volumes that may molder in a forgotten trunk in a Bavarian basement or be recycled into the grease-stained paper wrapped by Victorians around their cheese, or simply sit mutely on my shelves, makes me suspicious of Wellmon's emphasis on reading. It is not much of a challenge to the narcissistic sovereignty of scholarly reason to replace the old dream of a philosophy that could master the world with a new theory of books. Vladimir Putin steps down as prime minister to become president and a philosopher-poet politely declines to claim knowledge of the Absolute, only to feign blushing astonishment that *books* turn out to provide privileged access to reality. I understand the generous reading of course: books are only the starting point in the revolt of things. Wellmon's Novalis emphasizes books because it is the fastest way to unseat the smug certainty of his educated readers. After all, if books—the most basic tool of our trade, the object of our study, and the harvest of our labor—can escape us, what does that mean about the subjects we actually write about? Stressing the alterity of books, in this interpretation, really displays the profoundest humility, rather than the self-absorption I so uncharitably ascribe to the enterprise.

Bracketing the issue of whether or not the generous reading is correct, the question remains: *does* Novalis really privilege the material book as offering unique access to our contingency and, by extension, revelatory contact with an ungraspable whole? Might there be another encounter with contingency, another set of motivations for grappling with our fragile place in time and space germane to a less rarefied and less literary crowd? I believe so. Books and the moods in which we encounter them are central to Novalis's account of contingency, but they belong to a much deeper experience of contingency rooted in the science of the senses during Novalis's era and, crucially, the suffering of the sickened body.

In particular, to understand what Novalis meant by touch, and how it came to assume such a central place in his epistemology, I want to spend some time with the work of Albrecht von Haller (1708–1777) and John Brown (1735–1788), two scientists Novalis mentions explicitly in *Das Allgemeine Brouillon* who offered a tactile model of illness, energy, and neurosis. Haller, the elder of the two thinkers, was a Swiss poet and physiologist. On April 22, 1752, he presented his most famous scholarly paper to the scientific society at Göttingen, *A Dissertation on the Sensible and Irritable Parts of Animals*. Starting in 1746, Haller experimented on 190 different animals, ranging from goats to dogs to frogs. After six years of burning skin, lacerating tendons, severing nerves, opening the skulls of conscious dogs, and pouring acid on their uteri, Haller emerged with a new theory of sensation and motion. He proposed two main properties of muscles:

irritability and sensibility. "I call that part of the human body irritable, which becomes shorter upon being touched," he begins, before continuing:

> I call that a sensible part of the human body, which upon being touched transmits the impression of it to the soul; and in brutes, in whom the existence of a soul is not so clear, I call sensible, the Irritation of which occasions evident signs of pain and disquiet in the animal. On the contrary, I call that insensible, which being burnt, tore, pricked, or cut till it is quite destroyed, occasions no sign of pain nor convulsions, nor any sign of change in the situation."[48]

The nerves and, above all, the skin were the site of sensibility in Haller's account, just as the muscles were for irritability. The two properties never coexisted in the same organ. A nerve, no matter how plucked or prodded, never contracts in pain, while muscles continued their irritable spasming often long after death itself. "Irritability," Haller concludes, "therefore is independent of the soul and the will."[49]

Haller's research prompted a new set of investigations into the nervous system during the 1750s and 1760s, with particular attention to the role of nervous disorders in the genesis of diseases.[50] One of Haller's followers was a professor at Edinburgh, William Cullen (1712–1790), who briefly taught John Brown and employed him as a tutor for his children. The relationship fell apart, however, when he accused Brown of plagiarizing his ideas. Brown eventually was forced to complete his medical degree at St. Andrews, in 1779, after nearly a decade studying at the University of Edinburgh. A year later he published *Elementa Medicinae*, the text that underlies so many of Novalis's theories.[51] Brown's work launched from Haller's distinction between irritability and sensibility. He wrote, "all states of life, man and other animals differ from themselves in their dead state, or from any other inanimate matter in this property alone: that they can be affected by external agents, as well as by certain functions peculiar to themselves."[52]

In contrast to Haller, Brown believed that organism are not solely passive. Instead, each at birth receives a certain degree of "excitability." As to what excitability was or how exactly it interacted with stimuli or "exciting powers," Brown pleaded ignorance. The exciting powers were a combination of external stimuli, such as heat, food, and air, and internal stimuli, including thoughts and the emotions. Excitability formed a triad necessary for life with the internal and external exciting powers. While the exciting powers fed on excitability, draining it faster than it could be renewed as life progressed, the cessation of either excitability or the exciting powers would result in immediate death. The powers that made life possible inexorably and directly ended in death; the only question was how quickly.

Health, then, depended on the proper balance of stimulation. Overstimulation resulted in sthenic diseases of exhaustion, while understimulation led to asthenic diseases that, at their extreme, culminated in death. Brown accordingly thought that diseases could be treated by adjusting the amount of stimulation the patient received. As he considered most diseases asthenic, he prescribed, in theory, spirits, and seasoned food. In practice, though, he usually recommended opium as a faster and much more efficacious remedy. Following his own advice too well, Brown eventually died wrecked by his drug and alcohol addictions.

Plausible or not, Brown's work matters to my account because, through its discussion of health, it introduced singularity and contingency into Haller's mechanistic, tactile account of the nerves. Haller's scientific model of irritability was always, at base, a tactile one. He pricked a muscle and it contracted; he plucked a nerve and it sent pain data to the soul. Haller's experiments were controlled, and the laws he derived from them were regular, mechanistic, and consistent. Brown kept the importance of touch, but introduced contingency into Haller's orderly account by pursuing sickness to its most individual level. Perhaps he might have avoided the philosophical embarrassment of inventing excitability if he had been willing to leave his theory of stimulation on a more general level and made the basic suggestion that health was determined by over- or understimulation. Instead, he asked a more personal question: Why am I prone to illness and another not? Why does the battering of my senses by a common world leave me exhausted and ill but another seemingly untouched? Why this disease? Why now? Why me? That was where his account broke down. That was where contingency entered in the form of excitability.

Brown's work began to gain popularity in Germany after 1795, when A. K. Weikard translated his *Elementa Medicinae* into German, but the theory of irritability circulated earlier, most notably in Herder's references to Haller in his 1778 *On the Cognition and Sensation of the Human Soul*. Herder taught in Jena alongside Novalis's teacher, Friedrich Schiller, and we know Novalis read Herder's work, based on the admiring references he makes to his prose in *Das Allgemeine Brouillon*.[53] The connection matters because Herder combined the British theories of irritability with a belief that the acuteness of the senses is historically and even biographically conditioned. Novalis would pick up on that set of concerns and go on to pathologize them. For that reason, I want to linger a bit longer on Herder before returning to Novalis.

In his 1778 piece, Herder turned to irritability in order to bridge the mind-body divide, casting the workings of the nerves as at once a physical and psychological phenomenon. In many ways, Herder's early writings on the senses anticipated Brown's notion of excitability by attributing the workings of the nerves to an unquantifiable sensitivity. In a 1766 essay, "On the Change of Taste: On the Diversity of Taste and of Manners of Thought Among Human Beings," Herder addressed the question of relativism in taste.[54] A philosopher, he observes, must be struck by the differences in taste across nations. Unlike Kant in his later work, however, Herder dismisses the effort to subsume taste under a universal standard and turns, instead, to differences in the sensitivity of the senses to account for these discrepancies. Herder believes in broad, national, racial differences in the senses, noting, significantly for our purposes, that Europeans have exceptionally weak senses because they are so accustomed to abstract thought. Yet senses also differed from individual to individual, for a combination of biological, autobiographical, and utterly unknowable reasons. "No human being," he insists, "is exactly in agreement in feeling with another, because it cannot easily be the case that in two human beings the whole structure of the nerves is *entirely* tuned in a single way. That is why so many people have a *stubbornly idiosyncratic* sense of feeling which noticeably deviates now in this matter and now in that from the sensation of another person."[55]

After musing on other examples of the singularity of nerves— one man's voluptuous thrill at caressing velvet, another's shudder at the yelp of a dog, a third's desire to jump out of his skin at the sight of a particular color—Herder asks whether or not it would be possible to prevent "such a *stubbornly idiosyncratic* sort of sensation."[56] Flicking the question aside, Herder rejoins, "hardly!," noting that so much depends on the structure of nerves. "Their fiber-web has so to speak received a pitch that is peculiar to it through a *contingent event*" that may have happened in the womb.[57] Which is not to say that the senses are wholly outside of individual control. Herder thinks social norms do a tremendous amount to shape the squeamishness or coarseness of individuals, turning the sensitivity of the senses into a mark of class and conformity to gender norms. I would need to climb into another woman's body to understand whether or not we really shared the same sense of touch.

Novalis follows Herder in insisting on the historical contingency of the senses as we now know them, yet goes even further by pathologizing them. Wellmon yet again offers the best account of Novalis's stance, this time in an article called "Lyrical Feeling: Novalis's Anthropology of the Senses." Like Herder, Novalis believes that the contemporary experience of the senses changes across time and space. Novalis goes even farther than Herder, though, by asking if our current division of the senses into five is constant throughout history. In his *Fichte Studien*, Novalis mulls over the possibility of a single sense that would preexist and ground the individual senses of touch, taste, sight, smell, and hearing.[58] When Novalis speaks of this originary, unified sense as grounding the others, Novalis means that touch, taste, and smell would be "modifications, individuations of the category sense." This "total sense" would be a product of the imagination, as opposed to the individual senses that belong to physiology. Yet the total sense can not be thought directly; it is, in Novalis's words, "negative material."[59] Any discussion of it must proceed apophatically, through the individuated senses we possess.

Nevertheless, the world Novalis dreams of, where we have access to a single, primordial sense, is not our own; rather, we live in one where bodily experience is rent apart at every turn. I mean the division into individual senses, yes, but also a more fundamental cleavage between the types of senses. Novalis believes we possess two separate sets of senses: an inner, which takes as its stimuli mental phenomena, and an outer, which responds to the external world. Borrowing from Brown and Haller, he maps this distinction onto the concepts of sensibility and irritability, so that sensibility perceives internally produced mental or nervous experiences, while irritability does the same for external, worldly events. The two types of senses exist separately, but can form any number of relations with each other. Ideally, the two would be in perfect harmony, with neither the inner nor outer sense dominating the other. In his fondest dreams, Novalis even imagines that they might harmonize together so well that the distinctions would be blurred and, in Wellmon's summary, "future senses would mediate not just from world to mind but from mind to world."[60] Or, put otherwise, the inner sense or mind, as Wellmon names it, would not simply perceive and receive mental or nervous phenomena; it would be able to actively change the external world through thought alone.

I will return to that startling thought in the final section of this chapter; for the moment, I want to stress the historical contingency of the relationship between the inner and outer senses. If historical and bodily contingency come together for Herder in imperceptible events in the womb that string an individual's nerves to a certain pitch, for Novalis the same occurs on a broader cultural scale when technological, intellectual, social, and spiritual developments come together to influence the balance between the inner or outer senses. Our senses—inner and outer—could be otherwise and have been otherwise, which must have been something of a relief for Novalis to conclude, since he firmly believes that the current state is in a rather bad way.

The contemporary world is sick, Novalis believes, from the intellectual culture of abstraction I opened this chapter by discussing. As he writes in entry 274, "Too much abstraction produces asthenia—too much reflection, sthenia. I must reflect a lot more and abstract a lot less. I already possess enough irritability. An acute thinker is a sensitive meter—an extremely subtle reactant."[61] In essence, the push of Enlightenment encyclopedists—of the entire intellectual culture of systematizing—is not a neutral one. Rather, it deadens our senses by pulling us away from the world or teaching us to see books as thoughts, not things. Yet we need a certain amount of stimulation by the world in order to remain healthy. We, as a culture, suffer from diseases of exhaustion and understimulation. Our inability to see the world of things we live in, to recognize the material basis of knowledge, is not a problem for simply philosophical or ideological reasons; it is actively making us ill.

Perhaps this chapter could end here, having suggested a reading of Novalis that makes the bodily, affective experience of contingency central to his critique of foundationalism and the abstract ordering of knowledge, the religious experience of pantheism, and his diagnosis of the illness of the modern European. But a diagnosis is not yet a cure. What that cure might look like and how it fits into his account of contingency will be the topic of my final section.

FAIRY TALES, MAGICAL IDEALISM, AND CONTINGENCY'S CURE

This section might initially seem undermotivated. After all, if Novalis believes that he, like his culture more generally, suffers from sthenic diseases and names the whole edifice of disembodied, placeless knowledge as a part of the cause, it seems we should return to an emphasis on the contingent, material book outlined in the first section of this chapter. The idea that an awareness of contingency has liberatory potential on both a physical and intellectual plane is consistent with the centrality I have given experience in his thought. Nevertheless, a problem remains: we suffer from understimulation of the senses, but if we were to go in the opposite direction and emphasize the awareness of the physical world contingency brings, what would prevent us from contracting a whole new host of diseases from overstimulation? The answer to that question lies in Novalis's theory of magical idealism, his skeletal, idiosyncratic philosophy that sought to gain total control over the senses, and, surprisingly enough, his theory of fairy tales. Combined, magical idealism and fairy tales provide something like an answer to Kant's famous question, "What can I hope for?"

Magical idealism, often uncomfortably skirted around or tactfully omitted from histories of philosophy, is at its center an answer to Kant's question; it tells us we can hope for health. But what was magical idealism? Where does it fit into Novalis's thought? Novalis makes only passing mention of magical idealism, mainly in *Das Allgemeine Brouillon*, but also in his *Vorarbeiten* of 1797. Contemporary scholars agree that Novalis considered it to be his own., personal philosophy, even calling it "Mein magischer Idealismus" at points.[62] There is less consensus on whether or not Novalis abandoned it in the final few years of his life, but for my purposes that is not terribly important. Despite the telegraphic nature of his remarks on it, a reasonably clear sketch of the system has emerged in recent years.

The main aim or hope of magical idealism is to gain the power to voluntarily control our senses in the same way we now direct our thoughts, will, and speech. This aspiration rests on the distinction between inner and outer sense that I mentioned in the previous section. Most discussion of this depends on entry 338.

> If you are unable to make thoughts indirectly (and fortuitously) perceptible, then try the converse, and make external things directly perceptible (and at will)—which amounts to saying, if you are unable to transform thoughts into external things, then transform external things into thoughts. If you are unable to make a thought into something independent, something separate from yourself—and *therefore* also something *extraneous*—that is, into an externally occurring soul, then proceed in the opposite manner with external things—and transform them into thoughts.
>
> Both operations are idealistic. Whosoever has both completely in his power, is a *Magical Idealist*. Shouldn't the perfection of each of these two operations be dependent on the other?[63]

As Frederick Beiser summarizes it, "Thanks to our powers of attention and abstraction, Novalis writes, we have control over our internal senses. We have the power to determine what we perceive within ourselves by abstracting from, or directing our attention to, some things rather than others."[64] If we can do so for our inner sense, the thought runs, why not our external senses?

In addition to mastering the senses, Novalis also suggests that the magical idealist should strive to increase the amount of internal stimuli he receives until it matches the external. "The external stimulus is already present in its immeasurability," he writes, "and is for the most part under the control of the artist. Yet how slight is the inner stimulus in contrast to the outer. Thus the main concern facing the artist of immortality is the gradual increase in the inner stimulus. In this regard, aren't we then justified in

pronouncing what the poets have already strangely foretold—
that the Muses alone grant immortality. The scholarly class too
now appears in a new light. My Magical Idealism."[65] Thinking
back on my earlier discussion of how Novalis imagines a world
where the internal and external senses are in harmony, it becomes
clear that the capacity to sense at will is grounded in the equi-
table and harmonious relationship between inner and outer sense.
We will never get to the state of willful control over the body
until inner and outer senses work so seamlessly in tandem that
the stimuli affecting one can affect the other. We are at the
moment too overwhelmed by the external, too little focused on
the internal, for all the abstraction of the Enlightenment
encyclopedia.

If this sounds like my discussion of Brown, it ought to do so.
Brown's influence—no matter how bad his science—does a lot
to make magical idealism more sympathetic as a project. Taken
cold, magical idealism sounds either like the most hubristic form
of mastery possible within the modern project or frankly absurd.
It would seem that Novalis's desire to direct his senses where he
willed would undermine the contingency of our contact with
knowledge that I began with in my discussion of the encyclopedia. What good would it do to rescue books from their liquida-
tion into abstract ideas if we one day hope to gain total control
over how we sense the books we hold? At least the roots of the
project in medicine remind us that the starting point for Novalis is sickness; at least Brown reminds us that Novalis was seeking health.

There are other reasons to hesitate before dismissing magical
idealism immediately; to start, the centrality of aesthetics to his
vision of the world we might create means that our new relation
to contingency and the senses is not nearly as soulless as might
be expected. Once we gain complete control over our senses,

Novalis thinks, we will be able to live in a world of our own creation. He means this in two different respects. First, Novalis
genuinely considers himself part of the tradition of Idealism
because he believes our perception depends on our own creative
activity. He happily follows Kant's suggestion that we never simply perceive something as it is; rather, we always bring something to perception, whether by synthesizing intuition and concepts, in Kant's case, or in voluntarily directing the senses to an
object, in Novalis's. Moreover, he follows Kant in arguing that
we know something because we make it. As he writes in his philosophical fragments predating *Das Allgemeine Brouillon*, "We
know something only insofar as we *express* it—i.e., can *make* it.
The more completely and diversely we can *produce, execute* something, the better we *know* it. We know a thing perfectly when
we can communicate it, arouse it everywhere and in all ways—
if we can produce an individual *expression* of it in each organ."[66]
(It is worth noting that "*express*" in this sentence is "ausdrücken"
in German, with *drücken* the same verb as "to print.") Given my
analysis of the encyclopedia thus far, I think the etymological
link points back to the material basis of Novalis's transcendental
project. It implies that "to express" is not solely an intellectual,
cognitive exercise; rather, it involves a material alteration of the
world, as when thoughts are transformed into printed books.
Under the influence of Fichte, however, Novalis holds that our
cognitive faculties obey the commands of the will. In essence,
knowing depends on making, and making depends on willing,
therefore the world in which we dwell depends on the will itself.

Second, fully realized magical idealism would not solely be a
state in which we would master and manipulate nature; rather,
it would mean becoming more receptive to stimuli. The end state
would be an aesthetic one where internal and external senses
would enjoy a harmonious free play with each other without

either losing its identity. Novalis, however, explicitly models his vision on the work of art, specifically the novel where "the voluntary appears like chance and the chance voluntary."[67] Controlling our senses is as much a creative, receptive endeavor as an effort of mastery. It involves passivity and manipulation all at once.[68]

Though the novel may model magical idealism brought to fruition, another literary genre, *Märchen* or fairy tale, serves the much more complicated function of coaching us on how to view our current era of suffering and contingency while also training us in how to emotionally orient ourselves toward the promised future. I want to end, then, by briefly analyzing the way in which fairy tales serve within Novalis's work to create an uneasy resolution between the revelatory and pathological connotations of contingency.

The link between contingency, fairy tales, and religion is relatively easy to establish. At the start of a chapter titled "Toward a Metaphysics of Märchen," Kristin Pfefferkorn offers a catalogue of the relationships between myths, *Märchen*, fairy tales, legends, sagas, and fables. The details are less important than her conclusion that the *Märchen* "is a secularized myth, which not infrequently serves the myth as graveyard."[69] The key feature of the *Märchen* in her reading is that it "matter-of-factly assumes and the proceeds to illustrate the sudden and inexplicable intervention of chance in the orderly affairs of man and nature."[70] Fairy tales are propelled by chance—chance meetings of old crones in the woods, chance conversations with talking frogs, and chance acts of kindness to helpless children or animals.

We can see the centrality of chance in Novalis's own definition of the *Märchen*. "A fairy tale, is really a dream picture— devoid of all coherence—an ensemble of wondrous things and happenings—a musical fantasy for instance—the harmonious

effects of an Aeolian harp—Nature herself." Pausing to medi-
tate on the structure of a fairy tale, Novalis continues, "If a story
is introduced into a fairy tale, then this is already a foreign
intrusion.—A series of clever, entertaining attempts, an alternat-
ing conversation, and a masquerade—are all fairy tales. We are
dealing with a higher fairy tale, if without putting to flight its
spirit, we introduce some element of understanding into it—
(coherence, meaning—etc.)"[71] At other places, he classes Goethe's
Bildungsroman, Wilhelm Meister, as a fairy tale of sorts.[72] Novalis
makes it clear that the world of a fairy tale is not our own. It is
a "dream image," a world of pure chaos where "the whole of
Nature must be interwoven in a wondrous manner with the entire
spirit world."[73] As such, it is absolutely opposite, though similar,
to the world of history and a "prophetic representation of a
world to come." None of this should sound particularly new. As
established, Novalis's ideal future is a world of wholeness where
inner and outer sense, spirit and nature, work and communicate
seamlessly in tandem.

As Pfefferkorn reads it, Novalis's fascination with the fairy
tale stems in part from the way it mirrors our own dual experience of time as quantitative and qualitative. On the one hand,
the fairy tale is nominally linear, and its plot depends on a fairly
conventional flow of time, where one event succeeds another. On
the other hand, it is shot through with moments of chance, when
liminal beings disrupt the steady march of minutes and jerk the
story sideways in order to briefly unveil divine meaning or order.[74]
However, while Pfefferkorn reads the temporality of fairy tales
as fundamentally descriptive of our inner lives, I would argue
that for Novalis it is also prescriptive.

Because fairy tales portend a future world, I believe they serve
a didactic purpose in Novalis's thought. They tell us something
about how and what we ought to will in order to emulate most

closely the world to come. The key way in which they do so is in modeling a version of synthesis effected by desire. Novalis's version of synthesis when discussing the fairy tale is very distant from the Hegelian version, where internal contradiction necessarily propels a concept to incorporate its opposite meaning. Rather, synthesis is only ever arrived at indirectly. When discussing synthesis in terms of theories, Novalis suggests that a higher synthesis of two opposing theories naturally occurs when each is brought to perfection.[75] In fairy tales two contradictory terms come together and a third results accidentally as an unexpected result of seeking and desiring another end altogether.

This synthetic structure becomes most important for my project in a passage Novalis writes advocating the application of the synthesis found in fairy tales to our feelings toward illness. "A significant feature in many fairy tales," Novalis muses in note 653,

is that if the impossible becomes possible—then immediately something else impossible also unexpectedly becomes possible—that if man overcomes himself, he simultaneously overcomes Nature—and a wonder occurs, granting him the opposite pleasure in the very moment the opposite displeasure becomes pleasurable. *The conditions for magic*, e.g., the transformation of the bear into a prince the moment the bear becomes loved etc. Likewise in the fairy tale of the two genies. Perhaps a similar transformation would take place if man began to cherish the *affliction* in the world—In the instant man became fond of the illness or pain, the most enticing desire would repose in his arms—imbuing him with the highest positive pleasure. Mightn't *illness* be the means to a higher synthesis?—The more terrible the pain, the higher the hidden indwelling pleasure. (*Harmony.*) Perhaps every illness is the necessary beginning of an inner union of 2

beings—the necessary beginning of love. Enthusiasm for ill-
nesses and pain. Death—an intimate union of loving beings.[76]

Fairy tales, with the religious data they offer us in their contingent encounters and the impossible synthesis always at their axis,
allow us to fumble after this impossible, desirable moment when
chance and necessity become indistinguishable. We are, perhaps,
in our own fairy tale, if we could only see it.[77] Our chance encounters are not with crones in the woods, but with sights and sounds
that strike our senses, bombarding and disrupting the order of
our fevered frames. And in this story we are not expected to
redeem a frog or a bear with our love but the suffering of our
bodies instead. Fairy tales are the models of the impossible synthesis we must perform.

Or, rather, fairy tales are the models of the impossible synthesis we must allow to happen of its own accord. Fairy tales,
and really the entire discussion of synthesis, counsel patience and
the restructuring of our desires. In the end, for all the talk of
magical thinking that makes our thoughts immediately affect the
world and the injunctions to bring our inner and outer senses
into equilibrium, the possibility of ever realizing the aims of
magical idealism hinges on a remarkably tenuous thought that
the final synthesis of inner and outer will happen of its own
accord. In the interim, all that remains is the attempt to love the
affliction of our contingent, suffering bodies in the hope that
pain will be snatched away and they will become lovable in truth.

In a century filled with grandiose and slightly mad philosophical projects, magical idealism has the distinction of being just
too strange for serious philosophical rehabilitation. Even Manfred Frank, the biggest living proponent of Novalis's philosophical significance, focuses on his critical work at the expense of

magical idealism.[78] But magical idealism makes clearest Novalis's ambivalence toward contingency and offers, in its own
strange way, his own best efforts to manage its darker aspects.
Any single moment when he mentions *Zufall* would make for a
neat but unfaithful story. The Novalis who bucked the Enlightenment ideal of education by arguing for the power of material
books to throw us back on our partial connection to a world knit
together by chance might amiably pass time with the Novalis
who insisted on the particularity of the philosopher's thought as
a revolt against the dream of a first principle for all philosophy.
Those two versions of Novalis might even find in the third's
insistence on contingency as a mode of connection to higher
being a way to add nuance and hope to their rebellion. It is not
so clear, though, that they would recognize the version of Novalis who found contingency in the pitch of our nerves that leads
one person, one culture, one race to respond to the touch of the
external world with equanimity and the other with disease. Only
magical idealism holds together those aspects of contingency—
its rebelliousness against the status quo, its reminder of finitude,
its wonder, its horror, its incomprehensibility. For that reason
alone, it is worth studying.

Magical idealism sums up many of the virtues and problems
with Novalis as a philosopher. Yes, the science he uses is obsolete, and, yes, the pantheism he espouses may ring as somewhat
messy, but his thought never gets lost in itself or in unbridled
abstraction. There is always *some* experience of illness or leafing
through a novel that grounds his thought. My book is a work
about the affective and bodily experiences that make up our concept of contingency. It is about the moments when we are
ambushed by feelings we can never control, touches that leave
us sometimes raw, sometimes open, sometimes connected, but
always aware of our fragility as unnecessary creatures who pass

in and out of being. We see our loved ones sicken, sadden, and die, and, when we write books, sometimes the rhythm of our prose keeps time to the mortality of those we love. Whatever his flaws, Novalis captures that experience. He knew what it felt like to feel the tenuousness and unpredictability of life through an attack on his body because he himself would be dead within two years of abandoning *Das Allgemeine Brouillon* of the same tuberculosis that shredded the lungs of his fiancée.

But sickness is only one moment where contingency shows up as a problem. It says nothing about what it means to witness another beloved person's decline and death, for all that Novalis knew intimately of that pain. Evil, and loneliness, are only problems for survivors. Those would be the worries of an acquaintance of Novalis whose manuscripts suffered their own collision with history.

2

LONELINESS

LONELINESS AND THE LIMITS OF THEODICY IN SCHELLING'S PHILOSOPHICAL FABLE

Nearly 150 years after Novalis abandoned his encyclopedia, another equally puzzling manuscript went up in flames. It was July 1944, the introduction to Jason Wirth's translation of Friedrich Wilhelm Joseph von Schelling's 1815 *The Ages of the World* calmly informs us, and a plane had just bombed Munich. There was more than one plane—it had been four years since Churchill instituted the retaliatory firebombing of German cities—but the editor is only interested in one. This particular plane struck the University of Munich's library where, five years earlier, in 1939, a German scholar named Horst Fuhrman had stumbled across a chest in the library's basement, haphazardly crammed with sheaves of previously unknown manuscripts written in the sharply slanted handwriting of Schelling. At the time, Fuhrman counted two set and corrected versions, as well as twelve substantially different handwritten versions, of Schelling's unfinished, restlessly rewritten magnum opus, *Die Weltalter*, henceforth *The Ages of the World*.[1] Prior to this, only one version had been known to scholars, an 1815 draft published posthumously by Schelling's son. After three days of firebombing, that number would shrink again to three: one from 1811, one from 1813, and one from 1815. Long overshadowed by his former friend and rival, Hegel, it would take another fifty years before the second draft of Schelling's strange fragmentary work made it to any significant scholarly audience in English, courtesy of a new translation, the patronage of Slavoj Žižek, and, perhaps, a few million dead.

These history-charred parchments tell a half-literary, half-philosophical myth about the origin of the universe and God, written in anticipation of an era when "truth becomes fable and fable truth."[2] In them an all-encompassing will fractures from longing and, in a completely undetermined, contingent act, sets off in search of a counterpart in a move that will eventually snowball into the creation of the universe.

For all their similarity in time periods and circles, the attitude toward contingency in the second draft of Schelling's stuttering, abortive story of cosmic beginnings could not be more distant from the one discussed in the last chapter of Novalis's encyclopedia. If Novalis meditated on the ways certain kinds of touch bring home the contingent, limited nature of knowledge—whether that meant abstract intellectual knowledge delivered by the books that chanced into his hands or the more visceral knowledge of why *these* stimuli caused *this* illness in me and not another—Schelling worried about contingency felt through the absence of touch in order to speculate on no less than the birth of God. While Novalis immersed himself in the enthusiastically pantheistic world of Jena and early German Romanticism at the end of the eighteenth century, fifteen years later, Schelling had begun the middle period of a work that reimagined questions from Christian theology, such as the viability of theodicy, the nature of evil, and the creation of the universe. Even as Novalis tapped into an old theological anthropology to imagine contingency as a distinctively human problem, Schelling, in the most radical move of his career, overturned eighteen hundred years of orthodoxy to attribute the contingency normally reserved for creatures to God.

This last point, that Schelling attributed contingency to God, has been noted in scholarship but rarely, I think, properly understood. Scholars such as Žižek and Gabriel Markus have observed that Schelling's cosmogony begins with an apparently uncaused, undetermined act, as what Schelling terms "the eternal will" breaks from the primordial "will that wills nothing." Yet, in noting the contingency at the heart of Schelling's story, they have tended to couch the problem in German Idealism's familiar terms of freedom and necessity, rather than relating contingency back to the broader theological anthropology that this book tries to reclaim.

I am not trying to claim that Schelling has no interest in freedom in his text—after all, his arguably best-known work, *Treatise on the Essence of Human Freedom*, had only come out four years prior—but I am saying that placing *The Ages of the World* in this broader tradition that thinks of contingency through the passions and the flesh provides a better explanatory framework for his narrative decisions. More specifically, reading his text through the lens of loneliness clarifies why the narrative unfolds as it does, provides genuinely interesting psychological insights (similar to recent work on solitary confinement), and ultimately explains why Schelling came to reject the possibility of any consolation provided by theodicy.

Grasping how loneliness holds his tale together, however, requires taking Schelling at his word that he wrote a theological fable. The best way to do that is to offer a literary analysis of the images he invokes, set against the debates raised in his tumultuous years in Jena at the end of the eighteenth century.

HISTORY AND BACKGROUND OF SCHELLING'S INTELLECTUAL DEVELOPMENT

At the time when he was composing the second version of *The Ages of the World*, Schelling could have foreseen nothing of false starts, endless revisions, conflagrations, and obscurity. Nothing in his early career suggested a future of dusty basements for his work, though perhaps the older, wearier Schelling of the 1840s, who wrote that "there is in every deed, in all the toil and labor of man himself nothing but vanity,"[3] might have guessed at it. Unlike Hegel, whose peers mockingly referred to him as "the old man" for his plodding, methodical nature, Schelling was all restless energy and precocity. Born in 1775 in Leonberg, Württemberg, he spent his early years first attending a monastery school, where his father was an Orientalist professor and pastor, and then a Latin school, before being admitted to the Tübinger Stift at the age of sixteen, a full four years younger than was typical. He graduated with a degree in theology, though his interests gradually shifted toward philosophy, particularly once he began reading the work of Kant and Fichte. After a few years of working as a tutor, Schelling was called to Jena in 1798 to serve as an unpaid professor of philosophy. He was only twenty-three and had just gotten a job at Jena, the center of everything.

Descriptions of Schelling at that time sometimes read like a bad romance novel, filled with remarks about his "stubborn chin, curly hair, and flashing eyes."[4] Nevertheless, even in a time and place filled with unorthodox thinkers and artists, Schelling was noteworthy. In those early years, Schelling shared an overlapping social circle with Novalis. Nearly all the great thinkers of early German Romanticism and German Idealism lived in Jena in the late 1790s: Fichte (1762–1814), who was at the time hailed as the heir to Kant; Hegel (1770–1831), without whom there would have been no Marx; the brothers August (1767–1845) and Friedrich (1772–1829) Schlegel, who started the avant-garde journal *Athenaeum*, which sought to combine the literary and philosophical 150 years before Derrida; and Dorothea Veit (1764–1839), daughter of the famous Jewish figure of the Enlightenment Moses Mendelssohn and a novelist in her own right, who scandalized society by leaving her first husband for Friedrich Schlegel. Even Goethe visited, often dropping by to see Caroline Schlegel (1763–1809), August's wife and cotranslator of Shakespeare into German (a thoroughly remarkable woman whose daughter from her first marriage recent scholars suspect may have been Goethe's).[5]

As with Novalis, it was the first of these figures, Fichte, who triggered the avalanche in Schelling's thought that would land him at the problem of contingency in 1813. I mentioned in the last chapter that Fichte had risen to fame in the 1790s by criticizing Kant's philosophy as insufficiently systematic and attempting to ground human knowledge in a universal principle, namely, the self's awareness of the self while thinking. Novalis and Schelling had slightly different problems with Fichte, however. While Novalis worried about Fichte's efforts to find a first principle from which all thought originated (ignoring in the process the irreducible individuality and contingency of any given philosophical system), it was the psychology behind Fichte's philosophy Schelling objected to, as well as its ethical implications for the treatment of nature.

Schelling, who had once been an ardent admirer of Fichte, had come to believe that the result of Fichte's philosophy was to make human perception the measure of all reality. Human subjectivity might be opposed by external forces, particularly nature, but ultimately nature only mattered insofar as it served the development of human consciousness. Fichte had full faith in humanity's right to subordinate nature to human needs. In a prescient argument, Schelling anticipated a long train of critics who would accuse modernity of instrumentalizing nature when he castigated Fichte for seeing in nature only lumber for human tools, rather than a subject of value in its own right.[6] As a recent essay by Bruce Matthews argues, "Cutting straight to the heart of modernity's capitalist ambitions, Schelling demands that we stop exploiting nature by making it subservient to our immediate 'economic-teleological ends' as if it had no inherent value."[7] Instead, Schelling reversed Fichte's relation between the subject and nature, imagining reality as an organism with the human subject as the highest manifestation of nature. We are not prior to nature or in a position of control; we are nothing less than nature's efforts to become aware of itself. Which is to say, our subjectivity, our awareness, always depends on nature, a much larger, independently existing reality we can never fully access. It was this intuition, I argue, that set up the turn Schelling's work took in his middle period, the years that interest me.

Three major events happened to send Schelling's thought skittering sideways from his early preoccupations. The first was a personal tragedy, the second was his renewed interest in theology, and the third was the onset of his famous feud with Hegel. When Schelling began work on the second draft of *The Ages of the World* in 1813, he was only thirty-eight, still a relatively young man, but his life and thought looked tremendously different from his years in Jena. The social circle that had seemed so promising when he was twenty-three was a wreckage. Novalis had died in 1801, Schelling had decisively fallen out with Fichte, and the Schlegel brothers had broken with Schelling altogether after he had a very public affair with August's wife, Caroline Schlegel, a woman ten years older than he. He eventually married

Caroline—though not before the affair made it to the newspapers, as colleagues accused Schelling of killing Caroline's teenaged daughter with his medical interventions—and moved from position to position, running into constant conflict with his Catholic colleagues. Then, in 1809, Caroline contracted a short illness and died.

The loss of Caroline was a profound one. To be sure, Schelling did remarry; the year before he began writing the second draft of *The Ages of the World* he wed a friend of Caroline's he sometimes seemed to confuse with his dead wife. Still, the brave, sharp, magnetic woman who had once written him letters daydreaming about greeting him some morning by tracing the sign of the cross down his face with soft kisses (forehead, lips, left eye, right) was gone, and by all accounts he never fully recovered from that loss. Even ten years after her death, Schelling declined her sister's request that he return some of Caroline's old letters, explaining that her memory was still too painful to allow him to go though her old belongings. He certainly never published again, instead writing and rewriting the same fragment of a story about a will that wanted to return to nothingness but was trapped by the demands of life.

His philosophical preoccupations looked just as different as his personal. The concerns that had once led him to accuse Fichte of having *Bauernstolz,*[8] the self-satisfied pride of a farmer who uses nature solely for his own crude ends, remained, but instead of looking for the unassimilable source of human subjectivity in nature, Schelling increasingly turned to psychological explanations as he became more and more interested in theology. The intuition at the base of both his early and middle periods remained the same: human subjectivity is grounded in, and originates from, some dark source that can never be made fully conscious. There is something in us, whether nature or will, that is other than us and yet makes our subjectivity possible. In another two hundred years, scholars would credit this insight for anticipating the psychoanalytic category of the unconscious; more immediately, that inaccessible ground of subjectivity would become for Schelling the site of contingency and, at least in 1813, the linchpin of his model of suffering.

His shift in interests to theology had begun before Caroline's death, starting with his 1804 work *Philosophy and Religion.* The really significant work, though, came in 1809 when he published a treatise, *On the Essence of Human Freedom,* in an effort to rehabilitate the project of theodicy.[9] It was the last piece Schelling would publish in his lifetime. A recent work by Michelle Kosch has persuasively argued that one of Schelling's major preoccupations was to reject the entire theological tradition that defined evil in negative terms, as lack or privation of goodness.[10] The most famous example of a privative account of evil was Augustine's argument that God cannot create evil, so all evil must be understood as a lack or disorder of the good, in the same way that blindness is a lack of sight.[11] Instead, following Kant's 1793 work, *Religion Within the Limits of Reason Alone,* Schelling defines evil as a radical choice to act against the moral law. Like Kant, Schelling locates that decision prior to time.

To give a very brief summary: there are, Schelling thinks, two forces, one light and one dark, in constant struggle from the beginning of time. Even God is implicated in the struggle. Within God, this struggle occurs between revelation (light) and concealment (darkness). Whereas, in humans the battle happens between the universalizing tendency of the good and the active self to preserve its particularity. People are free because they choose their own characters, which side will win in the struggle, in a decision outside time. If it sometimes seems as if the entirety of our history is the inevitable unfolding of our characters into

deeds and desires, it is because the only true moment of freedom came before our birth. We chose our destiny when we
opted for light or darkness. Everything that has come after is
the necessary consequence of that free choice.

Two consequences emerge from Schelling's version of theodicy that matter for my reading of contingency in *The Ages of the
World*. First, in locating the origin of evil in an undetermined
leap of the will, Schelling begins to think of the inaccessible
ground of reason specifically as contingent, with contingency
understood as a wholly undetermined choice. Absolutely nothing determines or even tilts the personality to leap for lightness
or darkness. The choice could have been otherwise, it was contingent, because no reasons, no preexisting inclinations or surrounding circumstances, necessitated or even conditioned it.
Second, in limiting contingency to a leap of the will, Schelling
begins to think of contingency in terms of personality and desire.
What is the opposite of the restraining force of reason, where the
regular demands of logic constrain our choices, if not the capri-
cious, unpredictable movement of desire? Where is true contingency if not in the limitless capacity to desire randomly at
will, for no reason, from no cause?

Schelling might have abandoned this equation of contingency
with desire if Hegel had not replaced Fichte as his main intellectual rival in the years after Jena and thus pushed him to expand
the role of contingency in creation. The story of the friendship
that would one day end with Friedrich Wilhelm IV summoning
Schelling to Berlin to "slay the dragon-seed of Hegelian pantheism" is much better known than the details of Schelling's work
at this point.[12] By 1813, the years when Schelling and Hegel had
roomed together in the Tübinger Stift, loathing the seminary
and enthusiastically following the latest news of the French
Revolution, were gone. Hegel was no longer the jovial older

friend, steeped in Rousseau and indifferent to Kant, who loved dancing and dreamed of making philosophy accessible to the public. (That is, when the night porter was not greeting him with the warning, "Oh Hegel, you're for sure going to drink away what little intellect you have.")[13] He was, by then, a formidable philosopher in his own right and had six years earlier broken with Schelling when he derisively called his version of the Absolute "the night in which all cows are black" in the preface to the *Phenomenology of Spirit.*

In many ways, *The Ages of the World* can be read as Schelling's most direct rebuttal to Hegel. While in 1807 Hegel was busy writing the bildungsroman of *Geist*'s necessary journey to self-consciousness through history, driven by internal contradiction, in 1813 Schelling offered a story that predates the birth of Geist where the central events hinge on accidents, misperceptions, failures, and chance. Thus *The Ages of the World* can be read as a critical prehistory to the *Phenomenology of Spirit.*

In writing *The Ages of the World*, Schelling was not claiming Hegel's depiction of reason as driven by internal contradiction was wrong; in later years he even accepted it as an example of "negative philosophy," explaining the logic of change. Rather, his argument was that, in starting with the necessities of reason as the basis for the development of the world and philosophy, Hegel failed to explain why there should be a developing world at all. There is simply no motivation internal to reason to be forever negating its definitions, seeking out contradictions, false premises, and otherwise unraveling at night the cloth woven during the day. Reason may offer us the tools to push beyond previous theories, but the motivation for doing so lies in psychological grounds. Only wanting, both in the sense of lacking and desiring something beyond itself, makes possible reason's capacity for self-negation and differentiation, its endless search for its immediate, incomprehensible, contingent basis.[14] In the absence of any such account, reason can never reach the comprehensiveness and clarity Hegel claimed for it. Hegel starts too late and, in so doing, leaves reason groundless.

More than that, in focusing on reason, Hegel misses the true object of philosophy. "Nothing is more comprehensible than the concept," Schelling would assert in his 1841 lectures, "and whoever takes this as the object of their development has chosen the most malleable material. . . . The world does not consist merely of categories or of mere concepts, but rather of concrete and contingent things, and what is at stake is what is not logical . . . but rather its opposite, which the concept, as it were, only unwillingly accepts." Not just Hegel's philosophy, he tells his students, but, rather, all sciences are based on presuppositions that can never be justified. Whether language, physics, or philosophy, all falter before the question of why there should be anything at all.[15] Taking as his example the existence of the ether thought to produce light, Schelling confesses, "It seems to me something so contingent that I cannot even comprehend it and thus cannot accept as actually explained any phenomenon that depends on it." To imagine otherwise is to fall prey to the narcissism of reason that tries to reduce the world to its image.

The Ages of the World was, at least in part, an attempt to correct the oversights of the *Phenomenology of Spirit* by fleshing out what it would mean to find the ground of existence and thought in the contingent movement of desire. Yet it is not enough to make a simplistic equation between contingency and desire for Schelling. If this book is grounded on any one insight, it is that a thinker's evaluation of the possibilities of contingency are a function of the scenarios in which it shows up as a problem. And for Schelling, even as he began writing and rewriting what appeared to be an uncomplicated cosmological fable, desire emerges in language borrowed from Christian theodicy. The pre-occupations from 1809 with the problem of evil remained, only this time contingency would be drawn into an argument about the impossibility of ever redeeming suffering.

DISEASED DESIRE AND SCHELLING'S CRITIQUE OF THEODICY

Parts of Schelling's 1809 theodicy peek through his drafts of *The Ages of the World* like an early, discarded portrait not quite painted over by a frugal artist. The figures seem the same with different names: an omnipotent will, a division within this will between light and dark, expansion and contraction, a groundless free choice that comes to determine everything. It would be easy to read *The Ages of the World* as an uncomplicated continuation of his earlier text, especially since the project seems barely more than an underpainting itself, all bones and shadows and the promise of flesh never really fulfilled. But more than names changed for Schelling between the two works. By 1813 the imagery that had been used to criticize a particular idea of evil as a lack had morphed into a full-throated rejection of theodicy. Like so many stances Schelling takes in his oeuvre, this position was not a definitive one. I am not interested in reconstructing here his final thoughts on theodicy. My argument is a much more limited one. I am saying that the particular form of desire, Schelling equates with contingency in 1813 borrows on the traditional imagery of theodicy, only to pathologize contingency and reject the possibility of reconciliation with suffering. The details of that rejection play out in the imagery of his narrative, which runs roughly as follows.

Prior to the creation of the world, prior to time, prior to God understood as a personal deity, there existed eternity. Eternity is neither a perspective on the entirety of time nor even a primarily temporal phenomenon. Rather, it is an inaccessible state where all time, space, matter, and possibility exist in potential form. It is a will, but a totally passive, inactive will, also called "the will that wills nothing." In this space outside time the "will that wills nothing" produces in itself the "eternal will." How or why remains unclear, but the eternal will is characterized by a blind, restless longing for the will that wills nothing, a yearning that all life shares. Everything living desires above all this return to stillness and nothingness. It is desire in its purest form, but blind desire that does not know what it seeks called *Sehnsucht*. Eventually, experiencing only emptiness and longing, the eternal will conceives of itself as pure negation or lack and is renamed by Schelling "the negating will." One way to read the negating will is as the active form of the will that wills nothing; whereas the first lacks any desire whatsoever, the second actively, nihilistically wills nothing.

Unable to find satisfaction within itself, the eternal will, now the negating will, assumes that its object must exist outside of itself as plentitude, the fullness to its emptiness. In so doing, it produces pure essence or the "affirming will." Yet despite thinking the fullness of essence would satisfy it, the negating will finds itself in conflict with it. Only with the perspectival shift that allows the affirming and negating wills to understand themselves as a unity do they reach any satisfaction. Together, the two wills form spirit, or Geist, simultaneously the link between life and eternity and at one with eternity. Once Geist comes into being, it too, in turn, seeks its complement. As the opposite of spirit is matter, Geist takes on a primitive body, making a spiritual-corporeal essence that shines through objects into the present. Spirit and matter are, at this point, two aspects of the same thing.

My analysis ends with the creation of this early matter, but, to give a very abbreviated summary, the rest of the narrative runs as follows. Geist shapes matter to reflect the possibilities latent in eternity and holds it up before eternity as a fleeting vision of its own essence. Gradually, spirit pulls eternity to itself, allowing eternity to recognize itself for the first time in the possibilities Geist holds up to it. This mirror draws it out of its passivity through this vision of itself and transforms it into an active will. At this point, Schelling retroactively—and opaquely—insists that everything he described in the relation between the negating and affirming wills had been passive. However, he insists that the struggle between the negating and affirming wills now becomes an active contradiction. The conflict sharpens, the negating will takes on the active, destructive character of wrath, while the affirming will or essence assumes the identity of love. Where the two contradictory wills exist, so too does the third will of their unity. This is the "absolute I of divinity."[16]

In a flash of decision, wrath gives way to love. "The Eternal takes that part of its essence which—although not in fact the less significant—it is freely persuaded by love to regard as the less significant and makes it into the very innermost and strongest force at the beginning of existence [*Daseyn*]."[17] Wrath, or the negating will, contracts, giving primacy to the affirming will of revelation and allowing creation to begin. This is the deed that must forever remain unconscious, the inaccessible ground of creation.

At the center of this story of wills that want is the first inexplicable break, in a moment of desire, of the eternal will from the will that wills nothing. It is an incomprehensible event, an unjustified moment that the text dances uneasily around and that Schelling himself will come to renounce by his 1815 draft, a fact I will return to later. Schelling himself labels it a mystery even in 1813, writing:

> Now the great riddle of all time originates precisely here, the
> riddle of how anything could have come from what is neither

externally active nor is anything in itself. And yet life did not remain in that state of immobility, and time is just as certain as eternity. Indeed, to the casual glance the latter even seems driven out by the former; a world full of movement, full of conflict and strain of all forces seems to have taken over the place where the highest indifference, eternal rest, and universal satiation once dwelt. There have always been those who claimed that this riddle was easy to solve . . . But these words are without sense.[18]

I take the eternal will's break from eternity to be the central moment of contingency in the text. It is the undetermined moment at the center of existence, the inexplicable, radically free break that grounds every necessity that follows in the world. I am not alone in this characterization of the text. As Žižek writes in his introductory essay, "Schelling's entire philosophical revolution is contained in the assertion that this act that precedes and grounds every necessity is in itself *radically contingent*—for that reason it cannot be deduced, inferred but only retroactively presupposed."[19]

A philosophical revolution is not necessarily a theological one, though. Žižek leaves us with the philosophical version of Schelling so often plundered by scholars hunting for a forerunner to Derrida or Lacanian drive theory or the Big Bang theory.[20] Even if scholars agree that "the necessity of contingency" is Schelling's central insight in this draft of *The Ages of the World* and beyond, that does not yet mean that his invocation of contingency in this text has any relationship to his previous work on theodicy. So what textual evidence do I have for reading it as interested in theodicy at all, much less a pointed rejection of the entire tradition?

The strongest support for my reading comes in a passage about the role and motivations of the philosopher. Early on, Schelling

characterizes thinkers as driven to philosophize about this "tran-
quil realm of the past" out of hope that they can "genuinely get
behind the great process in which they are partly spectators and
partly compassionate participants." Most, however, "lack the req-
uisite humility; they wish to begin everything straight away
with the highest concepts and bypass the mute beginnings of all
life."[21] In its German entirety the text runs as follows:

> Es hat von viele gelüftet, in dieß stille Reich der Vergangenheit
> einzudringen, und so in eigentlichen Verstand hinter den großten
> Proceß zu kommen, von dem sie theils Zuschauer, theils mithan-
> delnde und mitleidende Theile sind. Aber den Meisten fehlte es
> an der gehörigen Demuth, in dem sie alles gleich mit dem höch-
> sten Begriffen anfangen und die Stummen Anfänge alles Leb-
> ens überspringen wollten.

A few key things get lost in Judith Norman's 1997 translation of
this text. To start, the presence of community. In German, the
philosopher finds herself as *mithandelnde* and *mitleidende*, coact-
ing and compassionate, always as finite, thrown, and suffering
with another, even another as nebulous as eternity. Relatedly, the
language of *Proceß* could either be translated as "process" or as
"trial," suggesting the traditional project of a theodicy. Finally,
the term for "concepts" here is *Begriff,* the grasping concept Hegel
uses. By switching to an aural metaphor and claiming that the
true source of interest is "mute beginning of life," Schelling is
suggesting that the grasping, bad philosopher's conceptual mode
of knowledge is so inadequate to its object that it cannot even
begin to adequately address it. After all, how do you grasp silence
with a hand?

However unsuited most thinkers may be, the task of and
motivation for philosophy seem clear enough in this passage: the

philosopher writes out of a sense of suffering, hoping to find some solace in understanding the life she finds herself thrust into at birth. Not from love of wisdom or the desire for truth or from any of the other traditional justifications of philosophy—from suffering. The psychological motivations for philosophy turn out to be, at base, those of theodicy. Theology and philosophy are one.

Once Schelling collapses theology into philosophy, his description of the eternal will takes on new significance. As mentioned, he consistently describes the eternal will as driven by Sehnsucht, "blind desire." Given his long-standing discontent with privative accounts of evil, what else could this adjective be if not a deliberate reappropriation from theodicy of the metaphor of blindness as a lack of the good? Attributing blindness to Sehnsucht could be read as making a double argument. First, it is a radical rejection of the sort of transcendent God who could ever make contingency disappear from a certain vantage point. It even mocks this tradition, which finds it so easy to reckon with evil; the thinker who seeks reassurance in a divine vision of the goodness of the whole finds only empty longing and incomprehension. Second, Schelling is also trying to show the idea of lack or blindness as an active ill, not simply something passively suffered, in the way I might, say, consider my inability to fly a lack. God is broken, and everything—human, divine, or otherwise—is fractured, finite, and blind. Schelling's universe is broken all the way to the bottom.

The etymology of the word Schelling uses to describe the longing the eternal will experiences so blindly further bolsters my argument that—whatever he intended in 1809—Schelling had drifted into deep skepticism about the project of theodicy by 1813. Sehnsucht is the eternal's will's blind longing for something absent, namely eternity. To the non-native speaker,

Sehnsucht sounds like a combination of *sehnen*—to long or yearn—and *suchen*—to seek. The combination elegantly captures the main features of the eternal will's desire: its restlessness, its dissatisfaction, its constant search for an unknown desideratum. However elegant, though, *Sehnsucht* actually possesses a different etymology. *Sehnen* remains "to long or to yearn," but *sucht* turns out to stem from *Sucht*, which in turn derives from *siechen*, to sicken.[22] *Sucht*, then, is not a search, but rather an illness. The term had a dual connotation of medical and psychological illness, often with some sense of excess. So to be *fettsüchtig* would be to suffering from too much fat, to be *fallsüchtig* would mean to suffer from an excess of falling, which is to say, to suffer from epilepsy. The *schwindsüchtig* were ill with consumption, while the *wassersüchtig* had edema or dropsy. Terms such as *Tobsucht*, madness, and *Mondsucht*, lunacy, *Sucht* suggest a more psychological dimension to illness, while *Trunksucht*, or alcoholism, make explicit the a sense of unhealthy dependence. Today, in common parlance, to be *süchtig nach* something means to be "hooked on it." *Sehnsucht*, therefore, could be read in two senses. First, as an illness of excessive desire. Second, as an obsession. There is something, then, sick, excessive, pathological even, about this originary split.

Schelling explicitly recognizes this pathological dimension to Sehnsucht in his subsequent drafts. Describing the eternal circular movement of the three potencies—or, in the vocabulary of the 1813 version, the negating will, affirming will, and Geist the unity of the two—Schelling asserts, "In that eternally commencing life there lies the wish to escape from the involuntary movement and from the distress of pining. . . . The obsession [*Sucht*] abates into yearning [*Sehnsucht*], wild desire turns into a yearning to ally itself, as if it were its own true or highest self, with the will that wills nothing, eternal freedom."[23] The play between the sense of obsession and longing that had been implicit in the 1813 version of the text becomes fully visible in the 1815 manuscript.

If I stop here, Schelling's creation story is frankly brutal. We find ourselves thrown into a universe, forced to act, forced to suffer in a drama we can never fully understand. Our most basic nature is at once stricken with a pathological longing to return to nothingness and denied the fulfillment of that wish by an equally persistent desire for life. When the philosopher seeks to understand why she suffers, she is presented with a story about a completely free, contingent act at the beginning of time and is told the universe simply shares her pain without reason. Whatever commitments Schelling had to theodicy in 1809, by 1813 he has no space left in his story for reconciliation with suffering.

The two centuries since Schelling wrote have lent his rejection of theodicy the glow of moral common sense. The idea that a slow, frozen death in the camps of Kolyma or the instantaneous conflagration of Hiroshima might be adequately understood as a lack of the good is as foreign as any the history of philosophy can invite us to inhabit. Reading Schelling, I am sometimes tempted to make him over into an early version of Somerset Maugham, who rejected the entire tradition of theodicy more clearly than any philosopher I have ever read when he wrote:

Evils are there, omnipresent; pain and disease, the death of those we love, poverty, crime, sin, frustrated hope: the list is interminable. What explanations have the philosophers to offer? Some say that evil is logically necessary so that we may know the good; some say that by the nature of the world there is an opposition between good and evil and that each is metaphysically necessary to the other. What explanations have the theologians to offer? Some say that God has placed evils here for our training; some say that he has sent them upon man to punish them for their sins. But *I* have seen a child die of meningitis.[24]

Of course, it sometimes seems, Schelling thought a privative account of evil misunderstands the demand suffering makes on us; the real wonder is that anyone ever thought otherwise.

Yet characterizing the eternal will as blind, suggesting through wordplay that the desire driving creation is obsessive and pathological—these are still rhetorical moves on Schelling's part. They may indicate his disenchantment with theodicy but they tell us nothing about the deeper reasons why he chose to understand the contingent break of the eternal will as a movement of Sehnsucht, rather than a more benevolent form of desire that might have led to a positive valuation of existence. Piecing together those justifications requires revisiting Schelling's great rivalry with Hegel and ultimately interrogating the very content of suffering in *The Ages of the World*.

TWO THEORIES OF SUFFERING

If Schelling wanted another model of desire, he could have found an example easily enough in the term used by his old rival, Hegel: *Begierde*. In one of the most famous passages in the history of philosophy, Hegel invokes *Begierde* in the *Phenomenology of Spirit* when a rudimentary subject, or self-consciousness, approaches others solely through desire (Begierde). At that stage, self-consciousness wants to affirm itself as an independent being by negating or destroying the object of its desire. It finds, however, that destruction to be ultimately dissatisfying because self-consciousness still depends on the existence of the other, even in destroying it. There is no satisfaction of desire—however selfish or destructive that desire may be—without an other. Even tempered satisfaction is fleeting. Desire returns the moment it is satisfied, forcing the self-consciousness to seek out satiation yet again. This earliest form of desire morphs into a need for recognition from a similar self-consciousness, leading directly to the master-slave dialectic. Begierde in Hegel is not exactly healthy, or even necessarily likely to lead to a happier origin story, but it is an alternative that Schelling could have taken if he wanted. It shows that casting desire as Sehnsucht in Schelling's origin story was a choice, not the result of thoughtlessness or the constraints of language.

It would be simple enough to look at Hegel's use of Begierde and see an answer, not a question. Why, the line of thought runs, would Schelling decide to speak of Sehnsucht when Begierde was a possibility? Because Schelling hated Hegel. He chose Sehnsucht precisely because it contrasted with Begierde. I do think this reading is partially right. The differences between Sehnsucht and Begierde map onto the broader criticisms of Hegel that Schelling spent his life developing. Begierde, with its connotation of bodily lust, has an object that it focuses on, in contrast to the aimless longing of Sehnsucht. It responds to something present, even if that thing turns out to be inadequate. In the same way Hegel's history of the evolution of reason misses the irrational, contingent ground of being, Begierde presupposes an object, an other on whom to pin its desires. It fails to really grapple with the dislocation of desire at its most primal, when it longs without knowing what it seeks; it fails to grapple with the idea that desire sometimes simply exists with no object, with no idea of what its object might be. Even unhappy consciousness, the stage that would seem to have the greatest affinity with Schelling's depiction of Sehnsucht, is not blind in the same, aching way as the eternal will. Hegel's self-consciousness may be wrong about what it desires, and be forced onto another stage of development in the story, but that does not counter Schelling's basic point: Hegel fails to leave space for pure, blind, wandering desire. Hegel presupposes a world, while Schelling looks for a state prior to the world.

All of that may be right, but it is still a nonanswer. Even if Schelling had chosen Sehnsucht as a way of working through his criticisms of Hegel, that does not make Schelling's model of desire *true*. What, really, is the metric for judging a philosophical account of desire, if not the question, "Do I, as someone who has desired, sometimes wisely, sometimes self-destructively, sometimes desperately, recognize my experiences in this account?" And if that is the criterion, isn't Hegel arguably doing better phenomenology? Isn't Hegel right that we always find ourselves in a world, desiring objects and people we stumble across without quite knowing what we demand from them? Can we even access the sort of blind, wild, undirected longing Schelling describes in 1813, or does he have to set it in the context of a myth free from the lure of others we might mistake as the cause of our desire?

I would attribute Schelling's choice of Sehnsucht to some combination of temperament and spite, if not for the peculiar fact that in his 1811 draft he actually used Begierde instead of Sehnsucht. I do not think this is a meaningless shift in vocabulary or part of an evolving critique of Hegel. Instead, I think it marks a deep change in Schelling's understanding of suffering from 1811 to 1813.

Schelling's most evocative statement on suffering comes shortly after the eternal will breaks from eternity. Driven by diseased desire and blind intuition, the will comes to negate itself. In doing so, it creates the affirming will, the something to its nothing, but not before Schelling introduces one of the most interesting remarks in the entire text. "Wäre aber auch nicht dieses überfließende und sich mittheilende Wesen," he comments, "so wäre die anziehende Kraft leer und eigentlich wirkungslos, unerfüllt und sich selbst unleidlich."[25] Judith Norman renders this sentence thus: "But without this overflowing and communicative essence, the attracting force would be empty and genuinely ineffectual, unfulfilled and unbearable [*unleidlich*] to itself." Norman herself recognizes an inadequacy in her version by including in brackets the original of one German word: *unleidlich*.

While *unleidlich* can mean "unbearable," for the remainder of this chapter, I want to break from Norman's translation and hold, instead, to the root of the word, *leiden*, "to suffer," by rendering *unleidlich* as "insufferable." Though the change may seem trivial, a literal-minded fidelity to the German makes visible the question of what counts as insufferable in Schelling's text, and illuminates—however briefly and inadequately—the circumstances that drive the negating will to create its opposite, the next moment in this text. What follows, then, is in some sense an artificial abstraction from the narrative Schelling gives, a counterfactual reconstruction of what the negating will would look like before the emergence of the affirming will.

I call it counterfactual, because the moment is shuttled to the side as soon as it's raised through the subjunctive. "Es wäre sich selbst unleidlich": it *would be* insufferable to itself if not for its other, but the other is there, instantaneously, soothing and saving from the possibility of paralyzing, impossible suffering. A grammatical trick rescues Schelling from pursuing this claustrophobic thought and allows him to transform the stakes into those of the familiar drama of two forces circling, sparring and reconciling. *Krapp's Last Tape* becomes *Pride and Prejudice*.

At the root of the movement lies *leiden*, to suffer, and from *leiden* it is only an extra syllable to *leidenschaft*, passion. In both

English and German, the verb *to suffer* hovers between two senses: first, to bear or endure. I suffer an insult; I suffer through a meal, an evening, a night. It is suffering as sufferable. The second sense is what Emmanuel Levinas pointed to in his 1982 essay "Useless Suffering" when he described suffering as "the unassumable," *l'inassumabilité*. More than simple "sense datum," suffering is a "negative synthesis" of mental content, not just, "consciousness of rejection or a symptom of rejection, but this rejection itself: a backward consciousness, 'operating' not as 'grasp,' but as revulsion. A modality."[26] Suffering is what I cannot endure or take upon myself; it prostrates me. The two meanings are opposed, and yet united in experience. I continue to suffer my suffering even as it overpowers me at every moment. It is clear enough that the philosopher suffers in this ordinary sense, which holds the two experiences together. It is clear because she does go on.

This is not the suffering of the negating will in 1813, imagined as unleidlich, but it is a real form of pain nonetheless that Schelling took extremely seriously—seriously enough that in the first draft this first, ordinary form of suffering drives the originary forces to posit a primordial unity. The 1811 text develops this model of suffering at enormous length through a metaphor of the beating heart, tying it to love, desire, and fear. This early image will prepare the possibility of thinking the insufferable while expanding our understanding of the sufferable. And so, as is often the case in my reading of Schelling, I want to dwell with the familiar in order to open a way to the unthinkable.

The metaphor of the beating heart, and with it Begierde, emerge at roughly the same place in the narrative as Sehnsucht does in the later manuscript. Only, while Schelling in 1813 imagined the first moments of creation taking place in an all-encompassing, quiescent will, in 1811, the primordial will comes into existence split into three. The vocabulary differs slightly between the two texts. What is called "the negating will" in 1813 is "wrath," while "the affirming will" is "love," and "the existing will" binds the two together as subject and object.

Schelling goes on to explain the relationship between the three through the metaphor of the beating heart. That relationship is an unhappy one. Once joined in the will to existence, a "silent longing for the division [*Scheidung*]" of the two arises."[27] Yet this desire exists only so long as love prevails as the dominant feeling. As soon as its expansive, effusive nature moves the unity toward dissolution, wrath senses this division and, in terror of losing existence, draws the two back together. Love, then, assumes the outward, expansive movement of the diastole, while wrath becomes the contracting force of the systole. Meanwhile, the existing will, or will to existence, as the tie between the two, cannot leave the struggle between the two wills without forfeiting its existence altogether.[28] Thus "in the conflict between these two struggling wills it [the will to existence] loses its own freedom and becomes, as the first throbbing point, so to speak, the beating heart of Godhood, that in the never-ceasing systole and diastole seeks peace and never finds it."[29]

This push and pull of desire, the longing for and fear of self-loss, is the most basic dynamic underpinning creation for Schelling in 1811. It is this dynamic that denies us, as participants in this eternal drama, peace. It is this Begierde that makes us suffer. Given the dynamic Schelling describes, the choice of Begierde cannot be an accident. The blind, objectless longing of Sehnsucht would be all wrong for the relationship Schelling describes. Unlike Sehnsucht, love knows what it desires; it desires its freedom in response to the constricting presence of its other, wrath. That desire may be, in principle, impossible to fulfill, but it arises in relationship to an other, much like Hegel's self-consciousness and unlike Schelling's eternal will.

Schelling might have had other motives behind his choice of Begierde as well. It could be that Schelling used Begierde to underscore the corporeality of the heart metaphor. Alternately, it could be he had a static understanding of Sehnsucht throughout the three manuscripts and so deliberately chose Begierde to signal a more immediate, less pathological type of desire. If Schelling chooses a term for desire that lacks the morbid connotation of an illness, perhaps it is because he thinks the contracting will's momentary panic and hunger for existence is the absolutely appropriate response to its situation.[30] In its dark inward cringing, the contracting will understands what the expanding will does not: there is no existence without this struggle between love and desire. And yet, unlike the constant awareness of Sehnsucht that propels the later narrative, this knowledge fades in and out, remembered and forgotten with every pulse of the Godhead's beating heart.

In the pulsing imagery of the beating heart, he captures the constant and deeply conflicted vacillation between the desire to merge with another in love and the selfish, inward-drawing impulse to cannibalize the beloved. Implicitly underlying this struggle is another metaphor of the suffering heart: the broken heart. The rhythmic contraction and expansion of affirmation and negation, love and desire, is already a play between the metaphor of the heart as love and its biological dimension. And, as we have seen, Schelling does have a history of linking suffering to the language of biological infirmity, whether blindness or the Sucht of Sehnsucht. Thus, it is not so much of a leap to spend a few moments contemplating how and why biology, metaphor, suffering and philosophy come together.

To do that, I want to make a move that would please, I think, the thinker who once argued, "philosophy has acquired . . . such a deep and internal bearing on poetry, that from now on . . . the destiny of both can only be a common one."[31] I am going to turn now, for illumination, to a brief detour into the 1945 poem "Beethoven," by Albrecht Haushofer. Written while imprisoned for his part in a plot to assassinate Hitler, "Beethoven" was found on Haushofer's corpse by his brother, along with eighty other poems, called *The Moabit Sonnets*. It tells the story of a piano lesson from Haushofer's youth. Bored of the "throbbing triplets of Opus two," he played, instead, "Opus a hundred and eleven." "My teacher, a white-haired mistress of the art, / let me play on, just nodded, and—in reflection: 'The man who wrote that way was a deaf man. / You'll understand it only in later years.' / She was silent. 'When someday your heart is broken / and goes on beating and has to go on beating.'" His teacher seats herself, plays, and the poem ends with the narrator remarking, "Often during these days it comes into my mind / the way she played that time, my dead teacher."[32]

A broken heart is a cliché, of course—even the paradigmatic one—but in its banality it reveals something essential about suffering and its ordinary everydayness. To label suffering ineffable has become de rigueur, but, more often than not, that move smuggles in a sense of the spectacular. The catatonic becomes our model of broken speech, and we forget the other ways in which we mean or fail to mean, speak or fail to speak. We miss something vital when we allow the sufferer's stuttering to obscure the painful, unremarkable fluency of nonmeaning in day-to-day speech. Thus, it *matters* that Haushofer's imagery presses up against the limits of language, not by fractured syntax or cryptic allusions but by a cliché, a phrase so commonplace as to be emptied of content, and by reference to the rhythm of a heart.

These lines say nothing because both biology and banality murmur below the register of consciousness in their familiarity.

And yet, in this cross-fertilization of silences, the cliché briefly blossoms with content. The beating of the broken heart becomes both familiar and strange. Familiar, because what could be more intimate than my heart? Strange, because my heart becomes something that beats first despite me, then despite itself. German grammar makes this uncanny dimension even clearer. "My" heart is not broken; "das Herz," *the* heart, is broken to me. Abruptly, my heart reveals itself as something foreign, as biology strains against metaphor and discredits my identification of self with body. No matter how often I insist that my heart is breaking, my physical heart never stops from pain. Words do not do anything here; if any imperative exists, it comes from the opposing insistence that my heart "weiterschlägt, und weiterschlagen soll." Something in me refuses to recognize my suffering. This is what fills the cliché of the broken heart with content; this is what makes the exchange between the sufferable and the unassumable possible. The very rhythm of the lines, the parallelism of unequal length, echoes the uncertain ebb and flow of the beating, injured heart but also captures this movement of pain and contradiction, which nevertheless constitutes a unity.

This is important because it captures something commonplace. Yet, however illuminating, however interesting, this vision of suffering should not be conflated with what Schelling terms *unleidlich*. "The insufferable" is very close to "the unassumable" that Levinas mentioned earlier. Examined in more detail, it becomes clear that the language Levinas uses to describe the unassumable echoes Schelling's critique of the bad philosopher. "'Unassumability,'" Levinas begins, "does not result from the excessive intensity of a sensation, from just some quantitative 'too much,' surpassing the measure of our sensibility and *our means of grasping and holding*; but an excess, an unwelcome superfluity, that is inscribed in a sensorial content, penetrating, as suffering, the dimensions of meaning that seem to open themselves to it, or become grafted onto it."[33] Suffering cannot be grasped; in French it is what "passant la mesure de notre sensibilité et de nos moyens de saisir et de tenir," that which operates, "non comme 'prise,' mais comme révulsion." Just as Schelling ridicules the thinker who wants to begin by seizing the highest concept, *Begriff,* so too does Levinas suggest that it would be all wrong to think we could get a handle on suffering if only we could somehow be made stronger or more capacious. The unassumable eludes mastery as the radically heterogeneous in the same way the mute beginnings of life can never be held by concepts.

But if I hesitate to collapse the insufferable into the unassumable, it is because I think Levinas uses it far too freely. It is a real weakness in his analysis that he considers all suffering unassumable.[34] If this discussion about Schelling has made one thing clear, I hope it is that the interplay between the unassumable and the sufferable is a deep type of suffering in its own right. Schelling is more sophisticated than Levinas in this instance. He understands the difficulty of envisioning a type of suffering that is purely unassumable, insufferable, which is why he brackets his own vision of the unleidlich twice: once by placing it in a myth set before time and once by relegating that thought to a hypothetical through grammar. But if I am correct, what then makes the difference between the Levinas's unassumable and Schelling's unleidlich? In brief: the absence of an other. The eternal will is nailed to itself. It is suffering without an outside. And that is why it creates an other in the affirming will, so it can have an object, an escape. The form of suffering that drives Schelling's theodicy in 1813 is loneliness.

While this might seem speculation or eisegesis at its worst, reading loneliness as the paradigmatic form of suffering in 1813 resolves a number of mysteries about Schelling's text. It no

longer seems peculiar or undermotivated to describe that initial, contingent moment of desire through Sehnsucht. What
could better describe loneliness, *Einsamkeit,* than the eternal
will's longing for anyone, anything, to break through its isolation? Of course he abandoned Begierde, with its corporeality
and lustful response to objects that stray across its path. It is
simply the wrong term to capture sick, desperate pining for
companionship.

Reading the story Schelling tells in 1813 as a description of
loneliness makes sense even of the eternal will's split from eternity. As I briefly flagged while recounting the story, as written,
the break seems completely unmotivated. When the eternal will
gave birth to itself, it was already part of eternity. What could
have moved it to break from its state of quiescence and seek a
companion? How could the eternal will feel the lack of something to which it belonged? In 1813 Schelling names this moment
the greatest mystery of creation. So how is it that eternity was
there to be known yet felt to be absent? Why want something
you possess? *Intellectually,* the motivation behind this move is
unfathomable.

Psychologically, though, this is an incredibly common experience: it is the question of how it is possible to be lonely in a
crowd. There are others present who can be intellectually recognized, yet none are felt as present. The blindness of the eternal
will is affective, not conceptual, but at this stage there is no distinction between those two types of knowledge. The eternal
will has no conceptual knowledge at odds with or outside its feelings of longing. By depicting a state in which the inability to
feel the other as present collapses into the inability to know the
other as present, Schelling engages with the inexplicable disjunction between the objective presence of community and the
emotional sensation of isolation. It is an unanswered question in

his text: more a mystery than a problem. If the foundation of Heidegger's philosophy is wonder that there is something *rather* than nothing, the foundation of Schelling's thought in this book is wonder that we see something *as* nothing.

Moreover, textual proof exists that Schelling thought deeply about loneliness near the time he wrote this text. On his birthday in 1810, tersely noted in his diary as, "the first without Caroline," Schelling muses on the possibility of becoming so lost in mourning that the outside world ceases to register. "No passion is in itself unconquerable," he begins, in a telegraphic entry.

> The most wrathful can suppress their wrath in the presence of the king. The most sensual his sensuality before the eyes of chastity and virtue. In order to master his passion, man always needs something exterior that rattles him, occupies him, tenses him.— Will it always do this for him? . . . We remain unmoved by the most apposite warnings of Providence. Or these exterior counterforces are lacking. We languished in the most forsaken loneliness. Nothing comes to us that rattles us. When are we pulled away from the one thought that buries itself ever deeper inside us . . . no friend, no glance, no ray of outside help or hope stands us in good stead.[35]

The phrase, "the *most* forsaken loneliness," "der verlassensten Einsamkeit," as a superlative, suggests a gradation of loneliness, with the total absence of others at the extreme.

But what are these other forms of loneliness? The most obvious candidate for a contrasting understanding of loneliness would be one that contains a negative relationship to community, whether as something despaired over, hoped for, or lost. The touching that does not touch, the loneliness that has nothing to do with isolation, this can be the sense of forsakenness in the crowd, or the feeling that slips between two people in a moment of intimacy, when the faltering small talk of domesticity lapses into silence or recrimination. Vulnerability becomes suffocating; intimacy is snowed over with revulsion, boredom, and disgust. Yet loneliness only shows up in those moments as a problem because of love; loneliness here is a type of betrayal by love. However, there is also the loneliness of loss that shades into melancholy. Who could doubt that my loneliness at the death of a family member or the abandonment of a lover means something different than the bitter collapse of a marriage? But who would deny that it is loneliness all the same?

The loneliness of the negating will is something else altogether: a feeling of pure aridity, the gnawing absence of both affection and an object of affection. The negating will suffers not just from the absence of anything to love *it*, to disburden it of itself through distraction, or tenderness, or companionship; it suffers from a lack of anything to love. And not just anything to love—anything to hate, to desire, or to face with revulsion. Love cannot be a problem because we are not yet at the point where we can love. In this moment, when there is no distinction between affect and knowledge, when there is no conceptual knowledge of the other's presence to counteract the feeling of her absence, the negating will faces the possibility of total isolation and desolation.

While meditating on how best to read Hegel, Schelling once remarked that any truly generous effort to grapple with a philosopher required finding his first, most fundamental thought, "where he has not yet proceeded to the consequences; for against his own intentions he can go astray in philosophy, where every false step has infinite consequences, where one on the whole finds himself on a path surrounded on all sides by chasms."[36] I want to amend his statement to say instead, "If one wants to honor a theodicist, then one must grasp him there in his fundamental thought of suffering." Loneliness was that experience for Schelling in 1813. In honoring this thought, I want to end by doing something Schelling, in his endless revisions, never did. I want to argue that he gets something right by calling loneliness the deepest form of suffering.

CONTINGENT TOUCH, ABSENT TOUCH

The story Schelling tells fits together so beautifully that I am loath to trouble it. He comes to equate contingency with lawless desire, in part because of his feuds with Fichte and Hegel, in part because of his interest in theodicy. Only desire in the first moments before a life filled with constraints and predispositions and the problem of moral luck can be totally free, unnecessary, and unconstrained by the laws of logic. Yet the desire Schelling portrays in 1813 is not joyful or even neutral. It is sick, twisted longing, cloaked half-sarcastically in the language of evil as lack. Contingency serves a polemical purpose as part of a larger rejection of theodicy. The question then becomes why? Why choose such an unhappy, morbid vision of desire to set into motion the creation of the universe? Reading loneliness as the primal form of suffering answers that question. It offers a psychological explanation for why eternity would break from the will that wills nothing and explains the choice of Sehnsucht. Contingency is not cast as morbid Sehnsucht sheerly as part of a polemical rejection of theodicy. It is a deliberate choice, meant to bring nuance to a sophisticated, moving account of loneliness as the content of suffering.

And yet, in some respects, recognizing loneliness as Schelling's silent model of suffering merely punts on the questions concerning the justification of his depiction of contingency. Why pick loneliness as the primal form of suffering? Why should loneliness demand the rejection of theodicy? What makes loneliness so much more difficult to come to terms with than death or disease or despair or betrayal? Finally, to go back to one of my main questions in this book, does this account provide any political possibilities or space to think about how to live in the world?

Trying to answer these questions by creating a hierarchy of suffering or determining "the worst type of suffering" would be, frankly, nonsensical. There are too many variables to consider— the role of culture, individual temperament, personal history, the sufferer's social position, for a start. For all that, I think there are good reasons internal to Schelling's account that push him to focus on loneliness.

To deal with evil as more than just a metaphysical abstraction, as more than disordered loves or the absence of the good, Schelling needed the most difficult case of suffering he could muster. Loneliness served that function for him, not because loneliness does more to blight lives than poverty, mangled limbs, or a slow death hacking up shredded lungs from tuberculosis (Novalis's fate), but rather because the loneliness of the negating will is structurally incompatible with the philosopher's perspective. The philosopher is driven to think because she finds herself thrust into a situation she did not make, participating in a drama she only half-understands, surrounded by actors whose roles remain opaque. What would it mean to really understand the source of her trial? It would mean being able to inhabit a moment of isolation so total that the hope of a friend or a foe is not even a possibility. It would mean thinking herself out of her life, out of her subject position, out of the trials and questions that motivate her to search for the mute beginnings of life. The philosopher, by virtue of who she is and her place in the world, cannot access the experience of loneliness that drives Schelling's cosmogony. The project is incoherent; the philosopher always misses the problem.

When she does not miss the experience of loneliness, the philosopher betrays it. Schelling does not make this point, but it follows logically from his definition of loneliness as total desolation and his rejection of theodicies that privilege metaphysical accounts of evil over the lived experience of suffering. Let me explain. I could approach a person at the very moment she felt overwhelmed by pain or disease or fear and tell her that her suffering was due to free will or the need for moral development without necessarily calling into question the reality of her affliction. She might find my solution monstrously unhelpful and ask me, in the words of Ivan Karamazov, "But what do I care if [my tears] are avenged, what do I care if [my] tormenters are in hell, what can hell set right here, if [I] have already been tormented?[37]" She might find it unethical that I tried to offer her an explanation for her suffering, rather than the means to end it. She might even be right that theodicy is a completely untenable project for all the reasons just named, but, in that scenario, I would at least not be guilty of telling her that her suffering stems from a limited perspective on God's plan. I could not be accused of lapsing into a metaphysical account of evil that locates the true nature of suffering in the absence of the good or disordered love, rather than in her human experience of affliction. Her suffering would be honored as valid, and I would have to reckon with it as she experienced it, not explain it away as a problem of insufficient knowledge. I would avoid the type of theodicy Schelling found so problematic in 1809.

Not so with loneliness. Any theodicy I could offer the person suffering from the true loneliness of feeling that "nothing comes to rattle" her would necessarily involve telling a story about how her abandonment was never as total as it seemed. There was always a larger world, a larger plan to connect it to the suffering of others, a beneficent God to witness her isolation. It would, in short, involve telling her that her suffering could be explained as a mistaken perspective. If she only had the correct vision of the order of creation, she would understand she had never truly been abandoned and her loneliness would vanish. The act of telling her the good news might genuinely make her feel better by interrupting her isolation, but it would nonetheless deny her perspective on her suffering. The third-person account of theodicy has no space for the radically first-person experience of loneliness as Schelling formulates it in 1813, precisely because the defining feature of loneliness is the utter absence of a third person.[38] Any effort to incorporate the negating will's loneliness into a theodicy ends by lapsing into the sort of metaphysical accounts of evil Schelling struggled so hard to escape in 1809.

And yet, even if this is all true, why does it matter? Schelling can only imagine the pure loneliness of the negating will through a myth. He might write melancholic diary entries imagining himself left alone with his grief by all friends and foes, but somewhere a letter would start clattering its way toward him in a postman's coach from the woman who would become his new wife. The most forsaken loneliness as he imagines it is unsustainable in this world. We are the philosopher, not the negating will.

To further complicate the issue, not even Schelling's own text can sustain the gnawing loneliness of the negating will. Rather than face its own emptiness, the negating will creates the affirming will. Having created essence, or the affirming will, to provide some relief, the negating will is chagrined to find itself in opposition to it, condemned to be "strictness and severity as opposed to the mildness of the essence, to be darkness as opposed to the light, to be an eternal No that conflicts with the Yes."[39] Starting a new paragraph, Schelling goes on to say, "But the will seeks indifference—or rather it longs for indifference with a presentiment that is not knowledge. Thus, through a progressive effect of its desiring force, the will posits for itself indifference, or the unity that liberates it from conflict and allows it to recognize itself as one with its opposite."[40]

The significance of this passage cannot be overstated. The loneliness of the negating will is a mistake. Why else would the negating will abandon the affirming will to renew its longing for eternity, if not because it felt as if it had gotten something wrong? It misunderstood its object of desire and gave birth to the affirming will out of its misperception of what it really desired. It created an object to focus on in the form of the affirming will to interrupt its solitude and give it relief, even though it was never alone. The eternal will was part of the will that wills nothing until it began to desire. Everything was unified, prior to this mistake that took unity to be isolation, and then went out in search of an object it could desire and for which it could suffer. Desire effects loss; it does not stem from it.

Once it creates the affirming will, though, the negating will is stuck. It can never return to unmediated union with the will that wills nothing because it is bound to another, defined by its relationship to essence, not eternity. This mistake renders the alienation from eternity permanent. The constant emphasis on the yearning of creation for the quiescence of eternity points to a claim buried in Schelling's cosmogony: not only *could* creation have happened differently, or not at all, if the negating will had chosen otherwise at this juncture, but in some sense it *should* have happened differently.

Schelling himself tacitly backtracks on the entire 1813 narrative in his version from 1815. As he writes, "A transition from unity to contradiction is incomprehensible. For how should what is in itself one, whole and perfect, be tempted, charmed, and enticed to emerge out of this peace? The transition from contradiction to unity, on the other hand," he continued, "is natural, for contradiction is insufferable to everything and everything that finds itself in it will not repose until it has found the unity that reconciles or overcomes it."[41]

In this passage Schelling dismisses the previous narrative as misguided, even going so far as to reverse its basic premise. This move, I think, is interesting less because of the criticism of his former position than because of the vehemence of his rhetoric. So far as it goes, Schelling only notes the obvious logical flaw in his 1813 position. Yet what had been described in 1813 as the eternal will "giving birth to itself" becomes by 1815 a type of seduction. Singularity breaks from unity because it is "tempted, charmed, and enticed," and what had once been a fertile moment becomes a type of fall. The allusion to Genesis seems clear enough; equally clear are the ramifications of that language. Condemning his previous position as absurd did not satisfy Schelling. Rather, he had to transform the split of the eternal will into a moral failing.

I have no good explanation for the vehemence of Schelling's rhetoric. It could be that he balked at the darkness of his vision. In stressing that darkness, I want to resist the tendency to appropriate him too readily for postmodern concerns. Nothing would be easier at this point than to label contingency as moments of creative unsettling, the disruption that is the source of all invention. Everything horrifying and unsettling about these moments of disorientation would become affirmable as the condition for the possibility of philosophy or creativity, even if the experience itself proved ultimately unendurable. Schelling was writing about the creation of the world, but, in his ambivalence about this collapse of the original unity and the creation that comes from it, he captures something more broadly applicable: namely, if we believe the projects we engage in, in the hope of making the world a home, to be of some value—if, in short, we are more than simple nihilists—we ought to hesitate in affirming their destruction, regardless of what the outcome might be.

For the same reason, though, I am reluctant to follow him in abandoning his phenomenology of loneliness. I do not think it is reducible to a paroxysm of grief or a fantasy played out in myth. I think there is a real-world analogue to the total isolation of the negating will, with real-world stakes. It is a practice that started developing in the decade after Schelling wrote: solitary confinement. I want to end this section, then, by bringing Schelling's thought back to a world with bodies that touch.

The best account of the stakes of loneliness I have read comes in Lisa Guenther's remarkable 2013 phenomenology of solitary confinement, *Solitary Confinement: Social Death and Its Afterlives*. She opens the book with an observation, "There are many ways to destroy a person, but one of the simplest and most devastating is through prolonged solitary confinement."[42] Left too long without human contact, the imprisoned "see things that do not exist, and they fail to see things that do. Their sense of their own bodies—even the fundamental capacity to feel pain and distinguish their own pain from that of others—erodes to the point where they are no longer sure if they are being harmed or harming themselves." Fences waver, walls bulge, prisoners hallucinate companions where none exist.

For Guenther, writing in the phenomenological tradition, these prisoners are not simply becoming psychotic (as if there were anything simple about becoming psychotic). Deprived of human contact and, most important, human touch, their subjectivity is cannibalizing itself. In a careful chapter on Edmund

Husserl, she tries to give a phenomenological explanation for why solitude should lead to these sorts of hallucinations. For Husserl, she explains, our sense of selfhood is always nested. At the most abstract level, each of us has a transcendental ego. The transcendental ego is the sheer capacity for consciousness. It is not yet shaped by habit or life events or any identifying features. Despite its abstractness, it is nonetheless particular to me. No one else can inhabit my transcendental ego; it is my perception, my channel of consciousness. On a more embodied level, I also have a personal ego. This is my perception, or transcendental ego, transformed into a sense of self through its relation to the world and other egos. Guenther singles out two experiences central to the development and maintenance of a sense of personhood: touch and participation in a shared world with concrete objects.

More than any other sense, touch allows me to experience my body as my own. Were I merely a pair of eyes floating through space, I would feel myself a passive recipient of sights and sensations.[43] Were I a pair of ears, I might feel my body as a rickshaw that bears my consciousness as it navigates through the world. In touching, though, I can experience my body as something simultaneously under my control (I can stretch out my hand at will) and something passive, receptive to touch. (I touch the table and feel the swirl of a knot rough against my fingers, an interruption in its otherwise smooth, shellacked wood.) This duality of passivity and activity carries over to my relationship with my own body. In his most famous passage, Husserl meditates on the experience of grasping one's own hand. When I touch my own flesh, my hand may be warm and smooth to the touch, or perhaps chapped and chilled, with rough, uneven nails, but whatever concrete qualities I feel in it, I never confuse it with an object out in the world. I always feel my hand to be my own because only my hand can touch back. As Guenther neatly summarizes,

"At the same time I experience my left hand as warm, I have sensations of pressure on my left hand; likewise, if I shift my attention slightly, my left hand becomes the 'active' side touching my 'passive' right hand. . . . It is precisely the reciprocity of touch," she concludes, "that constitutes my body as mine."[44] This combination of passivity and activity is what it means to have a body; it's what it means to experience my body as a bounded yet permeable self.

A body is not yet a self in any robust sense, but it does provide the means to create one. I find myself in a world populated by chairs, jugs, books, and people. What makes this world show up to me as more than a solipsistic projection, a fantastic collection of objects with no depth or permanence in space and time, is the observation that other egos, lodged in other bodies, look upon the same objects from different perspectives. When I circle around a statue behind a black velvet rope, I know instinctively that there is more to the piece than the curve of the runner's arched foot directly before me, because I am aware of a toddler's dazed brown eyes wandering over its bent knee, her grubby fingers clasped in her father's hand while he surveys its aquiline nose. These differences in perspective are more than mere curiosities. They turn objects into part of a common world for me.

More than that, the presence of others gives me my first, earliest sense of personhood. Just as a baby's eyes track its mother's movement long before its recognizes itself in a mirror, so too do I come to know other, objective people first and only later, analogically, apply the idea of personhood to my own embodied consciousness.[45] Likewise, before I come to think of myself as an individual with a name, wants, needs, a family, an identity, I see the toddler and her father navigating through space. I see them as people, with connections to others, identifying features and wills of their own. I only come to know myself as a person by projecting the sense of personhood I gained from watching them back on to myself.

The testimony of prisoners in solitary confinement, Guenther thinks, allows us to see Husserl's model of perception as at once true and in constant need of renewal. Deprived of objects and people in a "common space," the grounds of personhood begin to collapse. No one comes to validate my perception of space by idly picking up an apple or propping their feet up on my bed. As she puts it, "Without the concrete experience of other embodied egos oriented toward common objects in a shared world, my own experience of the boundaries of those perceptual objects begins to waver. It becomes difficult to tell what is real and what is only my imagination playing tricks on me."[46] My body is included among those wavering objects. I may still be able to touch myself, but, without another person to confirm that I exist by brushing past me on the sidewalk or grasping my hand, my sense of touch becomes just as unreliable as my sight. I need another to reflect back my existence, not just as a human but also as an embodied consciousness with a bounded body and objective presence in the world.[47] Denied any other form of perceptual validation, prisoners sometimes produce others to populate their world through hallucinations, in the same way the negating will produced the affirming will to escape its solitude.

I started this book with a disclaimer and a set of questions. It may very well be, I acknowledge, that our choices and desires in life lack necessity, that history itself is a pileup of contingencies and catastrophes. It may even come to pass that someone will discover a philosophical argument to prove the contingency of history. I am not interested in that question. Instead, I want to understand the conditions under which contingency shows up as a problem. If contingency is the water we all drown in, why and when do thinkers notice it? What situations strike at the body and the passions in such a way that the tenuousness of my subjectivity, my existence, flash into focus?

Schelling and Guenther might have written in different centuries, in different contexts, but both give a similar answer. I feel myself most lost, most unstable, most subject to chance and change at the moment I am deprived of all others. To give my sense of self any stability or reality, I need to be anchored in objects and recognized by other people. I need the touch of others to give definition to myself and make my surroundings a world. The type of touch that triggers a sense of contingency, it turns out, is the absent touch.

Schelling did not remain in obscurity for the rest of his life, writing and rewriting his fragmentary fable. In 1842 he was summoned from retirement by King Friedrich Wilhelm IV of Prussia to take the chair of philosophy in Berlin previously held by Hegel, bearing instructions to "slay the dragon-seed of Hegelian pantheism" and lauded not as "a common professor, but a philosopher chosen by God and called to be the teacher of the age."[48] It was, as Karl Jaspers remarked, "the last great event of the German university that actually engaged the interest of the public."[49]

To a reactionary public, Hegel had become the enemy, with his tale of Geist coming to consciousness through history read as an effort to "reduce the human being to the immanent order of society, politics, or history."[50] Schelling, by contrast, with his talk of "the dark ground" of "personality" in creation, was received as providing a philosophical basis for Christian personalism, a nineteenth-century movement that broke from the eighteenth century's understanding of individuality in terms of an abstract citizen's or subject's possession of rights in order to return to a much more particularistic Christian conception of the individual as defined by unique capacities that ought to be cultivated through *Bildung,* "education" or "formation."[51] For a brief time, then, Schelling was hailed as the foremost thinker of Christian personalism and orthodoxy.[52] As Warren Breckman put it, for all of Schelling's "metaphysical pathos," his thought entailed some devastatingly reactionary implications.[53]

Reactionary or not, Schelling's rejection of theodicy in the face of a loneliness that undoes all ties was also prescient. In the decades to follow, Max Weber[54] and Theodor Adorno[55] would both argue that loneliness is the central condition of humans under capitalism, prison reform advocates and abolitionists would come to remarkably similar conclusions about the damage solitary confinement can do, and a growing clamor of voices would reject the possibility of any sort of grand reconciliation with a world of suffering. Among those voices would be an Austrian Jew named Hans Mayer who, in his reflections on multiple arrests, torture, and imprisonment in Auschwitz, noted with something approaching wonder that "the experience of persecution was, at the very bottom, that of an extreme *loneliness.*"[56] Whereas Schelling raised and rejected the possibility of reconciliation with God in the face of such isolation, Mayer pushed the question further and asked about reconciliation with his tormentors on earth.

3

VIOLATION

JEAN AMÉRY AND THE THEOLOGY OF NONFORGIVENESS

One hundred thirty years after Schelling drafted and then discarded his account of loneliness, which would so uncannily echo the experience of prisoners in solitary confinement, another man lay on a prison floor, smoking, with swollen, shaking hands, a cigarette butt a sympathetic guard had flicked into his cell. Earlier that day, July 23, 1943, a Gestapo officer named Praust had bound Hans Mayer's hands behind his back, slid the shackles over a long, broad hook at the end of a chain, and hoisted him up until he hung suspended a meter above the floor. For a few minutes Praust beat him with a horsewhip, demanding the names and addresses of his comrades in the Belgian Resistance, while he struggled to hold himself aloft through strength alone. Then: "there was a crackling and splintering in my shoulders that my body has not forgotten until this hour. The balls sprang from their sockets. My own body weight caused luxation; I fell into a void and now hung from my dislocated arms, which had been torn high from behind and were now twisted over my head. Torture, from the latin *torquere*, to twist—what a visual instruction in etymology!"[1] With that, claimed Mayer, reflecting from a distance of twenty years and the safety of his French pseud-onym, Jean Améry, the moment of torture was complete; Praust had effected the "transformation of the person into flesh [*Ver-fleischlichung*]."[2] This experience would linger with Améry, but not as a normal memory. Instead, it created a fundamentally different relationship to the body, permanently exiling him into a state of flesh. "If from the experience of torture any knowl-edge at all remains that goes beyond the plain nightmarish," he muses toward the end of the essay "Torture, it is that of a great amazement [*einer großen Verwunderung*] and a foreignness in the world that cannot be compensated by any sort of subsequent human communication."[3]

Améry marks a shift in the experiences of contingency dis-cussed in this book. In different ways, Novalis and Schelling worried about lack of contact creating a pathological experience of contingency. Like Schelling, who once dreamed of a force that might "rattle him . . . tense him," and by doing so pull him from his "most forsaken loneliness," Novalis imagines the European as sick with an excess of interiority. Her skin has hardened, leav-ing her insensible to an external world and withering away from lack of stimulation—Europe as a continent full of Brontë hero-ines. Recognizing contingency, for Novalis, means returning to the local, with its irreducible abundance of *things* that exist in specific *places*, not dispersing one's self in the abstract realm of thought. It means relearning how to be touched and moved by a world that exists without us so that we might be healthy once again. It means, above all, reordering the senses to dissolve hard-ened boundaries between sight and touch, interior and exterior, self and world. Desperate as they are for contact, he and Schelling simply have no space for imagining the sorts of disorientation and vulnerability that come from coerced, unwanted touch.

It would take a darker century, marked by psychological wards, war, genocide, and torture, to make the contours of that violating,

vertiginous version of contingency clear. That century would produce the starkest challenge seen yet to the dream that contingency
might prove marvelous, healing, revelatory. Through the work of
Jean Améry, Eugène Minkowski, and Maurice Merleau-Ponty, it
would raise a very different set of questions: What if we can only
experience the true vulnerability of contingency, of being flesh, at
the moment the last protective boundaries of place and personhood have been forcibly stripped away? What if contingency does
not simply ambush us or overwhelm us? What if awareness of our
contingency were so disruptive that we could only be made to recognize it by coercion? How would we evaluate contingency then,
and what might the repercussions of that experience be?

For Jean Améry, reflecting on his torture and abuse, both in
Breendonk and, after, in Auschwitz, that experience of contingency could only come after history, law, and, finally, violating
touch had transformed his experience of his body from a place,
protected by boundaries, into open, raw flesh. In order to tell the
story of that transformation and unpack the resonances of flesh—
Christian and otherwise—I want to begin by looking among
Améry's philosophical contemporaries for an account of how
normal and abnormal experiences of touch create the boundaries of the self.[4] To find that, my story begins in the first half of
the twentieth century at Sainte-Anne Hospital, a psychiatric
hospital in Paris, with the work of a largely forgotten philosopher-
psychologist, Eugène Minkowski.

MINKOWSKI, MERLEAU-PONTY, AND
SCHIZOPHRENIA'S SPACE
OF CONTINGENCY

Sainte-Anne Hospital was not a typical mental hospital in 1926,
when Eugène Minkowski first began making the rounds among

the mad who would become the basis of his work on schizophrenia, space, and time. To begin with, it was old, even compared with its much more famous sister hospital, the Pitié-
Salpêtrière, where Jean-Martin Charcot's treatment of women
diagnosed with hysteria drew a young Sigmund Freud in 1885.
The first hospital built on the current site dates back to the thir-
teenth century, receiving the name of Sainte-Anne in 1651. Up
until 1788, when it was rebuilt as a fully functional hospital,
Sainte-Anne's served as a working farm where the mad could
find some sort of normalcy and therapy in tilling the land. In
1863, Napoleon III designated it a mental hospital once again
and assigned Baron Haussman, the man responsible for much
of the massive nineteenth-century redesign of Paris, to find an
architect for its new grounds.[5] Despite the changes in psychiatric treatment in the century since Sainte-Anne's was farmed by
the patients, the grounds retained much of their idyllic character. The buildings, even today, retain the sweeping stone facade
of the Second Empire, while the grounds are filled with carefully manicured gardens, light-dappled verandas, and marble
statues of mermen, mischievous angels, and graceful headless
women.

While it may have been old when Minkowski began his peculiar mixture of phenomenology and psychopathology, it was
innovative. Patients were encouraged to learn manual trades,
such as carpentry, and to find grounding in the world through
the work of their hands. The doctors, particularly Dr. Gaston
Ferdière, encouraged artistic expression among inmates and even
went so far as to stage shows of their work, turning Sainte-Anne's
into a hub for artists affiliated with the Surrealist movement.
Andre Breton, Alberto Giacometti, Marcel Duchamp, and Joan
Miró all visited Sainte-Anne's in the 1930s and 1940s, while
any number of local artists attended Dr. Ferdière's lectures on

clinical psychiatry from 1934–1938. When the Nazis staged their exhibit of "Degenerate Art" in 1937, comparing modern art with the drawings of the insane, Sainte-Anne's responded with its own exhibit of over two hundred patient pieces.[6]

In short, Sainte Anne's was hardly the stereotype of an early psychiatric institution, filled with endless identical corridors, dark rooms, straitjackets, and doctors interested, at best, in restraining patients they saw as subhuman. It is more than a little ironic, then, that it was in this singular, vibrant place, founded on centuries of cultivating the earth, designed as a monument to the state, and transformed into a salon for the most daring artists of the day, that the Russian-born émigré Minkowski first noticed patients drowning in disorientation. It was there he came to the insight that would be central for Merleau-Ponty's account of contingency nearly a decade later: sanity is constituted by a normal affective relation to place and space, and the inability to recognize place is the essence of madness.

In his Sorbonne lectures of 1949, Merleau-Ponty would call Minkowski "the first 'witness among us'" of phenomenology in France,[7] but in 1926 he was only a new doctor, not altogether young, without much of a name for himself. Born in 1885 to a Jewish family in Saint Petersburg, he began a medical degree in Poland before antisemitism drove him to finish his training in Berlin. By the end of his degree, he had drifted nearly entirely away from medicine to the study of philosophy, eventually moving to Zurich with his wife, where they both studied psychiatry. During World War I, Minkowski served in the French army, even winning the Croix de Guerre for bravery. Eventually, after several years working in Switzerland, Minkowski found his job in Paris at Sainte-Anne's and began to publish pioneering work on schizophrenia. Then, in 1933, deeply influenced by the work of Henri Bergson, whom he knew personally, Minkowski published *Les Temps Vécu,* or *Lived Time,* his only work ever published in English.

By most standards, Minkowski's work was a flop. It was self-published in a limited run of one thousand copies, using a sum of money he pooled together with his father. *Les Temps Vécu* draws heavily on Bergson's work on the experience of time and Minkowski's own 1923 article "Étude psychologique et analyse phénoménologique d'un cas de melancolie schizophrénique."[8] At the center of the work is Minkowski's observation that his schizophrenic patients lack the capacity to project a future based on their present experience. While the healthy person can relate to the future through any number of acts, such as hoping, praying, desiring, expecting, and acting morally, the schizophrenic is cut off from those basic modes of being. Even more significantly, echoing Heidegger, Minkowski suggests that schizophrenia cuts subjects off from the confrontation with death that gives shape to the activity of becoming in our lives.

Although at least one scholar has voiced the suspicion that "Minkowski's phenomenology of time is nothing but a loan from Bergson,"[9] *Les Temps Vécu* broke from Bergson and offered genuinely innovative work in the book's second half where Minkowski offered an analysis of "lived space," or *espace vécu.* It is that section of analysis, with its emphasis on pathological experiences of space, that Merleau-Ponty would draw most heavily on in formulating his understanding of contingency as a type of primordial spatial awareness in his 1945 work, *The Phenomenology of Perception.*

Merleau-Ponty came to link Minkowski's thoughts on madness to the experience of contingency through a broad meditation on the phenomenology of space. We always find ourselves in space, he insists, with no possibility of stepping outside it. The most primordial type of space takes the form of depth that is not yet anchored in the particularity of things. As Sue L. Cataldi notes in her study on Merleau-Ponty's philosophy of embodiment, "On principle, the primordial spatial level, 'on the horizon of all our perceptions,' can never be reached. As the first level, it cannot be spatially particularized, because it cannot be referred to as preceding anchoring setting *'anywhere'* to be expressly perceived."[10] It always precedes any act of perception, but is in no particular place and cannot be expressly perceived or grasped. Space serves as the groundless ground of all perception, the perceptual analogue to Schelling's will.

Our first "hold" on the world is that of "blind adherence."[11] Merleau-Ponty terms this originary grasp on the world "contingency" and suggests that while we ultimately lose sight of it as we become increasingly well oriented in the world, it makes meaningful our subsequent perceptions of space. It also establishes a form of "communication with the world more ancient than thought."[12] This blind grasp of space, however, gives way to a more directed way of moving in space as we come to inhabit it through intentional grasping. As soon as actions begin to sync up with objectives, a new *sens*—a deliberately polysemous reference to a sense (as in the five senses) and sense (meaning)—develops, bringing with it a definite sense of direction. Cataldi notes that all we have to do is think about the struggle of babies to stand upright and coordinate enough with their surroundings to, for example, drink from cups in order to understand the transformation Merleau-Ponty sees in play.[13] Contingency, then, is a type of presubjective, borderless continuity between self and world that leaves us utterly open to any change in our surroundings.

There are a few different ways of understanding Merleau-Ponty's decision to equate this early experience of blind adhesion to space with contingency. The first has to do with the link between contingency and dependency. A baby's initial experience of space is wholly dependent on (which is to say, contingent upon) the surrounding world. And it is not only the baby who depends on the world to give it any sense of self—it is all of us. Merleau-Ponty explicitly rejects anything like Fichte's self-positing subject, with its claims to be sui generis; on the contrary, we are birthed to a world that precedes us and makes possible our sense of self as we navigate through its space. There is no sensation, no thought, without the material world that exists before us and will perdure long after our deaths. Insofar as Merleau-Ponty believes our ability to think of ourselves as a stable self—with boundaries and an identity separate from our physical experience of the world—emerges from our ability to grasp and manipulate objects, so too does the baby's own sense of self fluctuates from moment to moment. It *is* the hot sun that scorches it or the cold that rips through its swaddling. There is no chance to build up the various little illusions that there is some self existing outside the physical forces that impinge on it. The baby does not just think, abstractly, "Yes, I could have been born to a different mother and my life might have been otherwise," as an adult might. Its life *is* otherwise from moment to moment because it lacks any of the categories or physical capacities that allow it to think it has control over the world. A baby has no resources to deny the sheer lack of necessity in its existence when confronted with the unmediated world.

Philosophically, this abandonment of blind adherence to contingency in favor of directed grasping is also a shift from a pre-subjective openness to the world to the subject-object distinction. Part of the process of coming to believe that personal subjectivity exists in contradistinction to objects in the world involves acquiring a different sense of depth that allows for distance between things. In discussing the normal experience of depth, Merleau-Ponty frames his theory in contrast to the traditional empiricist account. Thinkers such as George Berkeley (1685–1753) had explained away the vision of depth as breadth seen from the side, arguing that depth would disappear altogether if we could only gain the proper perspective. For Merleau-Ponty, however, this explanation relies on a God's-eye perspective of space that the spectator can never assume. It also misses the basic experience of depth. While breadth and height contrast two discrete objects, depth blurs and envelops objects. Depth implicates and contracts both time and space in one process. As Cataldi parses Merleau-Ponty's position, "Phenomenologically, we see (or 'our gaze holds') something (in front of us) from *here* at its place *there—at the same time.* The here and the there are contemporary in our experience."[14] Whereas a physicist, Cataldi goes on to explain, "must separate the here from the there, both spatially and temporally, in explaining how the light there at location A at time t strikes the eyes here at location B at time t_1 . . . [for Merleau-Ponty,] it is possible to see things from here over there at the *same* time because they, and we, are held (together and apart) in the thickness, in the depth, of the same 'living present.'"[15] Depth unites and separates. At the same time that my here is linked to there, I also see that there is a place where I am not.

For healthy people, our orientation in the living present involves a mixture of what Merleau-Ponty calls "clear space" and affective attachments. Clear space is a type of public, impartial space, "in which all objects are equally important and enjoy the same right to existence."[16] For the normal person, all clear space is shot through with affective commitments that make particular places significant, drawing them closer. Merleau-Ponty traces the association of feeling and direction back to "primitive man," for whom, he writes, "There is a mythical space in which directions and positions are determined by the residence in it of great affective entities."[17] It would be a mistake, however, to imagine that any society ever outgrows this affective dimension of its topography. Merleau-Ponty cites a range of examples to prove his point, such as the common labeling of morals as either "high" or "low" and the shifting perspective of the villager who, upon hearing that his capital has been invaded, suddenly experiences the surroundings that had comprised his whole reality as an exile from the world. Our experience of space is always a mottled mixture of the personal and public; that is what allows us to navigate the world and experience it as meaningful.

On occasion, however, this careful combination of depth, distance, public space, and personal commitments, collapses, allowing something much closer to the experience of primordial depth, and its attendant experience of contingency, to reemerge. Merleau-Ponty discusses this phenomenon later in his chapter on space, when he turns to the writings of Eugène Minkowski. I mentioned earlier that Minkowski believed that schizophrenics were defined by their truncated sense of time. Merleau-Ponty, in the passages I am interested in, focuses on Minkowski's parallel observations about the schizophrenic's disordered, affective relation to space. In contrast to the healthy person, whose constantly shifting perception of depth always holds objects at a greater or lesser distance, the schizophrenic inhabits something that Merleau-Ponty alternately calls "pure depth," "dark space," or "absolute space."[18] Pure depth is felt as the confusion of the ego with the darkness that surrounds it, an impersonal space that, in Minkowski's words, "palpitates at the base of our being. . . . It seems to go beyond the ego, yet we feel it to be the true source of our life. Taken in itself, this depth appears to have something impersonal in it; however, it is, above all, when we strive to give to the world what is most personal in us that we feel our *élan* coming from the depths of our being."[19] In this space everything is too close, depth too tangible, too much "mine."

All of us, not just schizophrenics, experience some degree of this altered relation to space at night. Drawing on Minkowski, Merleau-Ponty writes:

> Night is not an object before me; it enwraps me and infiltrates me through all my senses, stifling my recollections and almost destroying my identity. I am no longer withdrawn into my perceptual look-out from which I watch the outlines of objects moving by at a distance. Night has no outlines; it is itself in contact with me and its unity is the mystical unity of *mana*. . . . It is pure depth without foreground or background, without surfaces and without any distance separating it from me. All space for the reflecting mind is sustained by thinking which relates its parts to each other, but in this case the thinking starts from nowhere.[20]

"The distress felt by neuropaths in the night," he concludes, "is caused by the fact that it *brings home to us our contingency,* the uncaused and tireless impulse which drives us to seek anchorage and to surmount ourselves in things, without any guarantee that we shall always find them."[21] Our sense of contingency and disorientation can be borne on the occasional dark night; the effects become devastating, though, when the schizophrenic is ejected from a common world and swallowed by dark space.

With the dissolution of distance between subject and object in dark space, the schizophrenic loses the ability to limit his awareness of touch. Merleau-Ponty's schizophrenic feels awareness everywhere, overwhelming him. He is like a man without skin, subject to touch he can neither distance himself from nor resist. At every moment, he experiences himself as utterly porous, his identity fluctuating as grass bends under foot, clothing rustles against his skin, shadows streak across his face. Merleau-Ponty can be read as deliberately referencing Roquentin in Sartre's *Nausea* when he describes this experience of contingency, particularly when he writes of contingency "as the vital experience of giddiness and nausea, which is the awareness of our contingency and the horror with which it fills us."[22] In the pages before Roquentin recognizes contingency as the key to understanding his nausea, he writes constantly, frantically, about objects growing strange in his hand and imposing themselves on his attention. He no longer feels himself as a man grasping a fork; instead, he becomes an extension of the utensil, "which now has a certain way of having itself picked up."[23] "Objects should not touch because they are not alive," he wails. "You use them, put them back in place, you live among them: they are useful, nothing more. But they touch me, it is unbearable. I am afraid of being in contact with them as though they were living beasts."[24] This is the experience of contingency for the unhealthy adult: the inability to shift our attention at will and decide what we will or will not register as touching us creates a destructive continuity between the self and the world. Sanity, healthy subjectivity, is founded on the ability *not to feel* touch, to become only selectively aware of what brushes up against us, to experience things as distant, manageable objects.

Merleau-Ponty neatly sums up the stakes of maintaining a normal experience of space, which is to say, the stakes of surmounting our contingency. "What protects the sane man against delirium or hallucination is not his critical powers," he insists,

> but the structure of his space: objects remain before him, keeping their distance and, as Malebranche says of Adam, touching him only with respect. What brings about hallucinations and

myths is a shrinkage in the space directly experienced, a root-
ing of things in our body, the overwhelming proximity of the
object, the oneness of man and the world, which is, not indeed
abolished, but repressed by everyday perception or objective
thought.[25]

Repressing awareness of our contingency does nothing less than
found the entire nonpathological experience of subjectivity.

Years later, Merleau-Ponty came to rework his language of
dark and clear space into his notion of flesh, *la chair*. As one
scholar summarized it, flesh is, "a pre-subjective, elemental corporeality of which the world is made before 'I' am there."[26] Echoing his engagement with Minkowski, Merleau-Ponty described
flesh as self-occluding, dark, voluminous, deep matter that creates perception by "folding over itself" and creating opening or
hollows for perception. "My flesh and that of the world therefore involve clear zones, clearings, about which pivot their opaque
zones."[27] These clear zones make possible vision of a common
world; without them flesh would remain obscure, dark, invisible.[28] Human perception takes place in one such clear zone of
flesh.

The concept is obscure, and reams have been rightly written
on it. I mention it only to say that even Merleau-Ponty could not
remain faithful to the darkness of his original insight. The great
virtue of *The Phenomenology of Perception*, the virtue missing from
Derrida, Nancy, and Merleau-Ponty's own later, related work on
flesh, is its ability to imagine, for a moment, hostile touch from
the recipient's end. By the time he writes *The Invisible and the
Invisible*, that sensitivity dulls. Dark space becomes flesh, and
the impersonal space "that palpitates at the base of our being"
ceases to be an object of horror and nausea. Under one reading,
flesh even opens up as a wonderful dimension of creatureliness

that allows me to recognize my personal history as always a continuation of a prepersonal world.[29]

All of which is to say that I think Merleau-Ponty's and Minkowski's discussion of contingency as dark space needs a different heir, with a different notion of flesh, if only because their account leaves open too many questions in its richness. Most pressingly, in framing the experience of contingency as the domain of "neuropaths," illness, and madness, Merleau-Ponty naturalizes dark space. (There is, after all, no pathology outside of the framework of an organism). In doing so, he at once renders the collapse of boundaries familiar—this repressed sense of space, like all forms of the repressed, threatens to return to us— and distant—in all probability, though, I am not singled out and prostrated by illness. That ambiguity of whether the experience of dark space is always pathological, always a sign of neurosis, points toward a different question: What, exactly, have Minkowski and Merleau-Ponty given us? Is it, as it appears, a phenomenology of madness, of schizophrenia, only applicable to a few, or is it a phenomenology of violation anyone might experience?

The question matters because, just a few years after Minkowski published his work on schizophrenia, history would intervene through the brutality of a hostile Reich that created a new class of people who could not will who and what touched them. Minkowski, who spent the war years helping Jewish children escape Europe, would personally come to see altogether too many other situations where things—or rather, people—do not touch with respect.

Those victims pose a new set of questions. If Minkowski and Merleau-Ponty really are describing violation, if dark space can swallow us all, given enough world-historically bad luck, how does that happen? After all, Merleau-Ponty's claim should not be understated: there is no subjectivity without the repression of contingency. So, given how central it is to Merleau-Ponty's account for the formation of the subject and sanity to keep objects at a proper distance, to disown our contingency, what would it take to make a person confront his or her contingency? How thin *are* the walls between our selves and our contingency? One answer lies in Jean Améry's account of torture from the beginning of this chapter, which turns out to have surprising parallels to dark space.

THE SELF AS HOME

In 1935, two years after Minkowski published *Les Temps Vécu* to an indifferent public, Améry, or Hans Mayer, as he was called then, sat in a Vienna café reading his death sentence in a newspaper. That, at least, is how he recounted that afternoon in later years when he wrote, "I do not believe that I am inadmissibly projecting Auschwitz and the Final Solution back to 1935 when I advance these thoughts today. . . . To be a Jew, that meant for me, from this moment on, to be a dead man on leave, someone to be murdered, who only by chance [*nur durch Zufall*] was not yet where he properly belonged."[30] In the end, it would be Améry's own hand that would end his life in 1978, twelve years after his radio broadcasts and essays about his experience in Auschwitz lifted him out of obscurity, but, for as long as he lived, Améry remained insistent that his vulnerability, his exile, the sense of statelessness within his own skin that made his death inevitable, began that day in Vienna.

What changed that day was not only Améry's sense of security or faith in the stability of the world, or even his assumption that his bodily autonomy would remain unviolated, though those beliefs would be stripped away in the years to come. Rather, I suggest in the following pages, the sense of foreboding and estrangement he felt that day marked the beginning of an impoverishment in his relationship to places that ended in his torture. This confluence of place and torture is not a coincidence. To Améry, driven from his country, home and exile would be the defining categories of his life.[31] Even his torture would be felt as a shrinkage of safe space, as the circle of the familiar contracted and transformed his body into the last place he could call his own in an increasingly impoverished and hostile world.

None of what I just described—the slow constriction of place, imprisonment, torture, rise to fame—seemed at all likely at Améry's birth in a small Austrian village in 1912. He was born into a nearly entirely assimilated Jewish family to a schoolteacher and soldier. As he would write in later years about his upbringing in his collection of essays, translated as *At the Mind's Limits: Contemplations by a Survivor on Auschwitz and Its Realities*:

> I see myself as a boy at Christmas, plodding through a snow-covered village to midnight mass; I don't see myself in a synagogue. I hear my mother appealing to Jesus, Mary, and Joseph when a minor household misfortune occurred; I hear no adjuration of the Lord in Hebrew. The picture of my father—whom I hardly knew, since he remained where his Kaiser had sent him and his fatherland deemed him to be in the safest care—did not show me a bearded Jewish sage, but rather a Tyrolean Imperial Rifleman in the uniform of the First World War.[32]

Améry encountered antisemitism in his upbringing, but did not think much about it either as a child or as a literature and philosophy student in Vienna, even when a student at university called him a Jew and knocked a tooth out during a fight. "Yes, we are Jews, and what of it?" he retorted to his schoolmate. "Today my tooth, tomorrow yours, and the devil take you, I thought to myself after the beating, and bore the gap proudly like an interesting dueling scar."[33] No one in the family, he would candidly explain, bothered to hide or deny their Jewish origin. He simply was a Jew, "just as one of my schoolmates was the son of a bankrupt innkeeper: when the boy was alone the financial ruin of his family may have meant next to nothing to him; when he joined us others he retreated, as we did, into resentful embarrassment."[34]

Whatever its intimations of darker events to come, Améry's upbringing sensitized him to the psychological importance of place and home. He was a man raised in rural Austria, fully steeped in folk traditions and rhetoric of the fatherland, and his love for that life shows unmistakably, if defensively, throughout his writing. Accordingly, his vision of a healthy relationship to place is tinctured with nostalgia in a way Merleau-Ponty's talk of dark and clear space simply is not. Out of that wistful remembrance of a lost home, Améry builds a larger theory where home serves three purposes: to make memory possible, to ground comprehension of human behavior, and to secure the individual from *Zufall*, chance, contingency.

Améry first addresses the role of home in memory in his essay reflecting on the inner life of the exile, "How Much Home Does a Person Need?" It is possible, he reflects, that one day everything making up a home—the countless different objects imbued with memory and emotions, the hammer handle worn away to fit the pattern of my palm—will become interchangeable, disposable, replaceable. A new generation may come that trades in houses the way we replace outdated cars, but home will mean something different for them, provided it continues to make any sense at all. For Améry's generation, though, home requires objects that tell stories, a table whose nicks bear witness to the local craftsman who sculpted and sanded it. Home "gives access to a reality that for us consists of perception through the senses."[35] Not just history, but also the senses themselves will become foreign when the future arrives, bringing with it cities understood as demographic tables and homes reduced to blueprints.[36]

It is easy enough to see how objects trigger memories (madeleine, meet Proust), but it is less obvious what Améry means when he says that that objects make memory possible. Fortunately, a recent scholarly conversation on the fate of place offers some leads. The most helpful book for thinking through this puzzle is Robert Pogue Harrison's 2003 book *Dominion of the Dead*.

Harrison belongs to a group of thinkers, largely influenced by Heidegger, worried about the erosion of place in the contemporary globalized world.[37] The way thinkers such as Marc Augé, Harrison, and Heidegger define place differs, but their nightmare vision of what replaces place is roughly similar to Améry's: it is a world of identical airports, stocked with McDonald's, that lead to highways marked with interchangeable billboards, that take you to buy anonymous kitsch.[38] Throughout the book, Harrison defines place by way of contrast with two opposites: space and wilderness. Space is a mathematical construct that allows for the plotting of points. For Harrison, the modern grid of city blocks presupposes an understanding of humans as inhabiting empty space that they shape according to the demands of logic, rather than in encounter with a world. Wilderness, by contrast, is placeless, not because nature has been eradicated by human mastery but because there it lacks all signs of human presence. Early on he asserts, "A place is defined by its boundaries, its intrinsic limits, its distinctly local 'here' that remains fixed in space even as it perdures in time. . . . Places are located in nature, yet they also have human foundations."[39]

As a way of explaining what he means by place, Harrison cites a Wallace Stevens poem called "Anecdote of the Jar." "I place a jar in Tennessee, / And round it was, upon a hill. / It made slovenly wilderness / Surround that hill. / The wilderness rose up to it, / And sprawled around, no longer wild."[40] The jar, Harrison suggests, provides a "measure of human containment," around which the wilderness converges. Yet a place does not just consist of boundaries or signs of human presence. That is what a place *needs*, but what it is, in a more fundamental sense, "is where time, in its human modes, takes place."[41] And this human mode is that of mortality.

In insisting on this, Harrison draws from Giambattista Vico's *The New Science*, specifically the passages where he describes the three defining features of human life as belief in Providence, the institution of marriage, and burial of the dead. The earliest inhabitants of the earth—giants, in Vico's narrative—lived in natural time, an endless cycle of birth and death. Gradually, though, the most pious began to bury their dead and mark their graves.[42] As the burial posts multiplied, humans began to attend more closely to their genealogies, in the process creating history, human time, and property. Graves created the first places; they tamed the wilderness, like Stevens's jar, and carved out a narrative or linear progression from the endlessness of wilderness. He even explicitly references the link between the home and the dead in antiquity when he claims that the hearth, in its original form, was the sacred fire on the altar of the dead. Citing Numa Denis Fustel de Coulanges's argument that the house had its origins in ancestor worship, Harrison writes, "The ancient house was first and foremost an institution by which, or *in* which, the dead were lodged and preserved in their being."[43] The descendants, the inhabitants of the house, thought of the hearth as the coals of the sacred fire on the altar, and the house's sheltering walls not as protection from the elements but rather as protection *by* their ancestors. "A house, in sum, was a place where two realms—one under and the other on the earth—interpenetrated each other."[44] In Harrison's account the private realm of the home is the quintessentially historical one where the dead are buried. Améry intuited that place makes memory possible; Harrison finds in Vico and the Romans historical practices and precedents for that thought.

In other ways Améry anticipates Harrison's concerns. He loathes and distrusts the slow erosion of place marked by memory, and its replacement with the abstract, mathematical space where citizens "settle at topographical points but are subject to eviction anyway," and who primarily relate to a city through "the statistical tables that anticipate demographic development."[45] He acknowledges the grounding presence of the dead when he insists on behalf of his generation that "we need a house of which we know who lived in it before us."[46]

Because of his forced ejection from home, however, Améry remains blind to the uncanny dimension of a home where the living and the dead "interpenetrate" each other that Harrison highlights. Remarkably, given that Améry and Freud overlapped, Améry never even mentions the idea of the *unheimlich*, the uncanny dimension that underpins the home. After all, as work by Anthony Vidler has shown, the *heimlich* and the *unheimlich* are inseparable in origin, with the concept of the *heimlich*, the homely, encompassing the cozy, the safe, the comfortable, *and* the brutal, hidden cruelties of a home.[47]

Améry's lack of interest in the uncanny dimension of home, and to the possibility of darkness within it, lead him to assign another function to home, beyond grounding memory.[48] As he would later write in an essay reflecting on exile, "Reduced to the positive psychological content of the idea, home is *security*."[49] Specifically, home offers the security of a framework for knowledge. Bodies, words, gestures were suddenly uprooted from all context, reduced to "sensory reality, but not interpretable signs."[50] To explain what he means, Améry relates one story, from his first days in Belgium, of sitting across a table from a large, coarsely built Flemish man, sharing a beer, and feeling utterly incapable of discerning whether his companion was a respectable bourgeois citizen or a thug about to punch him in the face and rape his wife. Every interaction had suddenly become inscrutable.

This inscrutability and perilousness of exile pushes Améry to his third realization: home is opposed to chance. "One feels secure, however, where no chance occurrence [*Ungefähres*] is to be expected, nothing completely strange [*ganz und gar Fremdes*] to be feared. To live in one's homeland means that what is already known to us occurs before our eyes again and again, in slight variants."[51] While a life spent entirely at home can be stifling and provincial, homelessness bewilders. With this discussion of home, the content of chance or contingency becomes clearer. Obviously, if Améry were claiming that the unexpected, inexplicable, or the "chance occurrence" could never occur in one's native land, he would be talking utter nonsense. Of course the unexpected and unnecessary come to pass at home. Since Améry is an exceptionally lucid thinker, however, it is more likely that when he refers to chance he has something much closer to my project in mind, namely a certain affective orientation toward the unnecessary and unexpected that makes it show up as such. Under this reading, the difference between the security of home and the disequilibrium of foreign lands is not so much a question of what types of events happen in each. Rather, the difference between home and exile is that home allows Améry to integrate unexpected events into a broader framework and, by doing so, dismiss anything unexpected about them. In exile, by contrast, chance events seem like the product of chance. As such they are frightening, upsetting, and incomprehensible. For Améry, contingency can only reveal itself as such at the moment when home as a category disappears for him.

Given the sheer range of meanings home has for Améry, however, no one single event is enough to destroy it. Home's different functions need to be peeled away before he is fully confronted with his own contingency. His sense of security first began to erode the day the Nuremberg Laws "made me formally and beyond any question a Jew," and thus "quarry of Death."[52] His formal exile to Belgium in 1938 uprooted him permanently from the objects that reminded him of his history and the interpretive framework that made his interactions with other people comprehensible. All of that is true, even obviously so, but even then the language he uses to describe home does not disappear fully until his torture; rather, the language of place gets redirected toward his body. When he is shut off from all other places, his body becomes a place.

To become a place is not the same thing as inhabiting a place or being understood through the metaphor of a place. To be a place, as in Harrison, Stevens, and Casey, the body would need some sort of boundary that marked the passage of mortal time. I contend it has one: the skin. This thought has a certain intuitive logic. As in English, German has a number of colloquial phrases tying the skin to home, such as "to feel at home in one's skin," with eyes as "the window of one's soul," and so on.[53] Likewise, in a very basic sense our skin is a record of our past, showing signs of age and damage; it wrinkles, spots, thins, tans, burns, scars, and stretches.[54] Moreover, biologically, the skin gives us over to life and to relation in the first moments of birth. As

Ashley Montagu notes in his review of the science of touching, the pressure on the fetus's skin as the mother's contractions force it out stimulate the respiratory system, making possible the transition into postnatal life, while the level of caressing immediately after birth could be correlated to the relative anxiety of the child in later life, with less contact associated with more emotional disturbance.[55] These are biological facts that nonetheless underlie the construction of the social.

For Améry, even after home has been stripped away through exile, unviolated, intact skin still ties him to a social world through "the expectation of help." So long as I can feel on my skin what I want, or, at any rate, objectify it such that I do not feel identical with it, I can maintain "the expectation of help." "The expectation of help," he writes, "the certainty of help, belongs to the fundamental experiences of men and also to animals. The expectation of help is even a constitutive element of the psyche."[56] The child who falls instinctively expects the mother to run to his aid, just as wounded soldiers await the sirens of the red cross.[57] The full, normal range of temporality, for Améry, is associated with the expectation of help. As long as I can expect at every moment someone will come to my aid, I remain connected to a past filled with loved ones and friends, as well as to a future from which help arrives. In that sense, Améry echoes Minkowski's point about the ability to project forward into time defining a normal psychic life. The inviolate skin belongs to the world of parents, friends, siblings, and lovers, but also to ambulances, pretty Red Cross nurses, and the wounds of war. That is to say, it belongs to biology, institutions, relations, history, and a world. It is, in some nontrivial way, *historical*.

Thus the skin acts as a boundary, preserving the individual's history, sovereignty, and even faith in social relations. As Améry writes, "the certainty that by reason of written or unwritten social contracts the other person will spare me—more precisely that he will respect my physical, and with it also my metaphysical, being. The boundaries of my body are also the boundaries of myself. My skin surface shields me against the external world. If I am to have trust, I must feel on it only what I *want* to feel."[58]

Even by Améry's own account, skin is only really the boundary of the self in exceptional moments. He states quite explicitly that in most circumstances when struck he can dissociate from his body or in striking back make the attack a reciprocal one. As he says, "I can expand in urgent self-defense, objectify my corporeality, restore the trust in my continued existence."[59] In his final essay of this collection, "On the Necessity and Impossibility of Being a Jew," he recounts a moment in Auschwitz when a Polish guard beat him for some trifle. In a moment of defiant clarity, he struck him back. "That it was I, the physically much weaker man, who succumbed and was woefully thrashed, meant nothing to me," he writes. "Painfully beaten, I was satisfied with myself . . . because I had grasped well that there are situations in life in which our body is our entire self and our entire fate."[60] This memory clearly figures as a revelation of sorts in Améry's narrative, one that breaks from the intellectual knowledge that the body and self belong together in a way reminiscent of his earlier remarks on language.

Yet sometimes, in the moment of total helplessness, objectification is no longer possible. For Sartre's Roquentin that moment came when he began to feel all the little lifeless things touching *him*, rather than just his body; for Améry it arrived with the first blow of the Gestapo after his 1943 arrest for distributing subversive pamphlets in Belgium. Handcuffed, unable to resist, he would feel the first blow as a violation, "a rape, a sexual act without consent," and, as such, "a physical overwhelming by the other [that] becomes an existential consummation of destruction altogether."[61] The violating touch of torture, I will argue in the next section, is what finally destroyed Améry's sense of home and place, propelling him into something very similar to Merleau-Ponty's notion of dark space by transforming his body into what Améry would call *Fleisch*, flesh.

VERFLEISCHLICHUNG

Verfleischlichung, the transformation from man into meat, begins with the first blow. With the first blow, the expectation of help that Améry found so crucial to the normal psychic functioning of humans and animals collapses. Everything the prisoner had anticipated as an abstract possibility suddenly becomes a present certainty. "They are permitted to punch me in the face, the victim feels in numb surprise and concludes in just as numb certainty: they will do with me what they want. Whoever would rush to the prisoner's aid—a wife, a mother, a brother, a friend—he won't get this far."[62] When that boundary is violated, the past and the relationships that shaped it recede to insignificance, and a new temporality is introduced—one first of numb expectation and then of no expectation at all. His entire history, his identity shaped by family, friends, loved ones, and commitments recede to insignificance.

This is the moment of violation. This is the moment of contingency, as Merleau-Ponty understood it, when the boundaries that make a body a place collapse, leaving open, empty, dark space. Améry himself says everything that came after—the splintering of his shoulders, the fall into a void, the uncertainty that would never, ever leave him—were just the logical continuation of the first blow. To feel hands on his body, knowing he had never invited them, never asked for them, never wanted them, and yet was powerless to push them away, was enough. Even if the miraculous had happened and his torturer had laid down his weapons, unshackled him, and walked him to the gate as a friend, he still would have left that day with his trust in the world destroyed. Not because the touch of another's hands was so objectively terrible, especially in comparison to what came after, but because with that touch he was ripped out of the normal network of human relations and restraints, completely abandoned. In that moment he knew that every boundary he had erected between himself and the world to guard his sense of subjectivity could have been otherwise. His sense of self as an inviolable, whole individual turned out to exist just as a courtesy from the surrounding world, and that courtesy had just been revoked.

But of course the torturer did not lay down his tools. If he had been the type to do so, perhaps he never would have picked them up in the first place. Instead, he picked up his tools and proceeded to complete the process of turning Améry into flesh. To become flesh, it is not enough to look at one's past as another, unreachable world; the world itself needs to be destroyed in pain. Drawing on Georges Bataille's work on the Marquis de Sade, Améry describes torture as the "total inversion of the social world," where the torturer seeks to "nullify this world . . . by negating his fellow man" because "he wants to realize his own total sovereignty."[63] To be sure, Améry admits, a world consisting entirely of torture, death, and destruction cannot sustain itself. The torturer, however, does not want to completely nullify the world; he wants to have the *power* to nullify the world.[64] It is enough that "a slight pressure by the tool-wielding hand is enough to turn the other—along with his head, in which are perhaps stored Kant and Hegel, and all nine symphonies, and the *World as Will and Representation*—into a shrilly squealing piglet at slaughter."[65] Mastery, true mastery, exists in the ability to torture and to choose when to stop torturing. Under that reading, the torturer dominates the prisoner by inflicting pain without being caught up in the dynamic of torture or dependent on the torture victim to reflect back his own mastery. When he has finished, Améry drily notes, "He himself can then smoke a cigarette or sit down to breakfast or, if he has the desire, have a look in at the *World as Will and Representation*."[66]

"It was over for a while. It still is not over."[67] With that, Améry was left with the question of how to understand the torture. Almost equally difficultly, he was left with the question of how to *write* about torture. In understanding torture as an expulsion from a common world, with its relationships, hopes, and references, Améry sets himself the problem of the apophatic theologian: how to describe something that transcends language or human comprehension. Attending to what he says about *Verfleischlichung* leads the reader part of the way but misses the significance of *how* Améry describes it. It misses the question of why Améry, a Jewish victim of Auschwitz, adopts the paradigmatically Christian language of "flesh" to depict his torture. It is impossible understand what Améry means and means to do with *Verfleischlichung* without understanding his attitude toward language.

Some of the problems Améry faces are well documented in literature on trauma victims. There is the issue of how to write about pain that Elaine Scarry describes so well in the opening pages of *The Body in Pain*, when she wrote: "Physical pain does not simply resist language but actively destroys it, bringing about an immediate reversion to a state anterior to language, to the sounds and cries a human being makes before language is learned."[68] Likewise, there was also the influence of trauma,[69] as

Améry set out "in search of the time that was impossible to lose, but had been difficult for me to talk about."[70] In Améry's case, trauma manifested less as blank spots in his memory than in fixed moments of brutal clarity that the thread of his life story kept catching on and snarling around. As W. G. Sebald astutely pointed out in his essay on Améry, "For victims of persecution, however, the thread of chronological time is broken, background and foreground merge, the victim's logical means of support in his existence are suspended. The experience of terror also dislocates time, that most abstract of humanity's homes. The only fixed points are traumatic scenes recurring with a painful clarity of vision and memory."[71]

While Sebald writes as well as anyone I have read about the texture of time in Améry, I think he misses what is unique about language in Améry's work when he broaches the subject elsewhere in the essay. For Sebald, Améry had to revive his atrophying German and relearn to write in the language of his torturers before he could speak about his past. He succeeds brilliantly but, in Sebald's eyes, slips constantly into protective irony, as when he ends his description of torture by apostrophizing, "Torture, from the latin *torquere*, to twist—what a visual instruction in etymology!"[72]

Unlike Sebald, I don't think Améry is raising a brittle shield of irony here or flinching away from the memory. Rather, I think he means exactly what he said: the experience of torture vivified his abstract knowledge of etymology and created a new relationship with language for him. Sebald is right that language does not always function that way for Améry. As alluded to earlier, Améry sets out a contrast between the form of knowledge we have when secure in the routine of everyday life. "I buy a newspaper and am 'a man who buys a newspaper' [*ein Mann der eine Zeitung kauft*]," Améry reflects. "The act does not differ from the image through which I anticipated it, and I hardly differentiate myself personally from the millions who performed it before me. Because my imagination did not suffice to entirely capture such an event? No, rather because even in direct experience everyday reality is nothing but codified abstraction. Only in rare moments of life do we truly stand face to face with the event and, with it, reality."[73]

So far as my research can tell, Améry never addresses the Saussurean linguistics that came to dominate so much of poststructuralism, where words gain meaning by way of reference to other words, but referents, things, lie beyond the system. Yet I think it is possible to understand Améry's remark about codified abstractions as pushing toward a similar point about how language ordinarily functions. Words never really sync up with things most of the time; we comprehend them but we never really *apprehend* them on a deep affective level.

Yet sometimes words flash up, made meaningful by chance or wonder or sheer, bloody bad luck. In those moments, the root of torture in *torquere*, to twist, syncs up with a falling, cracking body. The closest analogue to Améry's treatment of language here is Walter Benjamin's thoughts on history. For Benjamin, history largely proceeds in a monotonous, mythic time, where like succeeds like and nothing new ever arrives or is really experienced as present. Yet sometimes that dull, monotonous picture of time is punctured by curiously vivid echoes of the past. As he famously writes, "The true picture of the past flits by. The past can be seen only as an image which flashes up at the instant it can be recognized and is never seen again."[74] For Améry, language functions in much the same way. The body punches through abstraction just as the ideals of Rome punched through the consciousness of Maximilien Robespierre and became live once again in the French Revolution.

This is a corrosively anti-intellectual stance. In some sense, Améry thinks what it means to be an intellectual is to be able to glide from reference to reference, putting any event into a wider intellectual context. Intellectuals trade in references, and moments like torture short-circuit the entire process by bringing language back to the reality of bodies and things. Postmodern puns will never capture what Améry means. Words might give pleasure, conjure warm feelings about the fatherland, or evoke a sense of loss to the person still tied to the world, but faced with the brute, brutal fact of a body dangling from a meat hook, they fall silent. Faced with the "spiritually unhinged SS state," even their anesthetizing power fails. The skeptical humanist lacked the resources of the politically or religiously committed, whose "belief or their ideology gave them that firm foothold in the world. . . . They survived better or died with more dignity than their irreligious or unpolitical intellectual comrades; who often were infinitely better educated and more practiced in exact thinking."[75]

Fleisch straddles the two understandings of language, I argue. As in Améry's reference to *torquere*, the impact of describing his body as flesh is shocking in its immediacy. The word invokes the bloody, dripping image of meat, like a slab of steak a butcher might slap on the counter and watch ooze. He could have described himself as a body, using a term like *Körper* or *Leib*, but the appeal of flesh, rather than a body, is visceral. A body invokes the illusion of wholeness, boundaries, distinction. If you ask me how to define my body, I can count my fingers, touch my toes, and wrap my arms around my ribcage while I shiver. I never worry as I steer through a crowd that I might stumble into a stranger and lose track of where my body ends and another's begins. So long as I think of myself as a body, I think of myself as an individual unit, distinct from other individuals. I can imagine myself as a distinct agent, capable of mastery and control in my life.

Flesh is the body flayed for Améry. If I can all too easily slip into thinking about what it means to have a "good" body or a "bad" body, measured by social standards of beauty, with flesh I am surprised into silence by its vulnerability. Flesh is what remains after the adjectives and socialization of the body has been stripped away. In a key sense, it is the body outside of time. It is ripped from history and a possible future it might press into with hopes or fears or plans. Flesh is exposed, mute matter. "It is," as Sartre puts it, "There and there for nothing."[76]

I said that I think *Fleisch* straddles both Améry's theories of language, however, and flesh as meat only speaks to language in moments of extremity. Améry can try all he likes to force his reader to see what he sees, to sit with the reality of his body turned into a slab of meat, no different from any other butchered animal. By his own acknowledgment, though, most of us will fail to break out of our networks of codified abstraction. The intellectuals among his readers will fail even more spectacularly and inevitably start the process of looking for resonances between his words and other references. For those readers, Améry tacitly invites comparisons between his use of *Fleisch* and the Christian tradition of "flesh."

I feel self-conscious making this point because it seems so obvious. How could he not hear Christianity behind his language of a "man made flesh"? And how could he mean his words as anything other than a rebuke to the redemptive promises Christianity ties to the flesh of Jesus? Still, I think it is worth asking *which* redemptive promises Améry rejects, if only to set up my next and final argument about the ethical project he draws from his account of flesh. To do that, I want to spend a little time sketching different readings of flesh in early Christianity.[77]

In a recent book, *Poetics of the Flesh*, Mayra Rivera sketches out roughly three different typologies of flesh in the New Testament that continue to haunt the term today. The first in her account comes in the Gospel of John. From its famous prologue, when "word became flesh," John sets up flesh as unstable and transformative, in implicit contrast to the stasis of the body. In fact, as Rivera points out, the Gospel uses *sarx* (flesh), instead of *soma* (body) in every instance except when describing the corpse of Christ. Flesh circulates and unites, particularly as the narrative ties it to the language of food. As she quotes from the last supper, "For my flesh is true food, and my blood is true drink. Those who eat my flesh and drink my blood abide in me, and I in them."[78] Flesh is not rejected or sloughed off in the pursuit of spirituality here. Instead, Jesus speaks to his followers, in their carnality, to take him into themselves through his flesh. Miraculously, his flesh is never exhausted; it is absorbed by his followers, nourishing their flesh in turn. As Rivera summarizes, "Like bread, flesh is shared, becoming part of many bodies, transformed into the very flesh of those bodies that partake of it."[79] That flesh is always haunted by death, either in the image of the grain of wheat that dies to make bread or the prospect of Jesus's own impending crucifixion, but that mortality is the precondition for a community united by sharing in the flesh of Christ. Flesh, in sum, breaks down the isolation of the individual, giving her a new identity as part of a community that shares in the glory of God by imbibing his blood.

John offers one option for hearing the word *Fleisch* in Améry, though perhaps not the most immediately plausible one. Rivera's second thinker, Paul, might be a closer match. Unlike John, Paul sees bodies as much less firmly tethered to flesh. Rivera makes a nod to the difficulty of piecing together a comprehensive account of flesh in Paul, given the well-known problem that his letters were written in response to specific communities, but then launches into her analysis. The key distinction, for Rivera, is the one Paul makes between earthly and celestial bodies. All creatures have bodies of some sort. Celestial bodies, like planets or stars, have bodies made of ether, while earthly creatures have bodies of flesh. Unlike John, for Paul flesh does not circulate and break down boundaries. Each type of creature has its own distinctive species of flesh, and each type of flesh has its own glory. My flesh is a categorically different type of flesh than my dog's. Likewise, male, earthly bodies are superior to female flesh; though, in theory, spiritual bodies have no gender.

Flesh, for Paul, reeks of sin, death, passion, sense-perception, and the law, and as such "flesh and blood cannot inherit the kingdom of God."[80] It can never transform me or connect me with God. Rather, at every turn flesh betrays me. When I find myself calling out, like Augustine, like Paul, like Schelling's eternal will, that I cannot will what I will and have become a burden on myself, it is because my flesh thwarts me. Paul blames flesh when he writes, "I do not understand my own actions. For I do not do what I want, but the very thing I hate. Now if I do not do what I want, then I agree the law is good. But in fact it is no longer I that do it, but sin that dwells within me. For I know nothing good dwells within me, that is, in my flesh."[81] My willpower and my flesh war with each other. Flesh is at once vulnerable to sin and a wily tempter. Worse, in doing so, they compromise the body of the Church. When I sin, fail, and fornicate, it is not merely my flesh that I compromise; it is the collective body of the Church I implicate. The body of flesh must die for the spiritual body of Christ to live.

For all its influence, Paul's equation of flesh with sin created problems for his successors, including Rivera's last thinker, Tertullian. How, after all, could a good Christian reconcile the sacrality of Christ with the degradation of the body? If Christ really was without sin, and flesh as corrupt as he claimed, how could he possibly have been made flesh? More than that, how could the son of God have been born in a way that was so, well, disgusting? Tertullian wrote *On the Flesh of Christ* and *On Resurrection* to answer those questions. Sarcastically, Tertullian invites his readers to echo back the arguments he has grown so tired of hearing.

> Beginning then with the nativity you so strongly object to, orate, attack now, the nastiness of the genital elements in the womb, the filthy curdling of moisture and blood, and of flesh to be for nine months nourished on that same mire. Draw a picture of the womb getting daily more unmanageable, heavy, self-concerned, safe not even in sleep, uncertain in the whims of dislikes and appetites.

Christ was born in blood and feces and filth, covered in slime and pushed out of a woman's body, Tertullian insists. But so was everyone else. If "you hate a man during his birth," Tertullian asks, "how can you love any man?" True love means being able to accept and embrace everything abject and degrading about a loved one, including Christ. To reject the filth-ridden fleshiness of Christ is to dream of sterile, antiseptic love, free from the tug of origins. Flesh always "carries with it some part of the body from which it was born."[82] Christ's flesh belongs just as surely to Mary as mine to my mother. That maternal tie connects him to King David and the promise of Israel, and through Israel to God's hands as they shaped Adam out of clay. Flesh, stained with muck, carries the trace of God's hand as he shaped the first human out of the earth at the beginning of time. However, casting flesh as continuous with the earth was more than a simple rhetorical move for Tertullian. It was the strongest proof of

Christ's resurrection. Every day, nature plays out the cycle of death and resurrection. The sun dies at night, only to rise in the morning. Wheat crops died in the fall, only to regrow the following spring.

Admittedly, I am speculating about why Améry invoked the Christian imagery of "flesh." It might not have been a fully conscious decision or reducible to one motive. One reading is that he means it as a caustic commentary on John. Just as Jesus became flesh and died so that a community of believers might be established, so too did Améry become flesh in the service of creating a national German identity. Améry's incarnation would be a perverse mirror of Christ's, one stripped of any transcendent meaning or even the appearance of willing self-sacrifice. I am not wholly convinced by that reading, since Améry spends relatively little time thinking about his torture as a way of establishing a community. It could be torture establishes community, as a type of ritual sacrifice, but it could also be the outlet of an existing community's murderous impulses.

A slightly modified version of that interpretation seems more plausible. It could be that Améry identifies with Jesus, as one tortured Jew to another. He might also find something viscerally powerful in the Pauline association of flesh with filth and degradation. Those Christian resonances capture his sense that becoming flesh is a perversion contrary to a good, rightful order of affairs. His description of his torture as "falling into a void," while a literal account of what happened when his shackled arms gave out could also be read as an attempt to push the parallel further by calling on the imagery of the Fall.

I think there is some plausibility to each of these reading, but if I had to make my best guess as to why Améry invokes the imagery of the Fall and becoming flesh, I would say that he is priming the reader to expect some sort of redemption story. As Tertullian says, the story of the incarnation is the story of resurrection and redemption. We fall and Jesus dies, yes, but he dies in order to forgive humanity's sins.

It may be hard to entertain the possibility that he promises redemption through his imagery, but that is because his essays are relatively well-known today among anyone who has studied the Holocaust or torture. At the time he wrote them, though, he had never successfully composed anything about Auschwitz. He was a relatively obscure figure who made his living primarily writing reviews of popular music, including one book that he hoped "everyone would buy and no one would read." His audience would have had very little idea of what to expect, particularly since he first read the essays in a series of radio broadcasts. There were no critics who could read the book first and write reviews spoiling the main point. Everyone had to wait on him to learn where the narrative was going. If you read the first three essays, Améry makes it abundantly clear that he is a broken, damaged man, but for a German audience grappling with the Holocaust after twenty years of silence the depths of his despair might have made them all the more eager to grasp on to any possibility of redemption. What could be more powerful than good, Christian forgiveness from a man who had suffered as deeply as Améry?

The strength of that hope and need for absolution would make it all the more devastating when Améry denied forgiveness in his next essay, "Resentments."

WONDER AND THE THEOLOGY
OF NONFORGIVENESS

Torture ends—if it ends—with *großen Verwunderung*, great wonder. Wonder that, even after torture, "you still have a forehead that you can stroke with your shackled hands, an eye that can be opened and closed, a mouth that would show the usual lines if you could see it now in a mirror."[83] Wonder "also at the fact that what happened to you yourself, by right was supposed to befall only those who had written about it in accusatory brochures: torture. . . . The Gestapo tortures. But that was a matter until now for the somebodies who were tortured and who displayed their scars at antifascist conferences. That suddenly you yourself are the Somebody, is grasped only with difficulty. That, too, is a kind of alienation."[84]

It might seem as if this wonder is the start of wisdom or a new, more vulnerable, more fragile, more empathetic relation to the world. Every major development in continental philosophy for the last three generations supports that hope. Whether Heidegger's anxiety that modern technology has reduced nature and bodies to resources ordered into "the standing reserve," Derrida's endless efforts to disrupt pretensions to systematicity, or Judith Butler's refusal of gender essentialism, the tradition I am working in agrees on one point: ethics begins at the failure of systematic knowledge.

A 2008 work by Mary-Jane Rubenstein even ties that ethical hope explicitly to the power of wonder. In *Strange Wonder: The Closing of Metaphysics and the Opening of Awe*, she begins by citing an etymological connection between wonder, which derives from the Old English term *wundor*, and its German cognates *Wunder* but also *Wund*, or gash, wound.[85] She then lists a number of obsolete "phraseological uses," including "dreadfully, horribly, terribly." She concludes, "Wonder, then, is inherently ambivalent." Her analysis follows the role of wonder as a mode of attentiveness to "the stubborn inscrutability of the everyday," drawn in contrast to curiosity and puzzlement, which subside once the unknown is discovered and its causes or conditions brought to light.[86] While "the wound of wonder," as she puts it, can never remain permanently open, it plays a necessary ethical and philosophical role by unsettling pretensions to mastery. Wondering before the "groundlessness of things" creates the condition for the possibility of philosophy itself, even as the modern thinker seeks to shut it down in order to secure his or her thought.

For Améry, in the years after blood welled around his swollen, shackled hands, wonder *did* bring with it an ethical demand to remain faithful to his open wounds, albeit not the sort I think most postmodern philosophy of religion had in mind. In order to remain faithful to his wounds and his wonder, Améry espouses a moral obligation *not* to forgive.

Part of this conviction comes from Améry's notion of time. For Améry, the natural state of society, and of time more generally, is to move forward. Forgiveness comes inevitably, in the way time allows flesh to knit wounds, or the elements to erode the sharp edges of rocks. At best, a society may look back and ask how to prevent the recurrence of a crime, but its interests remain in the well-being of the group, not the injuries of the individual. The social response to atrocity may be natural, and it may be necessary for the good of the whole, but it can never be moral. In Améry's thought, natural time can never have moral content precisely because it forgets to enable the survival of the whole. Or, as another contemporary put the problem with relying on natural time to heal wounds, "Each spring the trees bloom at Auschwitz as they do everywhere, for the grass is not too disgusted to grow in those accursed fields; springtime does not distinguish between our gardens and those places of inexpressible misery."[87]

By contrast, the resentful individual resists the ameliorating effects of time. His position, Améry fully admits, is an absurd one. "It nails every one of us onto the cross of his ruined past.

Absurdly, it demands that the irreversible be turned around, that the event be undone. Resentment blocks the exit to the genuine human dimension, the future. I know that the time-sense of the person trapped in resentment is twisted around, disordered, if you wish, for it desires two impossible things: regression into the past and nullification of what happened."[88] And yet the resentful person is the only one who holds "the moral truth of the conflict."[89] He is the one who still feels violation reverberating through his flesh. He is the one who continues to revolt against the past, holding firm to the truth that "what happened, happened. This sentence is just as true as it is hostile to morals and intellect. The moral power to resist contains the protest, the revolt against reality, which is rational only as long as it is moral."[90]

But what would it mean to say with Améry that forgiveness misses the "moral truth of the conflict"? One possible answer is that the push to forgive people masks a cynical desire to smooth over social interactions. Under this reading, most of what we think of as forgiveness is some species of self-interest or capitulation to social pressure. Améry suggests as much when he remarks that society cares about the continued survival of the whole, not the suffering of the individual. There is something right in this criticism, I think. Vladimir Jankélévitch, a Jewish contemporary of Améry who spent the war working with the French Resistance, wrote that the refusal to forgive is the just response to *any* injury, since there would be no need to beg someone's pardon if the offense deserved to be brushed aside as a matter of course. Only the unforgivable needs to be forgiven. Anything else is either a social nicety masquerading as forgiveness or just the dulling of time. In order for forgiveness to be a meaningful gesture, refusing to forgive has to be a live, respected option. Forgiveness may be a great good, even greater than the justice, but true forgiveness is a decision taken to absolve another's iniquity out of desire to reestablish a relationship with the wrongdoer. A person can will herself to forgive another, chide herself for harboring rancor, reconcile herself to the evil done, or even cease to think of the wrong altogether, but ultimately the ability to forgive wholeheartedly descends, or not, in a moment of grace. If we agree with Jankélévitch, we make the gesture of forgiving people far more often than we forgive them in truth.[91]

That jaundiced look at the social pressures motivating forgiveness would also disqualify forgiveness motivated by a desire to "move on." This promise of forgiveness as a release from trauma for the victim is familiar from self-help books. So long as you hold on to your resentment, the argument goes, you will never be free. Resentment holds open the wound by bringing you back to prod at it. Forgive, if not for the sake of the other, then for your own sake. Forgive so you can move on.[92] This argument, if anything, is even worse than the openly self-interested pressure to forgive in order to preserve social harmony. It turns forgiveness into a selfish act that has nothing to do with a desire to reconcile with another. It also confuses rancor with trauma. Wounds can linger long after a victim forgives a perpetrator. Even if Améry forgave his tormentors, he would have still lost his home and his language. He would still have the memories and scars of torture.[93] He would still have the lingering feeling that he could never be at home in the world. Forgiving another does nothing to repair his material losses, much less his psychological ones. It cannot and it did not. And at the point at which he is still bound to his persecution, why release his tormentor from the event through forgiveness?

More pointedly, why release the tormentor from the event when the tormentor shows no signs of remorse or even awareness of his guilt? Forgiveness, perhaps, makes sense in a dispute between two individuals, but, as Améry puts it, "it seemed to me as if I had experienced their atrocities as collective ones. I had been just as afraid of the simple private in his field-gray uniform as of the brown-clad Nazi official with his swastika armband." Even bystanders were complicit in his persecution. "I also could not rid myself of the sight of the Germans on a small passenger platform where, from the cattle cars of our deportation train, the corpses had been unloaded and piled up; not on a single one of their stony faces was I able to detect an expression of abhorrence. Let collective crime and collective guilt balance each other and produce the equilibrium of world morality."[94] What would it mean to forgive a society for its silence and complicity? Most of the guilty are and remain strangers by necessity. There is no personal relationship to be reestablished.

Even if forgiveness were to descend on Améry in a moment of "grace," he would still be left with the problem pointed out in Dostoyevsky's *Brothers Karamazov*: we have no right to reconcile ourselves to another's pain. He might one day find himself capable of forgiving his torturers, but what about the other inmates that soldier beat or battered or murdered? What about the deaths that soldier witnessed silently? What about the other soldiers who watched the casual brutality of Améry's assailant? What right does Améry have to forgive that suffering? What moral standing could ever give him the right to forgive on behalf of those who died and are beyond forgiveness? Ivan Karamazov would say none, not even if the victims themselves were to forgive their tormentors.[95] As for Améry, though he never worries specifically about that dimension of forgiveness, I suspect he might agree with Ivan Karamazov.

Ultimately, these are all arguments for why Améry ought not forgive and, more generally, why forgiveness should be considered supererogatory, but they miss the more primal reason why

Améry feels he cannot forgive. In a moment of surprising vulnerability amid his spare prose, Améry admits that he is held back because "the experience of persecution was, at the very bottom, that of an extreme *loneliness.* At stake for me is the release from the abandonment that has persisted from that time until today."[96] Tellingly, the closest he ever gets to reconciliation comes when he discusses the execution of a soldier who had regularly beaten him with a shovel handle when he thought Améry wasn't working fast enough. At the moment the soldier was walking to his execution, Améry felt satisfied that the soldier had finally faced "the moral truth" of the atrocity he had committed and wanted the past undone exactly as much as he did. At that moment, Améry and the soldier were fellow humans, and Améry "was no longer alone with the shovel handle."[97]

The point about persecution as loneliness clearly matters to Améry. By my count, he only uses italics twice for emphasis in the entire book, and loneliness is one of the words singled out. At the same time, it is not exactly clear in the anecdote why he thinks of persecution in terms of loneliness. To be sure, I think it makes perfect sense that persecution would be lonely. As a Jew in the Resistance, he was singled out for death in multiple countries. It would have been impossible for him to trust anyone, and he would have been acutely aware that he was homeless—he *was* acutely aware that he was homeless. But it also would have been terrifying, enraging, anxiety-inducing, hopeless, and, ultimately, physically agonizing. Why summarize the experience as lonely "at the very bottom?" Schelling pointed out how loneliness could be destructive in the previous chapter, but that is still a strong statement.

I take Améry's experience of loneliness to follow directly from his description of becoming flesh and confronting his contingency. What, after all, began the experience of *Verfleis-chlichung* if not the first blow? The pain was as nothing for Améry when he thought back on those first moments of torture. Instead, he focused on the relationships stripped away. The moment of violation meant realizing that he was cut off from all hope of help. There was no past he could call on or a future from which he could expect salvation. The normal bounds of society dissolved, and he was left alone in the immediacy of flesh. How could the realization that every boundary he took for granted could have been otherwise help being a moment of loneliness? The relationships that gave him stability vanished into insignificance.

Améry never did find release from his desolation. On October 17, 1978, he checked into a hotel in Salzburg, wrote a letter to his wife, wrote another to his mistress, and swallowed a bottle of sleeping pills. The coroner ruled it suicide.

In the end, for all of the complexity of Améry's attitude toward place, space, flesh, and forgiveness, there remains something very simple about his discussion of flesh. He is writing about vulnerability. If he uses the word *flesh*, it is in part because it is the only word he has to capture his amazement that we are so thinglike and fragile at the same moment, with so little to stand between us and anything that might harm us other than a scrap of human hide.

The hopelessness of Améry's insight is never clearer than the moment he bursts out in his third and final autobiography, *Örtlichkeiten (Places)*: "This poor bundle of all too vulnerable flesh, intangible emotions and impressions, this poor human skin that wants only to protect itself from icy cold and burning heat. One can never make enough allowances for mankind, whose physically vulnerable existence crushes and devours him from within."[98]

With that, Améry leaves us with the darkest meditation yet on the fragility of flesh and the costs of contingency. The only question left is whether that account of contingency is so dark as to foreclose any exit into a better world.

4

LOVE

INSIDE THE SHIPWRECK OF HISTORY: MICHEL SERRES AND THE ETHICS OF CONTINGENCY

Strangely enough, one answer to my question about contingency and the limits of despair begins with a sinking ship. Early in his lectures on the philosophy of history, Hegel mulled over the blind passions, selfish interests, and cramped, narrow-minded desires that served as "the springs of actions in this theatre of activity" as world history pushed ever closer to realizing its goal of perfect freedom.[1] Warming to the subject, he went on to write:

> Without rhetorical exaggeration, we could paint the most fearful picture of the misfortunes suffered by the noblest nations and states, as well as by private virtues—and with that picture we could arouse feelings of the deepest and most helpless sadness, not to be outweighed by any consoling outcome. We can strengthen ourselves against this, or escape it only by thinking that, well, so it was at one time; it is fate; there is nothing to be done about it now. And finally—in order to cast off the

tediousness that this reflection of sadness could produce in us and to return to involvement in our own life, to the present of our own aims and interest—we return to the selfishness of standing on a quiet shore where we can be secure in enjoying the distant sight of confusion and wreckage.[2]

History was "a slaughter bench," he concluded, "upon which the happiness of nations, the wisdom of states, and the virtues of individuals were sacrificed." Or, as he explained at other moments in the text, history is lived in the shipwreck, where every illness, unexpected death, and deep betrayal is experienced as a moment of contingency—as unplanned, unexpected, and unpredictable. Philosophy, by contrast, takes place from the safety of the shore, where distance dissolves the illusion of contingency and allows human suffering to be understood as part of a necessary movement of Spirit.

For all that I have spent the previous three chapters arguing against the Hegelian approach that treats contingency as primarily a matter of history, I have not managed to answer the question Hegel poses when he reproaches the spectator for wallowing in the contemplation of irredeemable suffering: Can contingency build anything? Does awareness of our contingency inevitably bring nausea and vertigo that we must repress in order to get on with the business of building a stable psyche, as in Merleau-Ponty's account, or can contingency itself found its own type of ethical relations with the world?

Instead, I have dwelled on the costs of contingency. To a large extent, the texts I have read made this choice for me. Ambivalence, if not outright horror, are built into the accounts of contingency given by Schelling, Novalis, and—above all—Améry. With illness, loneliness, and violation as their entry points into contingency, how could they not be? To an equal extent, though, my emphasis on the darkness of contingency has been a deliberate choice, made in response to the tendency within continental philosophy of religion to celebrate the irruption of the unmasterable and incalculable into daily life,[3] as a source of enchantment and even ethics.[4] I have tried to inject a cautionary, even skeptical, note into this conversation through my choice of figures, but in fairness to these thinkers, I have to follow them in asking whether its flux always destructive or is there, nonetheless, the potential for creating an ethics out of our vulnerability? If so, what might that ethics look like?

Shifting my attention to these questions brings me to the final thinker I will address: the French philosopher of science, Michel Serres (1930-present). If Hegel wrote as a spectator watching the wreckage of history safely from the shore, nearly 150 years later Michel Serres would compose his own meditation on contingency from the perspective of a sailor struggling to escape a blazing, sinking ship. Where Hegel sees the wreckage at a distance, Serres gropes his way through a dim smoke-filled room on his hands and knees. In the pages that follow, I will use this imagery of a shipwreck to pull out Serres's own sophisticated theory of contingency rooted in erotic touch and subjectivity. While that theory may seem to be a self-sufficient and fully realized account of the connection between contingency and touch, I argue that it poses problems for another main commitment in his work, reimagining the senses as mingled, nonhierarchical, and continuous with the external world.

SUBJECTIVITY AND CONTINGENCY AS COMMON TANGENCY

Unlike Hegel's account, the shipwreck story in Michel Serres's 1985 book *The Five Senses* begins with a literal sinking ship. Like much of Michel Serres's early life, the ship was shadowed by war.

Born to a bargeman in Agen, France, in 1930, his early years were marked by the catastrophes of the twentieth century. The Spanish Civil War occurred when he was six, the blitzkrieg when he was nine, the collaboration and deportation to concentration camps under the Vichy regime when he was ten, the Liberation and its score settling in France when he was fourteen, and Hiroshima when he was fifteen. Even eroticism in those early years was marked by death; the first woman he saw naked was a girl being lynched by a crowd.[5] Those formative years were followed immediately by the French colonial wars in Vietnam and Algeria. "In short," as he told Bruno Latour in a 1990 interview, "From age nine to seventeen, when the body and sensitivity are being formed, it was the reign of hunger and rationing, death and bombings, a thousand crimes." For the young Serres, it was "war, always war. Thus, I was six for my first dead bodies, and twenty-six for the last ones."[6]

Nevertheless, he continued to explain, "the son of a bargeman becomes a sailor," naturally, as a matter of course. So in 1947, lured by his native affinity for the sea and propelled by his more pragmatic need for a scholarship, Michel Serres joined the French navy. He remained there for another two years, until his scruples about serving the cause of violence in the atomic age drove him out in 1949 to study mathematics. The draw of the sea and deep uneasiness toward his occupation form the backdrop of the story he tells at the beginning of *The Five Senses* where he grounds his account of contingency in subjectivity and touch. Subsequent sections will probe the inconsistencies and commitments undergirding that account of contingency, but for the moment I am limiting my task to storytelling and explication.

The story begins after months of practice drills in the navy when Serres finds himself trapped in a ship on fire. He offers no explanation for the source of the fire, in keeping with the section's title "Birth," and writes with all the ignorance, immediacy, and limited vision of the present tense. All he knows is that there is smoke, followed by the noise of bodies rushing down the manhole, and that then, suddenly, terrifyingly, he is absolutely alone. The door barred, he realizes his only possible exit is the porthole. He crawls across the room under a thick layer of acrid smoke, reaches the exit, and begins to unscrew the rusty flanges that hold the glass shut. At first the screws resist him. Slowly they give. When he finally pries the window open, a blast of air and water floods in, whipping the smoke behind him into a suffocating whirlwind. He pushes his head through, only to recoil from the douse of wintry wind and water. Instinctively, his body cringes back inside, only to be driven out the porthole again almost immediately by the sound of munitions exploding in the background. With no other choice, he inches his head through, then one arm, then one wrist and then stalls, stuck. As he writes, "I remain there, motionless, vibrating, pinioned, gesticulating within the confines of the fixed neckpiece, long enough for me to think, no, for my body to learn once and for all to say 'I' in the truest sense of the word. . . . No mistake about it, since my life quite simply depended on this dark, slow, blinding meditation."[7]

He is inside, burning, about to die, with only his head and arms poking into the sea, when a giant wave comes and propels him forward, freeing him up to his waist. Almost as soon as he begins to praise God for his liberation, another wave crashes, tilting the boat over and jamming his ribs back in the porthole, leaving him trapped inside once again. With the ship on fire, and he himself half inside, half outside, trapped between suffocation and freedom, Serres comes to the first key insight for his argument: the self is only a point of awareness or identity. It is irreducibly bodily, but not coterminous with the body. If he were identical with his body, with his subjectivity evenly diffused from his feet to his forehead, he would have felt trapped until the moment he fought fully free. Instead, the crisis forced him to economize his sense of self, to recognize the exact point dividing his life from his limbs. After a few more waves shuttle him between inside and outside, Serres eventually escapes, propelled out by the force of the waves. "Since my near shipwreck," he concludes, "I have come accustomed to calling this point the soul. The soul resides at the point where the I is decided."[8]

While the shipwreck taught Serres to recognize the localized nature of the soul, quiet observation of his own body brought him to his second set of claims about subjectivity: normally the soul wanders under the influence of touch. There are limits to its travels, as Serres learned in his crisis. Not every place can be "the point where the 'I' is decided" in moments of extremity. Instead, our bodies are mottled with points of exquisite sensitivity, as well as parts too remote to ever become the site I call "I." As he notes, when I bend down to clip my toenails, the blade only ever touches my toes; I may feel as if I am grasping the scissors, but I never feel as if it is my self, my very being, touched by the blade.[9] But when I press my finger to my lips, my sense of self flits back and forth, with awareness at one moment entirely in the pads of my thumb as it bears down on my mouth, then the next in my lips as they kiss back my suddenly object-like hand. Physically, everything remains the same: fingers and lips meet. Yet "the I vibrates alternately on both sides of the contact, and all of the sudden presenting its other face to the world, or suddenly passing over the immediate vicinity, leaves behind nothing but an object . . . pure chance, each time."[10] My body becomes at once subject and object, with touch pulling my awareness behind it from spot to spot.[11]

French, perhaps, allows Serres to more easily think this idea through the construction, "Je me brosse les cheveux." Like

German, it suggests by way of a reflexive verb that whole regions of the body—the hair, the teeth—are impersonal, not me, for all that they grow in my head. English, by contrast, flattens the entirety of my body into a possession. In English, it is "my" hair, not "the" hair that I brush, even if I live my entire life feeling my hair as little more than an object. Which is not to say that Serres claims certain areas could never house anyone's awareness and sense of self; rather, he thinks each body is idiosyncratic in that respect. Each of us possesses "zones where this contingency does not"—and does— "come into play," which we could come to recognize, if only we accepted the idea that our bodies could be simultaneously subject and object.[12]

The language of "zones of contingency" brings me to the question of how Serres understands the relation between contingency, subjectivity, and touch in *The Five Senses*. Why, aside from the etymological roots of contingency in *tangere*, does he see any particular connection between touch and contingency? The answer, I think, has a few different, interlocking parts. Most obviously, the areas of potential subjectivity or objectivity are contingent, in that they cannot be universalized or located according to any unwavering, necessary law of sensitivity on the body. Rather, they are the product of a whole history of being injured, trapped, caressed, and otherwise touched that interacts with a native, idiosyncratic predisposition to feel places on the body more or less keenly. There is nothing necessary or predictable or determined about where I can feel my soul at stake. These zones are contingent because they bear the marks of history.

Moreover, these areas of sensitivity or dullness provide the landscape on which my experience of touch unfolds, and, for Serres, touch provides the basic intuition of unpredictability, flux, and connection underpinning the experience of contingency. That instability is the deeper point behind Serres's

example of the hand touching lips. Even in the most seemingly self-enclosed, static situation—a body touching itself,
motionless—the line between touching and touched travels.
Even if we were able to completely control or will what came in
contact with our body, as Novalis dreamed, the experience of
instability, flux, contingency would remain in the constant,
uncontrollable migration of the soul as touch alights on it in one
moment as an object of touch and in the next moment a subject.
Though Serres never bluntly states as much, in emphasizing the
link between touch and chance, he can be read as making the
argument that flightiness of feeling is a much more fundamental experience of contingency than the upheavals of history.
Long before we wake to awareness of the uncertainty of hopes
and plans in history, or the way that events depend on an unfore-
seeable chain of previous events, we find ourselves in bodies
that sting us to wakefulness with the sensation of feet that have
fallen asleep or blinding stabs of pain that momentarily jerk us
away from our thoughts and focus our awareness on a banged
elbow.

That being said, we do not live in some sensory deprivation
chamber, with nothing to observe except the feeling of our skin
folding over itself or our hands touching our lips; we live in a
world that constantly caresses, abrades, and wounds us. In his
clearest statement of the link between contingency and touch,
Serres writes, "The skin is a variety of contingency; in it, through
it, with it, the world and my body touch each other, the feeling
and the felt, it defines their common edge. Contingency means
common tangency; in it the world and the body intersect and
caress each other."[13]

I wrote a moment ago about pain as a form of contact with
the world, but, as his language suggests, Serres finds the paradigmatic example of contingency as common tangency in the

caress. Much of his analysis of subjectivity and contingency remains the same when he turns to the erotic encounter. Like the shipwreck, the point of perception or soul still travels, only this time his lover's caress drags awareness across the skin as a magnet does a pile of iron filings. At one moment the sense of self matches the staccato drum of his lover's fingers as they tap the ridges of his spine; at the next it rushes to his lips as he bends down to kiss her shoulder. Awareness orients itself around this unstable point, leaving tracts of flesh temporarily insensible as they fade to the background, only to be awakened in the next instant through some chance shift of skin.

Serres highlights the caress because it undermines even the pretense of controlling the conditions of sensation. The two bodies connect and disconnect in a series of movements that exceeds the sum of individual actions. One partner's decision to stoop down for a kiss shifts the balance of weight and the angle of contact for both, creating in turn a different vector of desire that pulls the soul in anew. The site of awareness, the soul, for both partners, is created in a common, contingent act; it changes through openness to each other and the world.

In his interviews, Serres often denounces polemical philosophy as an expression of the agonistic culture that bred the world tragedies of his youth.[14] All the same, his equation of contingency with the caress, and a very particular egalitarian version of the caress at that, *is* a polemic of sorts. He writes of the caress not as an act of a master attempting to dominate, subdue, and transform the other in a vehicle for his pleasure, as in Sartre.[15] Nor does he reduce the caressed feminine other to a passive recipient of his pleasure or occasion for his revelation of the infinitude of the other, as Derrida accuses Levinas of doing.[16] For that matter, he has no account of the violent, violating, or indifferent touch of others and things, as in Merleau-Ponty's discussion of the dark space of the schizophrenia sufferer. On the contrary, he actively rejects the moment of sadism underpinning so many accounts of touch in phenomenology, writing, "No, I do not objectify, freeze, ensnare or rape you as that tedious old marquis would have done. And I do not expect you to do as I do. For that you would have to become a ghost or an automaton."[17] Instead, the caress in its mutuality, gives birth to the soul.

I am not convinced Serres contributes anything particularly novel or subtle in his account of the caress, but his decision to feature the gentle lover's touch as the model of common tangency sets up the ethical project that drives his later work. I will address that project in the sections that follow; for the moment, I want to conclude with an argument for the novelty of the theory of contingency and subjectivity just explained, particularly given that Serres—strangely—is so seldom read as a serious philosopher. Recent literature discussing *The Five Senses* has focused on Serres's concept of the soul, specifically stressing its liminality, its ability to be at once on the edge of perception and the center of all sense of self, how it is born out of contact with others.[18] If Serres only offered the insight that the boundaries of the self are poorly defined, or subjectivity is created on the margins in contact with others, or even that my knowledge is always bodily, I would not be writing this chapter. Not because I disagree with any of those assertions, but because they would only amount to tinkering with insights that have long since become dogma in theory circles. Continental philosophers have spent the last two hundred years arguing against the autonomous self, whether in Hegel's vision of the creation of subjectivity through battling desires in the master-slave dialectic, or Kierkegaard's insistence on the self's constitution in relation to God,[19] or Freud's various iterations of the unconscious.

No, the interesting question is not "how is my capacity to know, to reflect, to feel myself any sort of subject created in conjunction with others and the world?" Rather, the novel question Serres poses is "*where* do I know?" Or, put more specifically, "where on my body do I know, where do I feel myself to be a self and where just a clumsy bundle of limbs?" What does it mean that I can feel parts of my body as vital to my life and identity, and others as expendable in the right circumstances? Serres poses this question in the form of the drowning sailor; I would recast it in the image of a crippled man dragging his nerveless leg behind him. What is that limb to him? Does he still feel it part of his very self, or does it register as a wooden object, his in the abstract, but an alienated, lifeless intrusion in practice? That insight works best on the level of phenomenology. The experience of the soul might not be comprehensive, it might not cover every situation or have much to say about moments of vertiginous self-dissolution, but it allows us to see *something*. The fact that it only allows us to see something about our experience of touch is not an oversight, as I will argue: it is a tactical decision that at once sets up and undermines the ethical commitments that Serres makes to history and the environment.

THE HISTORY OF THE SENSES, OR WHY TOUCH?

In one respect, it seems as if this work could stop here. Serres, more than any other thinker I have discussed, makes explicit the link between contingency and touch. When he writes that "contingency means common tangency,"[20] we know now that he is not trading in vague generalities or platitudes about the embodiment of the subject. He means that I experience myself as subject to chance, fragile, and contingent, not primarily because of an illness that devastates my family or an assault on my body (as in Novalis and Améry), but because I can recognize at every moment the way the point of my awareness, my soul, is jerked about my body with every passing, unpremeditated contact with another's hand. My sense of self is dependent—contingent—upon physical contact with the world. I find contingency in the topography of my body that has been stippled with points of sensitivity and hollowed with valleys of dullness from a lifetime of being touched or deprived of touch, all through the actions of others I cannot control. Finally, I feel contingency in the way touch itself vibrates, rendering one part of my body subject and the other object randomly, without my volition. Contingency is constant; I only have to focus to become aware of it at any moment.

There is, however, a crack in Serres's model of contingency that rumbles up from internal fault lines in his thought. We see it most clearly in the moment that he writes, "Things mingle together and I am no exception to that, I mix with the world which mixes with me."[21] Taken out of context, the lines seem a reiteration of the point made by his theory of contingency: subjectivity and objectivity mingle within my own body, making it impossible to distinguish between my self and some external, objective world. In reality, though, Serres is making the much deeper point that so long as we continue to believe that our bodies can be broken into separate, orderly spheres ruled by different senses, breaking down the idea of an autonomous subject is just cosmetic work.

The point is a logical continuation of his theory of subjectivity. How fundamental could any theory of mingling, blurred boundaries between self and world be that is grounded in the division of senses into five distinct spheres? It would be strangely incongruous to insist on the porousness of boundaries between self and world, or inside and outside, while quarantining the senses to their proper organs, such that scent belongs solely to the nose, sight to the eyes, and touch to the hand. If touch is so fluid, could it transgress more than the boundary between subject and object, or toucher and touched? Might it also spill over the distinction between touch and sight or touch and taste and sound?

There are good historical reasons for challenging the traditional division of the senses. Even a desultory skim through philosophy—much less psychology or neuroscience—shows alternatives to the current canonical senses of touch, taste, sight, smell, and hearing. Democritus thought all senses were a variation on touch. Aristotle modeled his senses on the four elements: vision correlated with water, smell with fire, air with sound, and touch with air, all the while flirting with a fifth *sensus communis* that mediated between the other four.[22] Francis Hutcheson argued in the eighteenth century for a moral sense;[23] Locke posited an "inner sense" that observed the self thinking;[24] and folk tradition, of course, holds to a sixth sense for perceiving the occult. To switch into Kantian language, the condition for the possibility of subjectivity may be touch, but touch must be historicized as one out of many possible senses canonized through the whims of history.

Moreover, the current division of the senses into five comes loaded with a history of colonialism, something Serres could not help be sensitive to as a man who insisted, "Violence was already the major problem—and has remained so, all my life."[25] As a number of scholars in the burgeoning field of the anthropology of the senses have noted, Western thought has privileged detached, abstracted sight among the senses, at least since the time of Plato. Sight, in turn, promoted a sense of distance from the surrounding society that fed into a colonial project. Timothy Mitchell, in his 2002 book *The Rule of Experts*, offers one of the best examples of this connection in his discussion of mapmaking in Egypt. Transforming Egypt into an abstract, easily calculable landmass that could be visually represented in a map was the first step toward mastering it. Once the entire country was transformed into an abstract visual representation, it could be subdivided. From there, the careful field-by-field representation of the entire country allowed administrators to see any irregularities in tax rates as they were applied to adjacent fields. Once pinpointed, those tax discrepancies could be corrected, increasing the amount of wealth flowing into colonial coffers. All of which leads to Mitchell's basic point that there is a straight line from the colonial privileging of sight to the economic management of Egypt.[26]

Sight was not the only sense implicated in colonialism, however. All five of them were, in different ways. Colonial scholars have often attributed lesser keenness to the senses of indigenous people—particularly the sense of pain—to provide biological grounding for their racism or, alternately, have projected unparalleled sensitivity on "primitive man" as a basis for their mythology of civilization's fall from some romanticized state of nature.[27] This argument has cropped up in chapter 2 in my discussion of Herder's belief that contemporary Europeans lack the same degree of sensitivity as Africans.

While Serres makes both these criticisms of the senses more or less explicit throughout his work, his most pointed engagement with the history of the senses comes in his allusions to the 1754 *Traité des sensations* (*Treatise of the Sensations*) by Étienne Bonnot, Abbé de Condillac. The treatise was a thought exercise intended to examine "the senses one by one, distinguishing precisely the ideas we owe to each, and observing how they instruct us."[28] It took as its means the fantasy of a statue possessing the human senses latently, only waiting to have them awakened one by one. The first third of the book runs relatively quickly through smell, hearing, taste, and sight, attributing memory to smell, bodily pleasure to hearing, hunger and increased delight to taste, and color, without space, to sight. In each of these four modes, the statue identifies what it senses with itself. Rather than smelling something, it believes itself to *be* smell, and so on for hearing, taste, and sight.

Touch, however, is Condillac's true interest, taking up half the book. With touch, Condillac's statue learns for the first time how to distinguish itself from others. In the first moments, the statue begins to touch itself and to touch objects, gradually learning to distinguish itself as a discrete body. "When it comes to learn that it is something solid, it is, I imagine, much surprised not to find itself in all it touches."[29] It extends its arms outside itself, not knowing what it will meet. This moment of surprise turns quickly into anxiety, then a desire to know where it is in space. It grasps itself and objects, gradually coming to understand the dimensions of space. As its sense of self becomes clearer and clearer, its emotions turn outward. "Its love, its hate, its fear, have no longer its own modifications as sole object: there are tangible things which it loves, hates, fears, desires and hopes for."[30]

Some of Serres's other criticisms of Condillac are easily guessed. For Condillac, touch separates, stabilizes, and—after a brief rush of anxiety—gives the statue the means to settle into a stable ego amid discrete objects. Obviously Serres has little use for such a model of subjectivity or the idea that touch serves to separate us from our environment. I believe his deeper, more fundamental objection, however, comes down to the limitation of the senses to particular organs, most clearly in the case of touch.

Condillac belongs to a long tradition of thinkers, from Gregory of Nyssa to André Leroi-Gourhan, who locate touch primarily in the hand. At one point, musing on the finitude of touch, Condillac imagines a fantastical hand with even finer motor control and even more surface area. "Ought we not suppose that the hand would be of still greater value were it composed of twenty fingers, each with a greater number of articulations?" he asks. "And if these were an infinity of parts all equally mobile and flexible, would it not be capable of a kind of universal geometry?" Reluctantly, he dismisses the idea, writing:

> It is not enough that the parts of the hand should be flexible and mobile, the statue must also be able to notice them one after another, and form exact ideas of them. What knowledge could it gain of bodies by means of touch if it had only imperfect knowledge of the organ it uses in touching? And what possible idea could it have of that organ if its parts were infinite? It would pass its hand over an infinity of little surfaces; but what would be the result? . . . The study of its hands would be too vast for it; it would use them without ever knowing anything about them and would only acquire confused ideas.[31]

Upon first reading this fantastical passage—which sounds so much like an image out of a Salvador Dali painting—it is not immediately clear why equating touch to the hand should be problematic. After all, Condillac explicitly denies the reduction of touch to grasping or molding the world. Serres would likely object to the implication that we can know even the limited hands we have, but, whatever his prejudices, Condillac does not subscribe to some caricatured Enlightenment belief in the possibility of total knowledge or mastery over the world. We have the hands we deserve: seeking, searching, but circumscribed.

A generous reading might even put Condillac in a line of thinkers who have linked touch, technology, and biology in the figure of the hand.[32] In part, this tradition of thought can be attributed to Heidegger's influence. In *Being and Time*, when he sought to describe the subject's relation to objects in everyday life, he famously turned to the language of tools and hands. In everyday life, *Dasein* (Being) experiences tools as a seamless part of the world, *zuhanden* (ready-to-hand); it is only when they break that *Dasein* experiences them as objects, existing in opposition to itself.[33] In equal part, though, this trend can be attributed to the influence of the French anthropologist André Leroi-Gourhan. In 1964 Leroi-Gourhan argued that the human brain was able to develop to its current level of sophistication because—to grossly abbreviate his argument—once our species began walking upright our hands were freed for grasping and manipulation.[34] Under the dual influence of Leroi-Gourhan and Heidegger, a number of thinkers began associating the hand's use of tools with a distinctively human way of being in the world that challenged the old Cartesian subject-object divide. Instead of using tools as an expression of our mastery over a world apart and subordinate to us, the argument goes, we create technology as a type of prosthetic to compensate for our physical and instinctual weakness. We lack the defined features, such as claws, that make other animals so exquisitely suited for their environment. Our clever, clawless, multipurpose hands have no choice but to create spears and knives and ploughs to compensate for our relatively defenseless bodies. In making, we are made by our surroundings. Technology becomes an expression of human fragility and heteronomy, rather than the tool of an autonomous, dominating subject.

It seems as if Serres's version of contingency should slot quite nicely into this tradition of theorizing the hand. What could be a better example of the bodily experience of flux, finitude, and coconstitution with the environment than a theory of evolution that attributes language and thought to the work of our hands?

Nevertheless, Serres makes remarkably few references to the hand in his discussion of touch in *The Five Senses*, I think because he believes *any* account that confines a sense to a particular organ has already gone astray, in the same ways isolating the senses creates the wrong anthropology.

In thinking of touch primarily in terms of hands, we implicitly assume the position of the one initiating touch, whether in building, molding, crafting, or caressing. Even granted that touching means being touched in turn, localizing touch in the hands leaves the movement far too unidirectional for a thinker who attributed the discovery of his soul to the heaving of an inanimate metal ship. Emphasis on the hand as the organ of touch, or, correspondingly, eyes as the organs of sight, creates the wrong sort of subject for Serres. It overemphasizes our agency by obscuring the vast expanse of flesh that can manipulate nothing. It separates out part of the body as the locus of touch at the expense of a more integrated account of the senses.[35]

Instead, Serres privileges the skin over the hand. As Steven Connor explains in *The Book of Skin*, the skin, for Serres, has a unique place because, unlike the other organs, it extends over the entire body. It is neither localized in place nor limited in function. Rather, it is the "milieu" of all the other senses. "If all the senses are milieux, or midplaces where inside and outside meet and meld," Connor explains, "then the skin is the global integral of these local area networks, the milieu of these milieux."[36] The senses are already the place where the internal organs of the body meet the external world. Sound meets the ear drum in hearing, sweet or savory foods meet the tongue in taste, and so on. The skin, however, goes one further; it provides the meeting place for all of the senses.

Serres offers the clearest example of the senses mingling in his description of Pierre Bonnard's oil painting, *Nue au miroir*

(1931). In the passage, he follows a woman tracing her lips with lipstick, her cheeks with rouge, her eyes with shadow. He writes: "With cosmetics, our real skin, the skin we experience, becomes visible. . . . The ordered, chaotic, unruly nude wears on her skin the fleeting common place of her own sensorium—hills and dales on which currents from the organs of hearing, sight, taste or smell, ebb and flow, a shimmering skin where touch calls forth sensation."[37] Her lips become at once an object of touch as she smooths her lipstick and a visual marker of where she hopes to be touched and tasted by her lover later that night. The act of applying makeup has become so banal that we fail to see it as signaling the mingling of the senses, as Serres does, or a way of highlighting the multifarious sites where the body receives the world.

In writing about Bonnard's painting, Serres speaks of the model's act as a form of "cosmetography," highlighting the etymological tie between "cosmic" and "cosmetic" in the ancient Greek *kosmos*, "to order." The wordplay neatly highlights the ontological and even theological stakes underpinning Serres's insistence on the mingling senses. The point is not just that the senses simply do not work in a neatly divided way and that bad phenomenology would to pretend that they do. Nor is his objection solely the moral one that we *ought not* subscribe to an understanding of the senses that allows us to compartmentalize our experience of the material world. Rather, his point is the much stronger ontological one that if the senses—and by extension our body—were to be neatly segregated from each other, that isolation would be at odds with the basic structure of existence as Serres imagines it.

His emphasis on the link between cosmic and cosmetic suggests at minimum a mythological strand to his project. Serres's book *Angels* adds a theological gloss to his discussion of mingling. *Angels* is a 1995 coffee-table tome filled with images of angels

and architecture, interrupted by a conversation between two airport employees who are also lovers. "I see angels—which, incidentally, in case you didn't know, comes from the ancient Greek
word for messengers," the woman remarks to her lover. Then,
meditating on her job as a physician within an airport, she
continues,

> Don't you see—what we have here is angels of steel, carrying
> angels of flesh and blood, who in turn send angel signals across
> angel air waves. . . . . All we really are is intermediaries, eternally
> passing among others who are also intermediaries. But the ques-
> tion is, where is it all leading? Because I spend my life here, in
> this never-ending flow of passengers, communications, convey-
> ers, messengers, announcers and agents, because my work is at
> this intersecting point of a multitude of networks all connected
> to the universe.[38]

Everything mingles; everything is forever passing from one place
to the next without ever arriving, the senses as surely as ships.
This egalitarian mingling and traveling from connection to connection, place to place, is not a merely embodied experience of
the senses; it is the most basic structure of the universe.

Yet these reflections on cosmology and cosmetics alike leave
us with a problem. What does this theory of mingling senses
mean for Serres's account of contingency? If the division of the
senses is arbitrary, both historically and conceptually, why think
of contingency primarily in terms of touch, rather than touch-
sound or touch-taste? After all, take Serres's favorite example of
two lovers: how do you differentiate between the touch of lips
against another's flesh and the taste of the salt of sweat on skin?
Moreover, *all* senses, according to Serres, involve the mingling

of inner and outer, self and world. If we were cut off from touch, if we were lepers, we would not suddenly be inured to the unpredictability of sudden shifts of our environment. We would still have the daily ritual of eating, with its sharp shock of flavor, followed by satiation, and a renewal of appetite. What testifies more completely to our bodily dependence on the world than hunger pangs interrupting work? Alternately, why not locate the experience of contingency in sight? The constant movement of our landscape evokes a sense of transience and finitude as surely as touch. Or why not write a theory of contingency told through the sensation of sound whizzing by us? Which is to say, what makes the project of reading contingency as tangency—that is, *my* project—anything more than the cheap exploitation of etymology?

CONTINGENCY AND/AS
THE CLINAMEN

The problem I have arrived at, then, is this: everything Serres writes can be read as a protest against the crass reduction of the material world to a vehicle for thought. He begins by attacking the degradation of objects outside the body to mere tools for a human knower by reimagining subjectivity as generated through touch. Step 1 of his argument undermines the self-contained subject by insisting that there is no knowledge without contingency and no contingency without touch. I cannot be a sovereign subject lording over a mute world of things when at any moment my own body can become dead weight or wake to awareness only through the touch of others and objects. Step 2 uses that same logic to take aim at the entire history of thought that reduces the organs *within* the body to vehicles for senses. Serres castigates the tradition of Condillac that divides the senses, quarantining taste to the tongue, sight to the eyes, and touch to the hand. He wants a promiscuous theory of the senses where all sensations run together; he wants a respectful theory that does not reduce the organs to vehicles for the senses; and he wants an egalitarian theory, free from the baggage of the Western tradition that is forever imposing hierarchies among the senses, most often with sight as queen.

These commitments are at odds. They are at odds because of the mechanics of his arguments—practically speaking, Serres never does mingle his account of contingency as common tangency with any other sense—and they are at odds because his theory of the tactility of contingency is so central to his understanding of what it means to know and exist as a self that questioning the link between contingency and touch would introduce a deep arbitrariness into the center of his work. If contingency, subjectivity, and his entire challenge to the separation between self and world necessarily grow out of the experience of touch and only touch, there is a hierarchy of divided senses. His egalitarian ideals of mingled senses become lip service that simply obscure the reinstantiation of the old model, albeit with the new twist of making touch the top sense, rather than sight. Alternately, if I can arrive at his theory of contingency and subjectivity slotting in any sense I please, I am both admitting the essential arbitrariness of his work and making the senses interchangeable in the service of a preconceived theory. In that case, Serres is not really dealing with the specificity of each sense and has just as utilitarian an attitude toward the body as the most vulgar caricature of an Enlightenment thinker.

Accordingly, this section investigates how deep Serres's commitment to thinking of contingency through touch actually goes, and whether or not the apparent pride of place given to touch in his theory of contingency can be reconciled with the egalitarian impulse behind his discussion of the senses. I will attempt to answer those questions by placing *The Five Senses* in line with an earlier work by Serres that attempts to combine contingency, touch, and science, this time by rehabilitating one of the earliest accounts of contingency in philosophy, the Epicurean atomic swerve, or the clinamen.

The book I am speaking of, *The Birth of Physics* (1978), belongs to an earlier stage of Serres's career when he often wrote monographs on single figures, such as Émile Zola (1840–1902) and Gottfried Wilhelm Leibniz (1646–1716). This particular work centered on Titus Lucretius Carus's poem, *De rerum natura,* or *On the Nature of Things*. Rumored for centuries to be a Roman citizen driven mad by a love potion and only capable of writing in fits of lucidity, Lucretius (c. 99–55 BCE) composed his sole surviving work on the topic of Epicurean atomic physics.[39] The poem has six books, covering the basic principles of atomism, the mind and soul, theories of sensation and thought, the emergence of the world, and explanations for various celestial phenomena.

Historically, the poem has been more often praised for the fineness of its Latin than the subtlety of its science. Some of the disdain for Lucretius's version of science stems from the history of atomism common during the time that Serres composed his study.[40] While modern atomism has mathematical principles to support it and raise it to the level of a universal science, the story goes, ancient atomism was little more than a lucky guess, arrived at solely because thinkers sought a maximally reductive explanation for the behavior of the universe. The greater reason for the skeptical eye cast on Lucretius, though, comes from one particular doctrine within the text: the clinamen, or "swerve," which, significantly for our purposes, introduced contingency, in the sense of indeterminacy and unpredictability, into the Epicurean cosmogony.

The clinamen developed as a response to a fundamental problem in the Epicurean account of creation that runs roughly as follows. Epicurean thought imagined creation as beginning in a void filled with eternal atoms, impossibly small particles of all shapes and sizes. In everyday life, matter is never destroyed or created; rather, new shapes and creatures are born out of different configurations of colliding atoms. In the void, however, all things fall in parallel at equal speed. Since parallel lines by definition never meet, how did atoms begin to collide and create the world as we experience it?

The swerve was meant to answer this question. "When the atoms are being drawn downward through the void by their property of weight," Lucretius writes, "at absolutely unpredictable times and places they defect slightly from their straight course, to a degree that could be described as no more than a shift of movement. If they were not apt to swerve, all would fall downward through the unfathomable void like drops of rain; no collisions between primary elements would occur, and no blows would be effected, with the result that nature would never have created anything."[41] The clinamen, then, is this imperceptible inclination or swerve that allows for the creation of the world.

While the general point of the swerve seems clear enough, scholars continue to question the details. What causes the swerve? Is it the uncaused cause, as Cicero once derisively remarked,[42] or does it derive from a separate cause, in the way weight and speed do? How often do atoms swerve? Did it happen once, setting into motion creative chaos, or do atoms swerve constantly? Can Lucretitus's insistence on sensory experience as our only path to knowledge ever be reconciled with the argument for the swerve, which insists that "it is a plain and manifest matter of observation that objects with weight, left to themselves, cannot travel an oblique course when they plunge from above—at least not perceptibly; but who could possibly perceive that they do not swerve at all from their vertical paths?"[43]

Lucretius deals explicitly with none of these worries. Instead, after stressing the incalculable nature of the swerve, he imagines how the colliding atoms form new shapes, tastes, smells, and textures, depending on the different shapes of the interlocking atoms. For example, Lucretius imagines, water must be made from rounded, smooth atoms linking together in order to be so liquid and silky. By contrast, salt or vinegar, things that taste pungent or sharp derive, from jagged atoms that hook together and pierce the tongue.[44] All our sensations can be traced, in one way or another, to the collision of atoms and their impingement on our senses. In this respect touch is by far the most important sense for Lucretius, which he admits when he writes in a moment of unusual rhetorical grandiosity, "For the holy gods are my witness that touch, yes, touch, is the sense of the body, when something extraneous insinuates itself into it, or when something born within affects it . . . or again when, in consequence of a collision, the atoms are disturbed within the body itself and the commotion confuses our senses."[45] Even sight depends on the passage of atoms through the retina; even taste requires the abrasion of particles against the tongue.

Once he has explained the senses, Lucretius then goes on to make the most perplexing claim for the clinamen in the work. Not only does the swerve lead to material creation, somehow it also makes possible volition that cannot be strictly explained by the determinism of circumstances. If there were only the endless mechanical chain of atom hitting atom, Lucretius reasons, every action would be determined from the ground up by the orderly and inevitable chain of atomic collisions. Yet experience tells us that we humans, as well as "living creatures all over the earth," possess wills that "enables each of us to advance where pleasure leads us, and to alter our movements not at a fixed time or place, but at the direction of our minds."[46] We can see the power of volition everywhere, from the horse who has to pause before exiting a suddenly open stall, as it waits for its will to be translated into movement, to the power we feel within our breasts to resist the jostling of the crowd. Since nothing can come from nothing, there must be some sort of cause that allows for freedom and indeterminacy in action. This factor, Lucretius concludes, "that saves the mind itself from being governed in all of its actions by an internal necessity, and from being constrained to submit passively to domination, is the minute swerve of atoms at unpredictable places and times."[47]

Reams of scholarship have been written on the question of how Lucretius's libertarianism fits in with his account of atomism, if at all.[48] For Serres, though, that question primarily serves to shuffle the swerve sideways into questions of subjectivity, free will, and agency at the expense of the more profound scientific insight. More to my point, it also corrals the concept of contingency into a relatively constricted conversation about necessity, freedom, and indeterminism at the expense of the more material definition that Serres has been pursuing. Instead, he begins *The Birth of Physics* by claiming he wants to rehabilitate the Lucretian swerve from the charge of being a logical absurdity or moment of pseudo science based in metaphysical speculation rather than mathematical laws.[49] That dismissal of Lucretius grows naturally out of our post-Newtonian world. Serres thinks we have been trained by Newtonian sciences to think of physics as

first a science of solids. After all, the discovery of the rotation of
the planets began as a calculation of how solid bodies influenced each other's orbits through gravity, while the basics of the
atom are still taught to schoolchildren as a question of how the
nucleus, the center of an atom's mass, attracts or repels neutrons
and electrons. It seems natural enough to assume that the atoms
should be the linchpin of ancient atomism as well and, by that
metric, judge the theory wanting. Under Serres's reading, though,
that assumption gets ancient atomism exactly backward. There
is no atomism without the atom, of course, but the atom matters
less than the swerve, which *does* have a mathematical basis, not
in geometry or calculus, but in the differential mathematics of
Archimedes.

Specifically, the swerve comes from a treatise written by
Archimedes about whether a tangential line touches a circle at
more than one point. He ultimately proves that the two only
touch at one infinitesimally small point and, in the process, created the smallest possible angle. In ancient Greek treatises this
imperceptible, incalculable slant where circle and tangent touch
is called the angle of contingency; we might think of it instead
as the swerve. In Serres's reading, this confrontation with the
immeasurably small angle of contingency is even more basic,
more infinitesimal than the atom itself. The atom should not be
understood as a free-standing concept that suddenly, arbitrarily,
has the idea of an erratic, unobservable angle inserted to smooth
out the flaws in the Epicurean creation myth or to erect a pseudo
origin for free will. Rather, the true mathematical basis for Epicurean physics that gives the whole enterprise rigor comes from
this debate about the angle of contingency.[50]

Moreover, *The Birth of Physics* offers a second set of reasons
why the swerve seemed plausible at the time, rather than simply
the philosophical embarrassment it has largely become. While

we assume physics describes the motion of solid objects, Greek physics, more often than not, had in mind fluid mechanics. While the swerve may seem absurd in abstraction, Serres explains, read as an observation about the flow of water, it suddenly becomes much more plausible. Serres cites the example of water running through a glass pipe. As we watch it flow, occasional eddies appear. We can at best chart the statistical likelihood of their emergence, but we cannot predict them in advance or say with any certainty what specific confluence of factors cause them to emerge. We cannot, in short, explain why *this* eddy emerged in *this* space *now*. As he writes, "For it to carry weight, knowledge should have nothing to say about chance distribution. What Lucretius says, however, remains true—that is, faithful to the phenomenon: turbulence appears stochastically in the laminar flow. Why? I don't know why. How? By chance, with regard to space and time."[51]

While Serres's reading may seem a relatively low-stakes effort to rehabilitate an unjustly derided author, the beginning sentence of this quotation—"For it to carry weight, knowledge should have nothing to say about chance distribution"—introduces the real stakes of his argument. *The Birth of Physics* rails against nothing less than the whole model of science that invests truth in unchanging laws at the expense of unruly reality. From the Renaissance forward, Serres argues, science has implicitly drawn a distinction between laws and events. Laws say that gravity necessarily pulls objects directly downward; the event disrupts that trajectory with a slight eddy. The law says a light comes on when I flick a switch; the event happens at the moment when the bulb unexpectedly blows out. The fact that we consider the predictable action to be a law, fundamental to the working of physics, but chance turbulence an aberration says more about our model of laws than the nature of the universe. Lucretius appeals to

Serres precisely because he elevates the event, the chance disruption to the status of a law. Under his reading, building the
swerve into the Epicurean creation story should not be read as
an absurdity or moment of outmoded science; rather, it should
be understood as a sign of a drastically different set of priorities
about what phenomena are basic enough to the world we live in
to count as a scientific law. And for Lucretius—or at least Serres's
Lucretius—contingency, chance distributions, and stochastic
turbulence in the laminar flow all count as fundamental.

Serres wrote *The Birth of Physics* in 1978. I have no doubt a contemporary scientist could take issue with his characterization of
science, particularly given advances in the last thirty-five years.
I am also sure a conscientious Lucretius scholar would find plenty
to contest in his reading of *De rerum natura*. But, as Rousseau
once said, "Let us therefore begin by setting aside the facts, for
they do not affect the question."[52] Whether or not Serres gets
Lucretius "right" matters less than figuring out what he gets out
of Lucretius and, equally important, what he discards.

So what does it mean for a twentieth-century author to
argue that we need to study the physics of ancient atomism,
practically speaking? It certainly cannot entail swallowing
Epicurean cosmogony whole, with its account of jagged atoms
held together by interlocking edges. Michel Serres first trained
as a scientist; he knows the developments of subatomic physics
as well as anyone, along with all the reasons why Lucretius's
account cannot hold. And yet Serres undoubtedly thinks
Lucretius gets something profoundly right about knowledge
and our most fundamental experience of the world as one filled
with chance fluctuations. How much he thinks Lucretius gets
right depends on whether you commit to a strong or weak
reading of the connection between *The Birth of Physics* and *The
Five Senses.*

In the strong reading, the language of "tangency" from *The Birth of Physics* seamlessly becomes "common tangency" in *The Five Senses*. In this version, there is nothing arbitrary or incidental in his account of touch's role in the formation of subjectivity. Rather, since his early days, when he used the tangency of Epicurean atoms to challenge the systematic exclusion of chance from scientific laws, Serres has clearly been fascinated by the capacity of the slightest touch to send bodies and events tumbling askew. His work on Lucretius expands the role of touch and contingency in Serres's thought, from issues of where and how I know to questions about the inadequacy of scientific explanations and the space for suffering. Any work he does on the senses simply makes explicit the implications of earlier work; the experience of touch is one instant in a universe defined and created by colliding, connecting, contingent atoms.

In the weak reading, Serres's account of touch, subjectivity, and contingency in *The Five Senses* supersedes his discussion of the clinamen. The physical dimension of contingency remains a constant preoccupation, of course, but *The Five Senses* draws out the role of touch that had been previously implied while simultaneously restricting the scope of contingency. Undoubtedly, structuring subjectivity and undermining the distinction between the self and the world are tremendously important roles for contingency and touch, but not when compared to the earlier implication of the clinamen in questions of cosmology and the limits of science. At best, the uncaused cause, the unpredictable shift of the atom, finds a new home in the example of touch wandering from finger to lips. The real paradigm of cosmology for Serres moves to the woman applying makeup in the mingling of senses. The contingency of touch becomes one among many ways of relating to the world.

Both readings, however, dodge the question I ended the previous section with: is touch the only sense that can build this bodily account of contingency? I have established that Serres has good historical precedent for drawing an account of contingency out of touch. Any number of thinkers, from Spinoza to Sartre to Merleau-Ponty, has explicitly or implicitly drawn on the etymological roots of contingency in *tangere* to build accounts of being at once connected and disconnected, rooted and uprooted, dependent and fragile. Serres even has strong reasons for positioning himself in the tradition of Lucretius specifically. Lucretius draws on a mathematical definition of contingency that moves the conversation away from academic distinctions between freedom and necessity to the concreteness of a mathematical problem; he validates or grounds Serres's belief that the experience of contingency is a function of touch by offering a model where everything comes back to the chance touch of atoms cascading into atoms; he offers an alternative model of science that grows out of the unpredictability of the event, rather than the idealized regularity of laws.

Historical precedent and logical necessity are not the same, though. Even if Serres wanted to use this tactile theory of contingency in touch as a starting point, nothing mandates that his account of contingency must draw *solely* on touch, particularly given his insistence on trying to mingle senses that have historically been held apart. So why not give an account of contingency rooted in a truly mingled sense of sight-sound-taste-touch? The answer, I think, goes back to the theory of subjectivity I outlined in the first section of this chapter. Touch teaches us to recognize not just the instability of our world but also the mobility of our selves. Go back to the initial definition of the soul as "the place where the 'I' is decided." How would that work with the senses of sight or sound or taste? We can experience ourselves as both subjects and objects because our soul wanders, leaving at one minute an expanse of our skin as the site of all selfhood and subjectivity, at other moments a wooden object. A more comprehensive understanding of touch could perhaps include the touch of food on the tongue, or noise on our eardrums, and thus amplify the experiences that contribute to our sense of contingency, but it is not so clear that the other senses could be equally expansive. Serres likes the skin precisely because of its promiscuity. The skin is the most fundamental site of mingling, the place of the mingling of mingling. So why shift the site of contingency, of mingling between self and world, to another, more localized sense?

I, frankly, cannot see any other option than to follow the strong reading of Serres's connection to Lucretius. I think Serres's early and later treatment of touch is continuous, and that he follows Lucretius in understanding contact as fundamental to the operation of all the senses. The senses may mingle for Serres, but only because they meet at the skin. His language, with its emphasis on skin and boundaries and tangency, traps him into imagining the senses as only capable of mingling under the auspices of touch. It might be a version of touch that contains the other senses—it certainly is a version of touch that has moved far beyond simple images of hands grasping hammers—but that move nonetheless reasserts a hierarchy of the senses, with the problematic historical associations that invokes. It would seem the senses in that scenario are not mingling so much as subsumed under the sense of touch. Why Serres feels justified trading his dream of an egalitarian theory of mingled senses for the hegemony of touch remains a question for the following final pages.

CONTINGENCY AND THE NATURAL CONTRACT

Contingency may be basic for Serres, found in everything from the touch of a lover's hand, which draws out our sense of self, to the swerves and collisions of the clinamen in the center of matter, but it does more than create us or overawe us or render us vulnerable to the world. Contingency is *the* central religious experience for Serres, and religion does not end with creation or even the communication of technological angels. Rather, everything in his thought, from his theory of subjectivity to his tactile version of contingency, to his philosophy of mingled senses, pushes him toward a new theology grounded in an ethical obligation to the world. It is for this theology that he sacrifices his egalitarian vision of mingled senses. Consequently, it is with this trajectory of his thought that I want to end, beginning with his definition of religion and the reasons he attributes to our alienation from it, before concluding with his ethics of contingency.

Religion in Serres does not look much like any of the canonical theories. He does not make the mistake of simplistically equating religion with beliefs or reducing it to community-building institutions among humans. Nor is he particularly interested in traditional terms such as the *sacred* and the *profane*. Instead, midway through his 1990 book *The Natural Contract*, he comes to define religion through a reflection on the superciliousness of the modern age in which thinkers address the rites, songs, and prayers performed in secret by priests and monks. "Amnesiacs that we are," we imagine that the priests who dressed and fed and coddled their icons mistook out of childlike simplicity the statue for the divine and adored it as a god.[53] But, he goes on to write, "No: they were giving to the thing itself, marble or bronze, the power of speech, by conferring on it the appearance of a human body endowed with a voice. So they must have been celebrating their pact with the world."[54] Likewise, we forget why the Benedictine and Carmelite monks arose before dawn to sing, "matins and lauds, the minor hours of prime, terce, and sext."[55] They were not marking the passage of time in the day, "they were sustaining it."[56] Without their rites, they believe, time itself would break. Their prayers and verses carried each moment into the next, sustaining the world, weaving together the continuity of time.

We could read the monks as madmen or as wild narcissists who believed they had the power to make God stone—if not flesh—and propel the Earth each day in its orbit around the Sun. To make that ungenerous dismissal, though, misses the very roots of religion in thought. According to experts, Serres argues, the word *religion* has two possible roots. The first is the Latin word *religare*, to attach. The second, more plausible word, which Serres never names, means "to assemble, gather, lift up, traverse, or reread."[57] But these experts, he continues, "never say what sublime word our language opposes to the religious, in order to deny it: *negligence*. Whoever has no religion should not be called an atheist or unbeliever, but negligent."[58]

We, the amnesiacs, look with incomprehension on the old religion of responsibility at least in part because language alienates and stands between us and the physical world. Language abstracts, dealing with the senses only to point out their inadequacies and failures, as when Descartes doubts his hand. Yet, unexpectedly, Serres also believes language once constituted the original insight of religion. Over and over, different cultures and cults have announced their idiom as the fulfillment and perfection of all language. In Genesis the word becomes the breath, the spirit moving over the waters before the first day of creation. In John the word becomes flesh, the incarnation of God.

The inspired nature of language has begun to wane, though. In linguistics and forms of analytic philosophy, however, language is categorized and described "scientifically using algorithms, equations, codes, formulae." Or, "in any case," Serres writes in a jab at the contemporary fascination with language among the followers of Derrida and poststructuralism more generally, thought "excludes from philosophy everything not related to language."[59]

In our current moment, words anesthetize us. They fill our bodies and blunt our experience of our surroundings. Serres first introduces this thought early into the second chapter of *The Five Senses*, returning to the imagery of the ship. This time, instead of throwing him in contact with his soul, the ship is a metaphorical one made of language that disrupts his peace by carrying a buzzing, squawking, rumbling herd of tourists. Their language encases them like the hull of the ship, gliding through the air like water. Encased as they are in thoughts and words, exclamation, and excerpts from guide books, the tourists do everything but arrive and observe. "Bathed in silent air, yellow and blue, alone, outside, I give a chance to the given, which the collective ruckus expels; I give a chance to those senses anesthetized by language. The group devotes itself to its own din, revels in its own roar, notices little outside of itself. It resembles a sick body, rumbling from the clamor of its own organs. What health would it recover if it were one day to fall silent?"[60]

Yet, in the fascination we have with language, Serres reads signs that this religion of the word will soon pass. "Today we take an active interest in this constant law because we are beginning to lose it. We are witnessing the last reverberation of the centuries-old shock which caused us to be born at the same time as language; we are witnessing it in its death throes."[61] The increasingly grandiose claims made for language in the 1980s reflect the orgiastic period of decadence before the collapse of an era. We can see the signs of that collapse coming in the decline of prose, Serres believes. Whereas once even farmers spoke with a degree of eloquence, today the most educated alternate between stammering out rambling nonquestions and luxuriating in the technical voluptuousness of jargon that deadens thought. We are writing badly because old-fashioned precision of language is beginning to feel strange in our mouths as we tumble into a new regime of thought.

Is this sentiment rank nostalgia? Of course. Philosophers, at least, have been writing terribly for centuries, and, decades before Derrideans came to be, George Orwell felt comfortable starting an essay with a matter-of-fact observation, "Most people who bother with the matter at all would admit that the English language is in a bad way."[62] Although the constant volley of clichés in the public pains Serres, he welcomes the end of language. "Being enclosed in language," he thinks, "stops us from seeing that the noise that it makes veils and and overwhelms the things which compose our world, and causes them to vanish."[63] By contrast, science, data, and the paradigm of thought he imagines coming next share with the soothsayers of antiquity an attentiveness to the natural world. Like the haruspices of Rome who watched the birds for signs of the time, scientists assume a world that exists without them and whose meaning endures regardless of whether or not the collective can ever give voice to the logic that governs its motions.[64] The future is a messianic one: when science fully arrives and "word becomes flesh," we will be freed from the narrowness of anthropocentrism, the anesthetizing function of words, the sickness of constant divisions into disciplines, categories, organs, abstraction.

In later years, in *The Natural Contract*, Serres suggests we will be rescued from abstraction and anthropocentrism despite ourselves. Regardless of the trends of technology or the internal necessity of thought, with the advent of climate change he argues that we *must* attend to the global or perish. He opens this argument with an image of two fighters grappling in quicksand, taken from a painting by Goya. "With every move they make, a slimy hole swallows them up further, so that they are gradually burying themselves together. How quickly depends on how aggressive they are: the more heated the struggle, the more violent their movements become and the faster they sink in."[65] The plight of the combatants increasingly reflects our own. After centuries of profound indifference to the natural world on the part of Western society, "the mute world, the voiceless things once placed as a decor surrounding the usual spectacles, all those things that never interested anyone, from now on thrust themselves brutally and without warning into our schemes and maneuvers."[66] Climate change has forced us to make the modern equivalent of Pascal's wager: we either believe in it, and we create a natural contract that recognizes the same obligations to the earth that the social contract demands for fellow humans, or we disbelieve in it and carry on with our lives as before. In the first case, if we are wrong we lose nothing, but if we are correct we win the right to continue on as agents in history. In the second case, if we are right we win the ability to carry on with the status quo, but if we are wrong we suffer a catastrophe and potentially lose everything.

The problem, the danger, the possibility of this wager comes down to the same point made by Maurice Blanchot forty years earlier in an essay wonderfully titled "The Apocalypse Is Disappointing." Reviewing a recent work by Karl Jaspers about the necessity of a new global politics to combat the dangers of a nuclear apocalypse, Blanchot mused about why such works—so unobjectionable on the surface—always seemed unsatisfactory to him. He concludes that they presupposed a unified global citizen, as if humanity had magically become a gigantic Hamlet pondering whether to be or not to be. And yet nothing justified that assumption. Countries remain engrossed in their own self-interests, sometimes hostile, sometimes conciliatory toward their neighbors, while individuals continue to cheerfully pursue their own desires, hatreds, and demons. In the absence of a genuinely unified humanity that could make decisions about the future of the world as a whole, the apocalypse remains a monstrous banality, capable of wiping the earth out randomly, thoughtlessly, for reasons abstract and peripheral to most of those who would die. In the face of such meaningless destruction, Blanchot concluded, what could we say except the trite but true phrase "It would be better to prevent it."[67] The global subject Jaspers and now Serres envisioned has yet to be created.

To create that global subject, we need individual subjects who recognize their environment as more than something that surrounds them at a distance; we need subjects who recognize they are coconstituted with and shot through by the material world. In short, we need something very much like the theory of subjectivity Serres developed in *The Five Senses*. Much like Hegel in *The Phenomenology of Spirit*, Serres writes in such a way that each level of his thought is isomorphic with the previous one. His environmentalism is really his theory of subjectivity writ large. Drowning in quicksand is not equivalent to a caress, of course, but both examples assume reciprocity in touch. The lover cannot shift his weight without having his partner's skin flow to meet him in turn, and humans cannot emit carbon into the air without it, in turn melting our icecaps. In each scenario, Serres imagines a type of radical equality where the binaries of subject-object, man-nature, and lover-beloved all dissolve and reform in turn. There can never be an untouched toucher or a fixed, stable subject amidst a world of contingency. His demands for a new natural contract depend on this assumption, which allows him to position his ethical demands as grounded in the pragmatic fact of our co-implication with the physical world.

Until that moment comes—when language gives way to science and we recognize ourselves as subjects with skins, imbricated in a world brimming with things that shape us, slap us, caress us, bruise us, trip us, birth us, and bury us—Serres can at best compose a transitional book, hemmed in by the words he struggles to escape. Writing in 1985, he wants no truck with contemporary scholarly movements that think of language, or, worse, literature, as a matter of semiotics, with words referring to words and signs to signs, theoretical movements that saturate every crevice of the world with words. He seeks, instead, in the words of one commenter, "a geography, an earth-writing, a writing that mimics the autography of the earth."[68] He wants a language of things and a literature of stories, not signs or symbols, a language that might model the new, healthier relation between thought and things that he thinks we need in order to save ourselves from the apocalypse.

Above all, he wants his writing to be a map. Not a map in the sense that the encyclopedists of Novalis's day imagined it (as a sort of abstract overview of scholarly terrain that allows for careful navigation among prescouted trails), but a map as tattered reflection of the landscape. For Serres, a map is not a photo that might dream of capturing the world as it is and reduce the user to an impartial spectator hovering above it. Instead, a map traces and creates a world as much by leaving out detail as by faithfully following it. A cartographer may decide to compose a map of roads or rivers, mountains or trains, and in that sense impose her vision on what she draws, but at some point her license ends. A map unmoored from the world as it finds it is not a map; it is a painting. The true writer who manages to escape the sterile repetition of books and ideas always in some sense follows the cartographer in her fidelity to the found. Late in *The Five Senses* the cartographer and the writer even blur together as Serres plays

on the dual meaning of the Latin *pagus* as "page" and "field."[69]
"What world is created by the rag stitched patiently from thousands of already ploughed pages and by the thousands we hope
are ahead of us," Serres asks, "what country is embellished by
them, what land do they map, what body do they dress? . . . How
is this map to be stuck on the countryside, to the ground of moving flesh, to erectile spring growth, in celebration of sensation,
for it is thus each page is erected. A work of art is dead without
this conjunction, sterile without this bracketing together," he
judges, before concluding that "pages do not sleep in language,
they draw their life from the *pagi*, the countryside, the flesh and
the world."[70]

The writer-as-cartographer echoes or even mimics the structure of touch in his composition. Just as touch bring together
points of sensitivity and dullness, subjectivity and objectivity, so
too Serres sees his work as basting words and the world together.
His favorite tactic is that of the long variegated list, where clauses
nestle within clauses and metaphors abut and abrade without
ever losing sight of the driving point. Take, for a moment, the
sentence just cited: "What world is created by the rag stitched
patiently from thousands of already ploughed pages and by the
thousands we hope are ahead of us, what country is embellished
by them, what land do they map, what body do they dress?"
Images of sewing, writing, plotting, and adorning all blend
together, but thoughtfully, all descending from the play he makes
on *pagus*, the page, and *pagus*, the countryside. These images are
scenes that make no pretense of being a comprehensive image of
the whole, but they are not, for that reason, fragments either. The
sentence sutures together the images like touch, and touch, in
Serres's words, "involves stitching together, place by place. Poin-
tillist, if you like, or impressionist, moving between sections
and localities, it creates maps, varieties, veils."[71] Or again, as he
writes a few pages later, "Touch involves local patches activated

or created by contact and brought together into an ocellated fragment, and skates about in flattened out dimensions of irregularly shaped patches and imprecise tacking."[72]

It would be a mistake to imagine that Serres does not recognize the tenuousness of his hope that humans may recover from their negligence in order to recognize their responsibility, their continuity with the natural world, their contingency. His entire philosophical project grows out of a commitment to uncertainty and finitude; the insight most basic to understanding subjectivity is that we are constituted by chance contact we can neither control nor will. Philosophizing about science can even be seen as the greatest commitment to finitude a thinker can make. Years will roll by and some unknown percentage of the theories that seem so certain today, just like mesmerism and irritability in Novalis's and Schelling's day, will be radically revised or discarded or proved to be deeply, definitively wrong. Yet, unlike the frequently despairing, internally oriented line of Protestant thinkers, stretching from Jacobi to Kant to Kierkegaard to Barth, Serres does not leap into despair or anxiety or acceptance of his own unacceptability; he makes a fideistic leap into a joyful, pagan affirmation of the material world and our responsibility to it. As he writes, "Without being able to prove it I believe, like soothsayers and haruspices, and like scientists, that there exists a world independent of men. . . . I believe, I know, I cannot demonstrate this world exists without us."[73]

"THE OPPOSITE OF RELIGION
IS NEGLIGENCE"

Serres writes about the most optimistic type of touch I have addressed in this book. Unlike "that tedious marquis," touch does not violate or traumatize or casually upend lives. He speaks of the caress, not the blow, not the slap, not the grasp, to the clenched fingers wrapped white around another's arm. The difficulties and darknesses of his version of contingency are not the abrupt dissolution of self and sanity found in the dark space of Minkowski' schizophrenia patients. The responsibility demanded by his new religion depends on envisioning touch as the caress, the most reciprocal and egalitarian among the types of touch I have discussed.

Despite the temperamental differences between Serres and the figures discussed before him, in some sense he draws out the logical conclusions of many of their projects. It is no coincidence that Novalis dreamed of an alternate arrangement of the senses nearly two hundred years earlier or, for that matter, that this work began with Schelling and ends with Serres. More than the scholars who write monographs on Schelling's influence on psychoanalysis or deconstruction, more than all who write careful explications of Novalis's politics or histories of the influence of the French Revolution on the Schlegels, Serres is the real heir to those short years of intellectual ferment in Jena and to the inventive early years of psychology and phenomenology in the twentieth century. I can think of no other writer today who theologizes science and poeticizes philosophy in the same way. There are differences, of course, but there are deeper similarities in their striving after some revelation of an interconnected, unreachable whole from the position of a finite, contingent subject.

CONCLUSION

I opened this book with the story of Havi Carel, a woman forced to confront the contingency of her dreams through the sudden onset of disease in her youth. I want to close with a story from my own earlier years as a coda, meant to engage—though not resolve—some of the questions raised by Serres in the final chapter about how we might use this model of contingency going forward.

When I was twenty, I had a night job working for a domestic violence shelter. I was too young for the job, of course, and too eager to rush into sympathizing with my callers, rather than keeping the clinical distance my more experienced supervisors recommended. Over time, I fell into a friendship of sorts with a regular caller, A. The first night we ever spoke, like every other night we would speak, she called in the midst of a flashback. Huddled in the closet of her guest room, too ashamed to tell her husband what she was suffering, too frightened to leave, she relived her childhood abuse. This particular night she was trapped in an afternoon that had taken place when she was fifteen. Her basketball coach had chosen that day, in an empty classroom, amid graffitied desks, to carve his initials into her pubic bone with a penknife. I asked what she did, and I could hear her shrug.

"I taped a sanitary napkin over it and went home." She was twenty-seven when we spoke, but sounded like a child. He had begun raping her fifteen years earlier and his hold over her remained total.

If Novalis and Schelling are right that every philosophical endeavor begins with a personal intuition expanded into a system, this image of a woman still able to trace the scars of her rapist's initials on her skin is mine. That night was the start of my interests in the vulnerability of flesh and the way that touch can make or unmake a world, forever.

I often think of A. when I am asked the inevitable question: So if everything you say is true, what comes after genealogy? What comes after critique?

It is a question I have spent a fair amount of time thinking about in the years I have devoted to this book. There is no doubt that the analytical tools we have used to build most of the last generation's theories are becoming blunted and worn about the handles from overuse. My book is only one among an increasing number asking whether it is time to lay them aside. Most recently, in 2015, Rita Felski wrote an entire book, *The Limits of Critique*, arguing that the main trends in critique from the last decade are defunct, sloppy, predictable, or some combination of all three. Taking aim at these forms of critique, Felski argues that reading texts for gaps, fissures, and excess descriptors results in diagnosing all texts as hiding instances of domination.[1] She condemns the conflation of denaturalization and critique, accusing it of relying on the rhetorical denigration, the unjustified assumption, that anything taken for granted is automatically oppressive, and the author's implicit belief that she is more aware of her presuppositions than she actually is.[2] Finally, she accuses context-based reading of overemphasizing the historical origin of the text at the expense of its later significance, interpretations, and aesthetic value—an argument that resonates with my worries about assuming a book or critique will mean the same thing to readers in future decades as it did when published.[3] Talal Asad, meanwhile, has begun to question whether critique itself is secular.[4] And Eve Kosofsky Sedgwick anticipated these questions by fifteen years when she asked if the humanities had confused one particular affective mode, suspicion, with critical inquiry.[5]

For years, I have worried about the future of critique, convinced that some new set of tools or insights or questions was cresting toward us. At times, this conviction has been nothing more than a generalized feeling of dissatisfaction, a vague sense that the old questions were dying and had yet to be replaced with new ones. At other moments, particularly once the framework of this book solidified in my mind, the problems with relying on a particular type of historicization, as if it were not a product of its own time and subject change, became clearer. Throughout all these moments, the answer to "what comes next" remained intractable.

I have since come to think that the problem remained so stubbornly unsolvable because "what comes after critique" is the wrong question. So long as I was trapped by the dream of a new Foucault, a new Derrida, who could inaugurate a radically different way of viewing the world, I was still beholden to Foucault's idea of epistemic breaks. What could be more faithful to Foucault than an imagined future where suddenly, inexplicably, our ways of knowing shifted, leaving past modes of analysis foreign? Even my efforts to escape Foucault took place on his terms.

Worse, the question of what comes next implicitly contained a type of fantasy that a heroic new thinker would vault into the intellectual vacuum and save us from our milling uncertainty. This very dream was a renunciation of the responsibility to think through my present, partial and partially obscured as my gaze may be. It was a refusal to acknowledge that there might not be any way of untangling the muddle of problems that each of these thinkers has pointed to—the fragility of the sick body, the impossibility of forgiveness, the careening catastrophe of climate change.

None of this is to suggest that there is nothing to be done after Foucault or genealogy. No single theorist is that important. There are plenty of smaller, less ambitious theories that have been helping scholars think through the present. Not all of them necessarily reimagine the historical, political questions that have dominated recent decades or concerned me throughout this book . I am wholly sympathetic to the point raised by Felski and Kosofsky Sedgwick that there are any number of constructive projects that might be pursued that have nothing whatsoever to do with genealogy, politics, power, or historicization.

Among the theories that do resonate with my concerns about contingency, however, affect theory comes the closest to my work, and not merely because I have found Kosofsky Sedgwick enormously helpful in thinking through the shortcomings of genealogy. Writing along parallel lines to my own thought, some of the field's theorists have made explicit the connection between contingency and feeling. Sara Ahmed, for example, notes that certain feelings, such as happiness, are irreducibly linked to the contingent happenings of the world. The very etymology of happiness, she suggests, comes from the Middle English word *hap*, connoting chance.[6] Happiness is contingent by definition because the word literally suggests being favored by fortune or lucky, uncontrollable events. Donovan O. Schaefer expands on that thought, arguing that affect theory is valuable to religious studies precisely because it challenges functionalist definitions of religion. Rather than accepting religious actors as motivated by rational self-interest, affect theory depicts a world churned by a "spiraling current of accidents," where "bodies splash and splatter across the balance sheets of costs and benefits."[7]

At their best, affect theorists also attend to sudden, sometimes unexpected shifts in feelings with the deftness of novelists. Kathleen Stewart's *Ordinary Affects* is a wonderfully observed series of vignettes, beginning with dogs dashing through a park, energized by a flash of *something*, and ending with the image of her mother, recovering from a stroke, and her young daughter, both setting off to do some as-yet-undetermined tasks, reveling in "the palpable pleasure of the state of trying."[8] Likewise, the most interesting moment in Teresa Brennan's *The Transmission of Affect* comes at the beginning when she describes the sudden shift in feeling as a person walks into a tense room.[9] I admire these finely drawn portraits of the present and wish there were more of them in contemporary scholarship. It may be that my audience consists of people working in affect theory. If so, I hope they find something useful in my book.

That said, I am not persuaded that, in its current form, affect theory offers a compelling direction for my future scholarship. I have a number of concerns about it ability to address large, looming social questions. Its rhetoric of charges traversing bodies provides an excellent description of how people become caught up in the feelings of crowds and lose themselves in their intimate partners. Yet, in its insistence that the self is fundamentally porous, affect theory loses the ability to explain certain forms of violation. If we really are porous, if we really are bodies churned in a whirlpool of affects that are neither entirely inside nor out, what is the source of the horror that someone like Merleau-Ponty or Améry feels in viscerally recognizing there is no clear distinction between self and world? What are we to make of Minkowski, who thought the experience of total porousness was a form of psychosis? For that matter, what are we to make of Spinoza, the grandfather of affect theory, who recognized the contingency of feelings, recoiled, and wrote in response one of the great ethical treatises about how to control our feelings?

If anything, the politics of reimagining the subject as the porous way station for traveling affects are even worse than its phenomenology. Abby Kluchin sums up the problem with refreshing bluntness.

> The status of *subject* is one that is still not equally awarded. If one takes the long view of the history of Western philosophy, for instance, women became subjects approximately five minutes ago, and I am disinclined to give that status away to be equal with dolphins and housecats and power tools, to flatten out the differences between all these entities and think of them first and foremost as bodies that affect and are affected by one another.[10]

She goes on to argue that it is crucial to maintain the idea of the individual, *"regardless of whether that distinction is fictive or not."* The ideas of autonomy and boundaries "confer upon the individual the ability to say yes or no on her own behalf, to give or withhold consent. This would cash out, just to name a few, in terms of reproductive self-determination, in the ability to consent to or refuse a sexual encounter, to cast a vote—in other words, in the recognizable capacity to make an autonomous decision on one's own behalf."[11]

The other reason I am not personally interested in pursuing affect theory has to do with the dual imperative of this book. As in affect theory, part of this book aims to understand and sympathize with experiences of contingency. But the other part of this book explores what people do with their lives after feeling every certainty stripped away, and there affect theory fails to provide much help. Do they respond with complacence, a new politics, or a reactionary longing for stillness before time? Do they invent a new poetry, a new role for art? Do they seek vengeance or justice? Do they forgive or refuse to forgive? What ought *I* do with the recognition of my own precariousness? What do I care about?

The last question, at least, gives me an anchor.

I care about A.

Still, and after all these years, I care about A. I wonder about her. Did she have children? Did she stay married? Did she ever find a space outside her spare closet to voice her fears? Did she forgive him? Did she finally learn to hate him for what he had done to her? Is she happy now? Is she even still alive?

I wrote this book because of A. and in some ways for A., but it feels incomplete. The book is haunted by dead women—Novalis's Sophia, Schelling's Caroline, Améry's first wife, dead of heart disease while he suffered through Auschwitz—but there are no women's voices in its pages. I would like to rectify that.

I would like to write a book thinking about the women like A. who might have woken up every morning, read their rapist's initials scarred on their skin, and decided not to forgive. What might it look like to refuse, not out of weakness but out of principle, to forgive? Is forgiveness even the right framework, or is it too individualistic for scenarios where the perpetrator is experienced by the victim as representative of an unjust society, rather than as an individual committing a temporally bounded offense? Could deciding never to forgive give similar solace as forgiving? First Améry, and now A., have raised the possibility that in response to the violation of contingency a person might refuse to forgive, but there is still more to say. I care about these questions, especially writing in the closing summer months of 2018, after a year of revelations and opinion pieces about sexual assault as trenchant as any collection I have ever seen.

And, like Serres, I care about climate change.

Every day at noon, my funny little ginger pit bull leaps into the outstretched arms of a woman who sells bottled water in our local park. My dog writhes and wriggles and preens, sometimes knocking to the ground the damp washcloth the woman wears on her head during particularly sweltering days. I look at them, capering about like the oldest of friends, and can't imagine any academic conversation that matters more than the fact that the Manhattan park where they play will one day be under water.

Other readers will have their own responses and concerns after reading this book. On my part, though, I chose to end with Serres because, more than any of the other thinkers I addressed, he recognized the responsibilities and possibilities that come with our return to the world in moments of contingency. He would say, I think rightly, that my emphasis on the psychological costs of contingency throughout this book can only be half of the story. If we want to recognize the full breadth of contingency and imagine a different, more earthly, less negligent basis for religion than continental philosophy has provided to date, we have to begin by admitting something like this.

We live in a world of stones, saplings, lilacs, and books. When I rest my hand on the trunk of an old and time-weathered tree, its crumpled, roughened bark gouges momentarily whitened rivulets in my palm. And when I let my arm fall, those lines may stream off my wrist and vanish, and my forgetful flesh may plump out exactly as before, but the rock I stoop to pick up is smooth and warm from a private covenant with the sun it never asked me to witness. The flower sends out its scent without me and the book, no matter how many papers I write about the technology that produced it, or the networks of exchange that delivered it, still bears the whiff of cigarettes and the circles of scotch stains some stranger left on its jaundiced pages. It resists me. It exists without me. I may rip it, trample it, burn it, destroy it, but I am until the end articled to finitude, the same as it, a perishable creature no higher and no less vulnerable than the world of things that surround me.

NOTES

ACKNOWLEDGMENTS

1. Pablo Neruda, "Sonnet XVII," in *100 Love Sonnets*, trans. Gustavo Escobedo (Ontario: Exile, 2004), 35.

INTRODUCTION

1. Havi Carel, *Illness: The Cry of the Flesh* (London: Routledge, 2014), 4.
2. Parts of the following introduction were originally published as an article in *Method and Theory in the Study of Religion*. See Liane F. Carlson, "Critical for Whom? Genealogy and the Limits of History," *Method and Theory in the Study of Religion: Journal of the North American Association for the Study of Religion*, forthcoming.
3. Tomoko Masuzawa, *The Invention of World Religions, Or How European Universalism Was Preserved in the Language of Pluralism* (Chicago: University of Chicago Press, 2005); David Chidester, *Savage Systems: Colonialism and Comparative Religion in Southern Africa* (Charlottesville: University of Virginia, 1996).
4. Maurice Olender, *Languages of Paradise: Race, Religion, and Philology in the Nineteenth Century*, trans. Arthur Goldhammer (Cambridge, MA: Harvard University Press, 2009).
5. Daniel Boyarin, *Unheroic Conduct: The Rise of Heterosexuality and the Invention of the Jewish Man* (Berkeley: University of California Press, 1997).

6. Talal Asad, *Genealogies of Religion: Discipline and Reasons of Power in Christianity and Islam* (Baltimore: John Hopkins University Press, 1993).

7. The Oxford English Dictionary also offers this etymology: "French contingent 14th cent. (Oresme), or < Latin contingent-em touching together or on all sides, lying near, contiguous, coming into contact or connection, befalling, happening, coming to pass, present participle of contingĕre to touch together, come into contact, etc., < con- + tangĕre to touch." OED.com, s.v. "Contingent," http://www.oed.com.ezproxy.cul.columbia.edu/view/Entry/40248?redirectedFrom=contingent #eid (accessed August 16, 2011).

8. I am bracketing the question of causality because the thinkers I deal with, as well as most scholars working in the field of religious studies, tend not to deal with the details of causality when talking about contingency. They are interested in the fact that events, terms, and social institutions could have been otherwise, the politics of contingency, or the emotional stakes of recognizing one's own contingency, without being overly scrupulous about what the nature of causality is.

9. Michel Foucault, "Nietzsche, Genealogy, History," in *The Foucault Reader*, trans. Paul Rabinow (New York: Pantheon, 1984), 81.

10. Foucault, 76.

11. Foucault, 79.

12. Foucault, 80.

13. The quotation runs in full, "History becomes 'effective' to the degree that it introduces discontinuity into our very being—as it divides our emotions, dramatizes our instincts, multiplies our body and sets it against itself. This is because knowledge is not made for understanding; it is made for cutting." Foucault, "Nietzsche, Genealogy, History," 88.

14. Foucault, 88.

15. For more on the disenchanting, destructive aims of genealogy, see also book 2, section 24 of *The Genealogy of Morals*. "I end up with three question marks; that seems plain. 'What are you really doing, erecting an ideal or knocking one down?' I may perhaps be asked. But have you ever asked yourself sufficiently how much the erection of every ideal on earth has cost? How much reality had to be misunderstood and slandered, how many lies have been sanctified, how many consciences

disturbed, how much 'God' sacrificed every time? If a temple is erected, *a temple must be destroyed:* that is the law—let anyone who can show me a case in which it is not fulfilled!" Friedrich Nietzsche, *On the Genealogy of Morals and Ecce Homo,* trans. Walter Kaufmann (New York: Vintage, 1989), 95.

16. Colin Koopman, *Genealogy as Critique: Foucault and the Problems of Modernity* (Bloomington: Indiana University Press, 2013), 13–16; Raymond Geuss, "Genealogy as Critique," *European Journal of Philosophy* 10, no. 2 (2002): 209–15.

17. For an overview of affect theory and religious studies, see Donovan O. Schaefer, *Religious Affects: Animality, Evolution, and Power* (Durham: Duke University Press, 2015).

18. Kosofsky Sedgwick, following Silvan Tompkins, differentiates affects from drives. A drive, they argue, is instrumental and oriented toward a particular aim, such as sexuality. "Affects have far greater freedom than drives with respect to, for example, time (anger can evaporate in seconds but can also motivate a decades-long career of revenge) and aim (my pleasure in hearing a piece of music can make me want to hear it repeatedly, listen to other music, or study to become a composer myself). Especially, however, affects have greater freedom with respect to object, for unlike the drives, 'any affect may have any object.' . . . Affects can be, and are, attached to things, people, ideas, sensations, relations, activities, ambitions, institutions, and any number of other things, including other affects. Thus, one can be excited by anger, disgusted by shame, or surprised by joy." Eve Kosofsky Sedgwick, *Touching Feeling: Affect, Pedagogy, Performativity* (Durham: Duke University Press, 2006), 19.

19. Schaefer, *Religious Affects,* 65–68.

20. Bruno Latour, "Why Has Critique Run Out of Steam? From Matters of Fact to Matters of Concern," *Critical Inquiry* 30, no. 2 (Winter 2004): 225–48.

21. Hannah Arendt, *The Origins of Totalitarianism: A New Edition with Added Prefaces* (New York: Harcourt, 1968), 459. I am indebted to Daniel May for bringing this passage to my attention.

22. If this sounds implausible, think of Alasdair MacIntyre's work on virtue ethics. Much like Nietzsche and Foucault, MacIntyre believes there

are no universal, self-evident, timeless truths on which to ground ethics; there are only communities whose commitments are shaped by their particular moment in time. Unlike Foucault, however, MacIntyre then goes on to argue for a return to a Thomistic version of virtue ethics. His decision to do so is not a mistake or a misunderstanding of the force of genealogical arguments; it is the natural outgrowth of the religious commitments he brings to history. Alasdair MacIntyre, *After Virtue: A Study in Moral Theory*, 3d ed. (Notre Dame, IN: University of Notre Dame Press, 2007).

23. Foucault, "Nietzsche, Genealogy, History," 90.

24. For example, a genealogy might undermine the claims to authority grounded in origin stories, but a pragmatist account might be necessary to show that a particular way of parsing the separation of church and state leads to an unacceptable level of discord among minority religious groups, or an account grounded in virtue ethics might be needed to dismantle the rhetoric of human rights a state takes as its basis.

25. Koopman, *Genealogy as Critique*, 271.

26. Frederick Neuhouser, "The Critical Function of Genealogy in the Thought of J.-J. Rousseau," *Review of Politics* 74 (2012): 371–87.

27. Jacqueline Stevens, "On the Morals of Genealogy," *Political Theory* 31 (August 2003): 558–69.

28. Koopman, *Genealogy as Critique*, 7.

29. Geuss, "Genealogy as Critique," 209.

30. On the contrary, there is a distinct strain in Nietzsche scholarship that argues genealogy is a self-defeating project. The point is made most clearly in Robert B. Pippin, *Modernism as a Philosophical Problem: On the Dissatisfaction of European High Culture* (Malden, MA: Blackwell, 1999). Likewise, in *The Order of Things*, Foucault wrote as convincingly as anyone I can think of about the historicity of the reader. Michel Foucault, *The Order of Things: An Archaeology of the Human Sciences* (New York: Vintage, 1994).

31. "To expose the contingent acts that create the appearance of a naturalistic necessity, a move which has been part of cultural critique at least since Marx, is a task that now takes on the added burden of showing how the very notion of the subject, intelligible only through its appearance as gendered, admits of possibilities that have been forcibly

foreclosed by the various reifications of gender that have constituted its contingent ontologies." Judith Butler, *Gender Trouble: Feminism and the Subversion of Identity* (New York: Routledge, 2006), 45–46.

32. Cited in David Hume, *Principal Writings on Religion Including Dialogues Concerning Natural Religion; and, The Natural History of Religion*, ed. J. C. A. Gaskin (Oxford: Oxford University Press, 2008), 100.

33. Alvin Plantinga, *God, Freedom, and Evil* (Grand Rapids: Eerdmans, 2008).

34. John Hick, "Soul-making and Suffering," in Marilyn McCord Adams and Robert Merrihew Adams, eds., *The Problem of Evil* (Oxford: Oxford University Press, 1996), 168–88.

35. Augustine, *Confessions*, trans. Henry Chadwick (New York: Oxford University Press, 1991).

36. Gottfried Wilhelm Leibniz, *Philosophical Essays*, trans. Roger Ariew and Daniel Garber (Indianapolis: Hackett, 1989).

37. Gotthold Ephraim Lessing, "The Education of the Human Race," in *Gotthold Ephraim Lessing: Philosophical and Theological Writings*, trans. H. B. Nisbet (New York: Cambridge University Press, 2005), 217–40.

38. Jean-Jacques Rousseau, *Discourse Concerning the Origin and Foundation of Inequality Among Men*, in *Rousseau: "The Discourses" and Other Early Political Writings*, trans. Victor Gourevitch (New York: Cambridge University Press, 1999), 111–88; Jean-Jacques Rousseau, *Emile, or On Education*, trans. Allan Bloom (New York: Basic, 1979); See also Frederick Neuhouser, *Rousseau's Theodicy of Self-Love: Evil, Rationality, and the Drive for Recognition* (New York: Oxford University Press, 2008).

39. Immanuel Kant, "Idea for a Universal History with a Cosmopolitan Purpose," in *Kant: Political Writings*, trans. H. B. Nisbet (New York: Cambridge University Press, 2003), 41–53.

40. G. W. F. Hegel, *Introduction to the Philosophy of History*, trans. Leo Rauch (Indianapolis: Hackett, 1988), 24.

41. Spinoza distinguishes between two different senses of contingency throughout *Ethics*. The first usage, found primarily in part 1, defines contingency as whatever is causally undetermined. The second version in part 4 defines "individual things as contingent insofar as, in attending only to their essence, we find nothing that necessarily posits their

existence or necessarily excludes it." Benedictus de Spinoza, *The Essential Spinoza: Ethics and Related Writings*, trans. Samuel Shirley (Indianapolis: Hackett, 2006), 20. Or, as Steven Nadler parses that definition, something is contingent, "when it is neither necessary by reason of its essence (as God/substance is) nor impossible because its essence involves a contradiction." Steven Nadler, *Spinoza's "Ethics": An Introduction* (New York: Cambridge University Press, 2006), 105. The second version of contingency undoubtedly exists in Spinoza's determined universe. God or substance is the only necessary being. By contrast we, as humans, along with the rest of world, are contingent because we depend on God for our existence; we would not exist if God did not cause us to be.

42. Hegel, *Introduction to the Philosophy of History*, 23.

43. Anselm, *Anselm, Basic Writings*, trans. Thomas Williams (Indianapolis: Hackett, 1997), 84.

44. Anselm, 85–88.

45. Mark Molesky, *This Gulf of Fire: The Great Lisbon Earthquake and Its Aftermath* (New York: Knopf, 2015), 69–70.

46. Molesky, 81.

47. Molesky, 105.

48. Molesky, 78.

49. Molesky, 132.

50. Susan Neiman, *Evil in Modern Thought: An Alternative History of Philosophy* (Princeton: Princeton University Press, 2004), 1.

51. Voltaire, *The Works of Voltaire: The Lisbon Earthquake and Other Poems*, trans. William F. Fleming (New York: Dumont, 1901), 36:14.

52. Jean-Jacques Rousseau, "Letter to Voltaire," in *Rousseau*, 233.

53. Neiman, *Evil in Modern Thought*, 39–40.

54. Immanuel Kant, "On a Supposed Right to Lie from Philanthropy," in *Practical Philosophy*, ed. Mary J. Gregor (Cambridge: Cambridge University Press, 2008), 611–15.

55. Neiman, *Evil in Modern Thought*, 74.

56. Thomas Nagel, "Moral Luck," in *Mortal Questions* (Cambridge: Cambridge University Press, 2015).

57. Irving Greenberg, "Cloud of Smoke, Pillar of Fire: Judaism, Christianity, and Modernity After the Holocaust," in Eva Fleischner, ed.,

Auschwitz: Beginning of a New Era? Reflections on the Holocaust (New York: KTAV, 1977), 23.

58. Svetlana Alexievich, *Secondhand Time: The Last of the Soviets,* trans. Bela Shayevich (Random House, 2016), 193.

59. Primo Levi, *If This Is a Man and The Truce,* trans. S. J. Woolf (London: Abacus, 2003), 128.

60. Anne Applebaum, *Gulag: A History* (New York: Anchor, 2004), 181.

61. Varlam Shalamov, *Kolyma Tales* (London: Penguin, 1994), 457.

62. Carel, *Illness,* 36.

63. Carel, 31.

64. Carel, 16.

65. Carel, 36.

66. Carel, 37.

67. I am using *ethical* in the broadest sense of how one should live, rather than in the sense of adjudicating moral dilemmas.

68. Martin Heidegger, *Being and Time,* trans. John MacQuarrie and Edward Robinson (New York: Harper Collins, 1962).

69. Wayne Proudfoot, *Religious Experience* (Berkeley: University of California Press, 1987).

70. Martin Heidegger, "The Question Concerning Technology" in Martin Heidegger, *The Question Concerning Technology and Other Essays* (New York: Harper, 1982).

71. Ann Taves, *Fits, Trances, and Visions: Experiencing Religion and Explaining Experience from Wesley to James* (Princeton: Princeton University Press, 1999).

72. Joan W. Scott, "The Evidence of Experience," *Critical Inquiry* 17, no. 4 (1991): 773–97.

73. I am not alone in stressing the close connection between the history of Western philosophy and Christianity. There is a huge body of literature supporting the claim, from positive and negative directions. The four major loci for this argument are conversations in 1. political theology, 2. religion and postmodernism, 3. secularism studies, 4. works critical of philosophy of religion for being overly Christian in its concerns. For the key works in these various conversations, see the following. On political theology, see Carl Schmitt, *Political Theology: Four Chapters on the Concept of Sovereignty* (Chicago: University of Chicago

Press, 2008); Ernst Kantorowicz, *The King's Two Bodies: A Study in Mediaeval Political Theology* (Princeton: Princeton University Press, 1957); Paul W. Kahn, *Political Theology: Four New Chapters on the Concept of Sovereignty* (New York: Columbia University Press, 2013). On religion and postmodernism, see Mark C. Taylor, *After God* (Chicago: University of Chicago Press, 2009); Amy Hollywood, *Sensible Ecstasy: Mysticism, Sexual Difference, and the Demands of History* (Chicago: University of Chicago Press, 2001). On the link between secularism and Christianity, see Gil Anidjar, "Secularism," *Critical Inquiry* 33, no. 1 (2006): 52–77; Charles Taylor, *A Secular Age* (Cambridge, MA: Belknap Press of Harvard University Press, 2007); On works that take philosophy of religion's Christian bias as a problem to be overcome, see Kevin Schilbrack, *Philosophy and the Study of Religions: A Manifesto* (Hoboken, NJ: Wiley Blackwell, 2014); Talal Asad et al., *Is Critique Secular?: Blasphemy, Injury, and Free Speech* (Oxford: Fordham University Press, 2013).

74. Maurice Merleau-Ponty, *The Visible and the Invisible*, trans. Alphonso Lingis (Chicago: Northwestern University Press, 1969).

75. G. W. F. Hegel, *Phenomenology of Spirit*, trans. A. V. Miller (New York: Oxford University Press, 1977).

76. While there are obvious parallels with genealogies in this project—notably, my agreement with Nietzsche and Foucault that definitions and the social significance of a concept cannot be static across time—I think of the project as more a series of historical, philosophical snapshots than a historical narrative.

77. Kosofsky Sedgwick, *Touching Feeling*.

78. Rita Felski, *The Limits of Critique* (Chicago: University of Chicago Press, 2015).

79. Thomas A. Lewis, *Why Philosophy Matters for the Study Religion and Vice Versa* (Oxford: Oxford University Press, 2015), 43–61.

80. It is outside of the scope of this project to recount the significance of Hegel's impact on continental philosophy, particularly concerning history. For more on the impact of Hegel on French philosophy, see Judith Butler, *Subjects of Desire: Hegelian Reflections in Twentieth-Century France* (New York: Columbia University Press, 1987); Alexandre Kojève, *Introduction to the Reading of Hegel: Lectures on the*

Phenomenology of Spirit, ed. Allan Bloom, trans. Raymond Queneau (Ithaca, NY: Cornell University Press, 1993); Ethan Kleinberg, *Generation Existential: Heidegger's Philosophy in France, 1927–1961* (Ithaca, NY: Cornell University Press, 2006), 49–111.

81. Manfred Frank, *The Philosophical Foundations of Early German Romanticism*, trans. Elizabeth Maillan-Zaibert (Albany: State University of New York Press, 2008).

82. Frederick C. Beiser, *The Romantic Imperative: The Concept of Early German Romanticism* (Cambridge, MA: Harvard University Press, 2006).

83. Dalia Nassar, *The Romantic Absolute: Being and Knowing in Early German Romantic Philosophy, 1795–1804* (Chicago: University of Chicago Press, 2014).

84. Bruce Matthews, *Schelling's Organic Form of Philosophy: Life as the Schema of Freedom* (Albany: State University of New York Press, 2011).

I. ILLNESS

1. Terry Pinkard, *German Philosophy, 1760–1860: The Legacy of Idealism* (New York: Cambridge University Press, 2002), 7. Like Terry Pinkard, I am using *German* loosely to refer to the German-speaking lands of the slowly disintegrating Holy Roman Empire, since Germany, strictly speaking, did not exist.

2. Johann Georg Heinzmann, *Appel an meine Nation: Über die Pest der deutschen Literatur* (Bern, 1795), 125; cited in Chad Wellmon, "Touching Books: Diderot, Novalis, and the Encyclopedia of the Future," *Representations* 114, no. 1 (Spring 2011): 65.

3. Johann Georg Hamann, "Socratic Memorabilia," in *Writings on Philosophy and Language*, ed. and trans. Kenneth Hayes (New York: Cambridge University Press, 2007), 4.

4. Wellmon, "Touching Books," 65.

5. As Goethe remarked in his conversation with Johann Peter Eckermann, "I call the classic *healthy*, the romantic *sickly*. . . . Most modern productions are romantic, not because they are new, but because they are weak, morbid, and sickly." Johann Wolfgang von Goethe and Johann Peter Eckermann, *Conversations of Goethe and Johann Peter Eckermann*, trans. John Oxenford (Cambridge, MA: Da Capo, 1998), 305.

6. It would be 1929 before a restored version with subject headings was published and 1968 before a chronological reconstruction of the entries. David W. Wood, "Introduction," in Novalis, *Notes for a Romantic Encyclopedia: Das Allgemeine Brouillon,* trans. David W. Wood (Albany: State University Press of New York, 2007), xiv.

7. By singling out the significance of Hegel, I do not mean to claim that he was the only thinker concerned with the philosophy of history. The question of the meaning and end of history has been ably debated for centuries by figures ranging from Augustine, to Giambattista Vico, to Johann Gottfried Herder, to Hegel, to Friedrich Nietzsche, to Walter Benjamin, to Michel Foucault. I am highlighting Hegel because he looms particularly large in this tradition of contingency in the last century, in part because of his influence on Marx and in part because of his influence on twentieth-century French philosophy through the lectures of Alexandre Kojève. For more on the impact of Hegel on French philosophy, see Judith Butler, *Subjects of Desire: Hegelian Reflections in Twentieth-Century France* (New York: Columbia University Press, 1987); Alexandre Kojève, *Introduction to the Reading of Hegel: Lectures on the Phenomenology of Spirit,* ed. Allan Bloom, trans. Raymond Queneau (Ithaca, NY: Cornell University Press, 1993); Ethan Kleinberg, *Generation Existential: Heidegger's Philosophy in France, 1927–1961* (Ithaca, NY: Cornell University Press, 2006), 49–111.

8. See Ann Blair, *Too Much to Know: Managing Scholarly Information Before the Modern Age* (New Haven: Yale University Press, 2011).

9. Wellmon, "Touching Books," 65.

10. Cited in Wellmon, 68–69.

11. Wellmon, 72.

12. Cited in Wellmon, 82.

13. Wellmon, 83.

14. Novalis [Friedrich von Hardenberg], *Schriften. Die Werke Friedrich von Hardenbergs,* ed. Richard Samuel, Hans-Joachim-Mähl, and Gerhard Schulz, 6 vols. (Stuttgart: Kohlhammer, 1983), 2:662–63:31–35.

15. In German the passage reads, "Es geht dir und vielen, wie den Juden. Sie hoffen ewig auf den Messias, und dieser ist schon längst da. Glaubst du denn, daß Menschenschicksal oder, wenn du willst, die Natur der Menschheit erst nöthig hat unsre Hörsäle zu frequentieren, umzu erfahren,

was ein System ist. . . . Die Zufälle sind die einzelnen Thatsachen die Zusammenstellung der Zufälle—ihr Zusammentreffen ist nicht wieder Zufall, sondern Gesetz." Novalis, 2:662:5–12 (my translation).

16. Novalis, 2:663.

17. Novalis, 2:663:8.

18. Cited in Wellmon, "Touching Books," 84; Novalis, *Werke*, 2:663:5–8.

19. "Du sprichst, wie ein Religios—Leider triffst du einen Pantheisten in mir—dem die unermeßlichen Welt gerade weit genug ist." Novalis, 2:664:1–2.

20. Manfred Frank points out that the title is doubly ridiculous, since not only was Schelling not a Romantic but the Nazis hated the Romantics, seeing them (rightly) as forerunners of the avant-garde.

21. For more on this dispute, see Frederick Beiser, *The Fate of Reason: German Philosophy from Kant to Fichte* (Cambridge, MA: Harvard University Press, 1987).

22. Part of the confusion is due to Novalis's *Fichte Studien,* a notebook where he at times tries to work out the logic of Fichte's propositions and at other times tries to think through his criticism. Until Henrich and Frank, Novalis's formulations of Fichte's thought were taken as endorsements, rather than a working notebook.

23. Manfred Frank, *The Philosophical Foundations of Early German Romanticism,* trans. Elizabeth Millàn-Zaibert (Albany: State University Press, 2004), 31.

24. Cited in Frank, 32.

25. Frank, 9.

26. Novalis, "Logological Fragments I," in *Novalis: Philosophical Writings,* trans. Margaret Mahony Stoljar (Albany: State University of New York Press, 1997), 48.

27. Cited in Frank, 33.

28. Frank, 29.

29. For a broader discussion of Novalis's attitude toward Descartes, see Beiser, *German Idealism,* 428.

30. "Der Buchstabe . . . [ist] eine Hülfe der philosophischen Mittheilung, deren eigentliches Wesen in Erregung eines bestimmten Gedankengangs besteht. "Novalis, *Schriften*, 2:522. Cited in Wellmon, "Touching Books," 101.

31. Wellmon, 87.

32. Bernard Stiegler, *Technics and Time 1: The Fault of Epimetheus*, trans. Richard Beardsworth and George Collins (Stanford: Stanford University Press, 1998), 50.

33. Stiegler, 50.

34. For more, see Beiser, *The Fate of Reason*.

35. Novalis, *Notes for a Romantic Encyclopedia*, 161; Novalis, *Werke*, 3:901.

36. Gotthold Ephraim Lessing, "The Education of the Human Race," in *Lessing: Philosophical and Theological Writings*, trans. H. B. Nisbet (New York: Cambridge University Press), 238.

37. The confusion, David Wood writes in his introduction to the English translation of *Das Allgemeine Brouillon,* stems in part from an exchange Novalis had with Schlegel roughly at the same time he began work on his encyclopedia. Novalis was delighted to learn that, just as he was conceiving his own project, Schlegel was likewise thinking of beginning a bible of his own. However, while Novalis's book attempted to provide a "body" for the sciences, Schlegel wanted to write "a new Gospel." For all his enthusiasm about the sympathy between their minds betrayed by their simultaneous turn toward the idea of a bible, Novalis ultimately found Schlegel's project strange, remarking frankly that he thought it "illusory and obscure." Cited in Wood's introduction to Novalis, *Notes for a Romantic Encyclopedia*, xix.

38. "ENCYCLOPEDISTICS. Analogical analysis (Analysis—art of finding the unknown from out of the known). Analogical equations— and problems." Novalis, *Notes for a Romantic Encyclopedia*, 17; Novalis [Friedrich von Hardenberg], *Schriften. Die Werke Friedrich von Hardenbergs*, ed. Richard Samuel, Hans-Joachim-Mähl, and Gerhard Schulz, 6 vols. (Stuttgart: Kohlhammer, 1983), 3:98.

39. Novalis, *Notes for a Romantic Encyclopedia*, 34; Novalis, *Werke*, 3:233.

40. Johann Gottfried von Herder, "On the Cognition and Sensation of the Human Soul (1778)," in *Johann Gottfried von Herder: Philosophical Writings,* ed. and trans. Michael Forster (Chicago: University of Chicago Press, 2004), 188–89.

41. Battista Mondin, *The Principle of Analogy in Protestant and Catholic Thought* (The Hague: Martinus Nijhoff, 1963), 3.

42. Mondin, 4.

43. Mondin, 3.

44. Novalis, "Miscellaneous Observations," in *Novalis: Philosophical Writings*, 26–27; Novalis, *Werke*, 22:420: #23 (translation modified).

45. Novalis, *Das Allgemeine Brouillon*, 161; Novalis, *Werke*, 3:901. In German the sentence runs: "Aller *Zufall* ist wunderbar—Berührung eines höhern Wesens—ein Problem *Datum* des thätig religiösen *Sinns*."

46. Novalis, *Das Allgemeine Brouillon*, 44; Novalis, *Werke*, 3: 295.

47. Novalis, 161; 3:904.

48. Albrecht von Haller, "A Dissertation on the Sensible and Irritable Parts of Animals," *Bulletin of the Institute of the History of Medicine* 4 (1936): 658–59.

49. Haller, 678.

50. This approach was in conflict with the prevailing school of thought that attributed disease to imbalances in the humors. See John Neubauer, "Dr. John Brown (1735–88) and Early German Romanticism," *Journal of the History of Ideas* 28, no. 3 (July–September 1967): 368.

51. Neubauer, 368.

52. Neubauer, 369.

53. Novalis, *Das Allgemeine Brouillon*, 66; Novalis, *Werke*, 3:419.

54. Johann Gottfried von Herder, "On the Change of Taste: On the Diversity of Taste and of Manners of Thought Among Human Beings," in *Johann Gottfried von Herder: Philosophical Writings,* ed. and trans. Michael Forster (Chicago: University of Chicago Press, 2004), 247–56.

55. Herder, 251.

56. Herder, 252.

57. Herder, 252 (my emphasis).

58. Chad Wellmon, "Lyrical Feeling: Novalis' Anthropology of the Senses," *Studies in Romanticism* 47, no. 4 (Winter 2008): 460–62.

59. Cited in Wellmon, *Anthropology of the Senses*, 461.

60. Wellmon, 462.

61. Novalis, *Das Allgemeine Brouillon*, 41; Novalis, *Werke*, 3:274.

62. Cited in Frederick Beiser, *German Idealism: The Struggle Against Subjectivism* (Cambridge, MA: Harvard University Press, 2008), 421.

63. Novalis, *Das Allgemeine Brouillon*, 51; Novalis, *Werke*, 3:338 (emphasis in the original).

64. Beiser, *German Idealism*, 422.

65. Novalis, *Das Allgemeine Brouillon*, 62; Novalis, *Werke*, 3:399.

66. Novalis, *Novalis: Philosophical Writings*, 79.

67. Cited in Beiser, *German Idealism*, 424.

68. This is continuous with Novalis's stance on creativity and genius, namely it requires both the cultivation of exacting skill of one's craft and the chance breath of inspiration.

69. Kristin Pfefferkorn, *Novalis: A Romantic's Theory of Language and Poetry* (New Haven: Yale University Press, 1988), 150.

70. Pfeffercorn, 158.

71. Novalis, *Das Allgemeine Brouillon*, 171; Novalis, *Werke*, 3:986.

72. "87. ROMANTICISM. Absolutization—universalization— classification of the individual moment, of the individual situation etc. is the real essence of romanticizing. Cf. [Goethe's] Wilhelm Meister. Fairy Tale." Novalis, *Das Allgemeine Brouillon*, 14; *Werke*, 3:87.

73. Novalis, 35; 3:234.

74. Pfefferkorn, *Novalis*, 158–59.

75. See entry 488: "The syncritical operation is dealt with eo ipso—thus if all the conditions for its appearance are present, then the highest comes about of itself. (Indirect construction of the synthesis). (The synthesis never appears in concrete form).

   The critique is the thesis—theory and countertheory are the antitheses.— The complete development of the thesis—depends on the complete development of the theory and countertheory, and vice versa. With the final stroke of the pen, the syncritical operation—the regular development of the simple thesis—of the simple equation, is likewise perfected—to become the completely developed thesis— the developed equation." Novalis, *Das Allgemeine Brouillon*, 86; *Werke*, 3:488.

76. Novalis, 120; 3:653.

77. Novalis even says as much: "It is only because of the weakness of our organs and of our contact with ourselves that we do not discover ourselves to be in a fairy world. All fairy tales are only dreams of that familiar world of home which is everywhere and nowhere. The higher powers in us, which one day will carry out our will like genies, are now muses that refresh us with sweet memories along this arduous path." Novalis, *Logological Fragments II*, 68.

78. Frederick Beiser has a very good chapter on it in *German Idealism,* and most of the introductions to Novalis's translated works deal with it in passing.

2. LONELINESS

Parts of this chapter have been published in a different form. Please see Liane F. Carlson, "Loneliness and the Limits of Theodicy in F. w. J. von Schelling's 1813 *Ages of the World,*" in *Journal of Religion* 98, no. 4 (October 2018): 339–465, copyright © 2018 the University of Chicago.

1. Jason Wirth, "Translator's Introduction," in Friedrich Wilhelm Joseph von Schelling, *The Ages of the World. (Fragment) from the Handwritten Remains: Third Version (c. 1815)* (Albany: State University of New York Press, 2000), vii.

2. F. W. J. Schelling, *The Ages of The World* (1813), trans. Judith Normal, in Slavoj Žižek and F. W. J. Schelling, *The Abyss of Freedom/Ages of the World* (Ann Arbor: University of Michigan Press, 1997), 114.

3. F. W. J. Schelling, *The Grounding of Positive Philosophy: The Berlin Lectures,* trans. Bruce Matthews (New York: State University of New York Press, 2008), 93–94.

4. Xavier Tilliette, *Schelling: Biographie* (Paris: Calmann-Lévy, 1999), 63.

5. See Fiona Steinkamp, "Introduction," in *Clara; or, On Nature's Connection to the Spirit World* (Albany: State University of New York Press, 2002).

6. See, most famously on this point, Heidegger's essay, "The Question Concerning Technology," in Martin Heidegger, *the Question Concerning Technology and Other Essays* (New York: Harper, 1982).

7. Bruce Matthews, "The New Mythology: Romanticism Between Religion and Humanism," in *The Relevance of Romanticism: Essays on German Romantic Philosophy* (New York: Oxford University Press, 2014), 211.

8. Jason W. Wirth, *Schelling's Practice of the Wild: Time, Art, Imagination* (Albany: State University of New York Press, 2015), 233.

9. F. W. J. Schelling, *Philosophische Untersuchungen über das Wesen der menschlichen Freiheit und die damit zusammenhängenden Gegenstände (1809),* in *Schellings Werke,* ed. Manfred Schröter (Munich: Beck and Oldenbourg, 1954), 4:571–721.

10. Michelle Kosch, *Freedom and Reason in Kant, Schelling, and Kierkegaard* (New York: Oxford University Press, 2010), 44–49.

11. "We may find an analogy in blindness. Blindness is a defect of the eye, and that in itself indicates that the eye was created for seeing; and thus even by its own defect is shown to be more excellent than the other parts of the body as being capable of perceiving light, since that is why it is a defect in the eye to be deprived of light. In the same way the nature which enjoyed God proved that it was created excellent by that very defect, by the fact that it is wretched simply because it does not enjoy God." Augustine, *Concerning the City of God Against the Pagans*, trans. Henry Bettenson (London: Penguin, 2003), 1023.

12. Cited in Warren Breckman, *Marx, the Young Hegelians, and the Origins of Radical Social Theory: Dethroning the Self* (Cambridge: Cambridge University Press, 2001), 63.

13. Terry P. Pinkard, *Hegel: A Biography* (Cambridge: Cambridge University Press, 2010), 28.

14. Schelling, *Ages of the World*, 135–37.

15. Schelling, *The Grounding of Positive Philosophy*, 94.

16. Schelling, *The Ages of The World* (1813), 170; F. W. J. Schelling, *Die Weltalter Fragmente: In den Urfassungen von 1811 und 1813*, ed. Manfred Schröter (Munich: Bilderstein/Leibniz, 1946), 170.

17. Schelling, 181/181.

18. Schelling, 135/135.

19. Schelling, 41.

20. For more on the tendency to reinterpret Schelling through postmodern concerns, see in particular Andrew Bowie, *Schelling and Modern European Philosophy: An Introduction* (London: Routledge, 2016).

21. Schelling, *The Ages of the World* (1813), 148; Schelling, *Die Weltalter Fragmente*, 148.

22. Günther Drosdowski and Paul Grebe, eds., *Duden Etymologie: Herkunftswörterbuch der deutschen Sprache* (Mannheim: Duden, 1963), 694.

23. F. W. J. Schelling, *Ages of the World* (1813), 27–28; Schelling, *Die Weltalter Fragmente*, 610.

24. W. Somerset Maugham, *The Summing Up* (London: Penguin, 1992), 174. See also Kenneth Surin, *Theology and the Problem of Evil* (Eugene: Wipf and Stock, 2004).

25. Schelling, *The Ages of the World* (1813), 139; Schelling, *Die Welatlater Fragmente*, 139.

26. Levinas is explicitly contrasting this to the synthesizing function of the imagination in Kant. Emmanuel Levinas, *Entre Nous: Thinking-of-the-Other*, trans. Michael B. Smith and Barbara Harshav (New York: Columbia University Press, 1998), 91; Emmanuel Levinas, "La soufling's france inutile," in *Entre Nous: Essais sur le penser-à-l'autre* (Paris: Bernard Grasset, 1991), 107.

27. F. W. J. Schelling, *Die Weltalter (1811)*, in *Die Weltalter Fragmente*, 34 (my translation).

28. While recognizing that "the will to existence" and "the existing will" do not mean the same thing, Schellanguage switches back and forth between "Wille zur Existenz" and "existirende Wille" without differentiation. Consequently, my discussion follows the particular terminology in German of whatever passage I am discussing.

29. Schelling, *Weltalter 1811*, 35 (my translation).

30. This could be read as parallel to the moment in the struggle unto death in the *Phenomenology*, where the slave realizes for the first time that its entire existence is at stake in a moment of terror and so surrenders to the master.

31. Schelling, *Grounding of Positive Philosophy*, 97.

32. The German runs: "Die Meisterin der Kunst in weißen Haaren, sie ließ mich spielen, nickte nur und dann: 'Der so geschrieben, war ein tauber Mann. Verstehen wirst Du's erst in späten Jahren.' Sie schwieg. 'Wenn Dir einmal das Herz gesprungen und weiterschläagt und weiterschlagen soll.'" Albrecht Haushofer, "Beethoven," trans. M. D. Herter Norton, in *Moabit Sonnets* (New York: Norton, 1978), 40, 41.

33. Levinas, "Useless Suffering," 91; Levinas, "La souffrance inutile," 107.

34. Levinas, "Useless Suffering," 92.

35. F. W. J. Schelling, "Appendice I: Calendrier de Schelling pour l'annee 1810," in *Stuttgarter Privatvorlesungen: Version inédite, accompagnée du texte des Oeuvres*, ed. Miklos Vetö (Turin: Bottega D'Easmo, 1973), 214, my translation.

36. Bruce Matthews, *Schelling's Organic Form of Philosophy: Life as the Schema of Freedom* (Albany: State University of New York Press, 2011), 12.

37. Fyodor Dostoyevsky, *The Brothers Karamazov*, trans. Richard Pevear and Larissa Volokhonsky (New York: Farrar, Straus and Giroux, 2002), r 244.

38. I am indebted to Yonatan Brafman for helping me more precisely formulate the nature of my objection.

39. Schelling, *The Ages of the World* (1813), 143; Schelling, *Die Weltalter Fragmente*, 143.

40. Schelling, 143.

41. Schelling, 12/595. Schelling's use of *unleidlich* in this context reflects this shift in his narrative. Whereas in 1813 the most primal form of suffering was loneliness or absolute solitude, here it becomes the more quotidian conflict or self-hatred or even despair, and so the use of *unleidlich* shifts accordingly. This switch is part of the reason I have chosen to focus on the 1813 version.

42. Lisa Guenther, *Solitary Confinement: Social Death and Its Afterlives* (Minneapolis: University Of Minnesota Press, 2013), xi.

43. This line of argument has precedence in the Abbe de Condillac's 1754 *Treatise on Sensation*. Condillac, *Treatise on the Sensations* (Manchester: Clinamen, 2000).

44. Guenther, *Solitary Confinement*, 30.

45. Guenther, 33.

46. Guenther, 35.

47. Guenther draws the connection between lack of touch and the mental collapse of prisoners herself when she writes, "If the phenomenological account of embodiment has merit, then imagine the effect that prolonged sensory deprivation, especially the deprivation of touch, could have on one's embodied consciousness." Guenther, 31.

48. Cited in Breckman, *Marx, the Young Hegelians*, 63.

49. Bruce Matthews, "Translator's Introduction," in *The Grounding of Positive Philosophy*, 7.

50. Breckman, *Marx, the Young Hegelians*, 14.

51. For a much more comprehensive discussion of this, see Breckman, *Marx, the Young Hegelians*.

52. In part, Breckman argues, this was a philosophical argument about whether or not the subject was identical with the person. Strictly

speaking, as he notes, in Kant's philosophical usage the subject is "that conscious apperceptive unity which recognizes itself as the active agent of knowledge A tension between the concepts of 'subject' and 'person' began to appear once it was recognized that even if Kant himself conceived the subject as a conscious and autonomous human individual, in truth the concept of the subject *per se* says nothing about the *particular* identity of the subject. . . . Hence the ease with which post-Kantian philosophers could extend Kant's epistemological argument about the subject from the conscious human 'I' to 'God' or 'Absolute Spirit.'" Breckman, 12.

53. Breckman, 63.

54. Interestingly, Max Weber suggests that loneliness is the paradigmatic state of the Calvinist. He writes, "This doctrine [i.e., grace by election], with all the pathos of its inhumanity, had one principal consequence for the mood of a generation which yielded to its magnificent logic: it engendered, *for each individual,* a feeling of tremendous inner *loneliness.* In what was for the people of the Reformation age the most crucial concern of life, their eternal salvation, man was obliged to tread his path alone, toward a destiny which had been decreed from all eternity. No one and nothing could help him." Max Weber, *The Protestant Ethic and the Spirit of Capitalism,* trans. Peter Baehr and Gordon C. Wells (New York: Penguin, 2002), 73.

55. In *Dialectic of Enlightenment* Adorno claims that alternately Odysseus, Robinson Crusoe, and Leibniz all prefigured the role of the individual in capitalism. As he writes of Leibniz's monads, "The absolute loneliness, the enforced reliance on a self whose whole being consists in the mastering of material and the monotonous rhythm of work, spectrally prefigure human existence in the modern world." Theodor W. Adorno and Max Horkheimer, *Dialectic of Enlightenment: Philosophical Fragments,* trans. Gunzelin Schmid Noerr (Stanford: Stanford University Press, 2009), 187.

56. Jean Améry, *At the Mind's Limits: Contemplations by a Survivor on Auschwitz and Its Realities,* trans. Sidney Rosenfeld and Stella P. Rosenfeld (Bloomington: Indiana University Press, 1980), 70.

3. VIOLATION

1. Jean Améry, *At the Mind's Limits*, 32; Jean Améry, *Jenseits von Schuld und Sühne: Bewältigungsversuche eines* Überwältigten, in *Jean Améry: Werke*, ed. Irene Heidelberger-Leonard (Stuttgart: Klett-Cotta, 2002), 2:73.

2. Améry, 33; 2:74.

3. Améry, 39; 2:84.

4. I am putting Améry in conversation with philosophical contemporaries as part of a deliberate effort to reintegrate his work into the philosophical canon. Améry is best known within Holocaust scholarship, where he is read as a memoirist. That body of literature is outside the scope of my project, but I have no desire to challenge Améry's place in it. Rather, I want to expand his significance for my field. Améry was an extremely erudite man who read his philosophical contemporaries carefully and had genuinely significant, innovative things to say on subjects such as forgiveness. I think it is a loss to philosophy that we do not read him and would like to add him to our tradition, in much the same way literary scholars have tried to integrate Primo Levi's work into the literary canon.

5. "Centre Hospitalier Sainte-Anne: Historique," Centre Hospitalier Sainte-Anne, http://http://www.ch-sainte-anne.fr/Etablissement /Historique (accessed January 27, 2015). For more detail on the work and intellectual life during the era of Minkowski at Sainte-Anne, see Edward Shorter, *A History of Psychiatry from the Era of the Asylum to the Age of Prozac* (Edison, NJ: Wiley, 1997).

6. Lucienne Peiry, *The Origins of Outsider Art*, trans. James Frank (Paris: Flammarion, 2001), 51.

7. Herbert Spiegelberg, *Phenomenology in Psychology and Psychiatry: A Historical Introduction* (Evanston, IL: Northwestern University Press, 1972), 233.

8. "Etude psychologique et analyse phenomenologique d'un cas de melancolie schizophrénique," *Journal de Psychologie Normale et Pathologique* 20 (1923): 543–48, cited in Spiegelberg, *Phenomenology in Psychology and Psychiatry*, 238.

9. Spiegelberg, 243.

10. Sue L. Cataldi, *Emotion, Depth, and Flesh: A Study of Sensitive Space: Reflections on Merleau-Ponty's Philosophy of Embodiment* (Albany: State University of New York Press, 1993), 36.

11. Maurice Merleau-Ponty, *The Phenomenology of Perception*, trans. Colin Smith (New York: Routledge, 2002), 296.

12. In full, Merleau-Ponty writes: "Nor does this blind adherence to the world, this prejudice in favor of being, occur only at the beginning of my life. It endows every subsequent perception, of space with its meaning, and it is resumed at every instant. Space and perception generally represent, at the core of the subject, the fact of his birth, the perpetual contribution of his bodily being, a communication with the world more ancient than thought. That is why they saturate consciousness and are impenetrable to reflection. The instability of levels produces not only intellectual experience of disorder, but the vital experience of giddiness and nausea, which is the awareness of our contingency and the horror with which it fills us." Merleau-Ponty, 254.

13. Cataldi, *Emotion, Depth, and Flesh*, 43.

14. Cataldi, 42.

15. Cataldi, 43.

16. Merleau-Ponty, *The Phenomenology of Perception*, 334.

17. Merleau-Ponty, 332.

18. Merleau-Ponty's language leaves it ambiguous as to whether or not we are supposed to read this version of depth as the primordial depth that exists at the horizon of all perception. He writes that "this primordial depth confers upon the other its significance" (*The Phenomenology of Perception*, 310). However, as Cataldi notes, the "other" is ambiguous. Read in reference to the preceding pages, it seems to be claiming that the relational depth experienced by the living body is primordial for the unsatisfactory, mathematical version of Berkeley and the other empiricists. However, if read with reference to the discussion that follows, "other" may mark a transition reintroducing the primordial notion of "pure depth" that confers significance to the relational depth just described. For a number of reasons that seem convincing—most importantly that the description of relational depth does not satisfy his criteria for the primordial spatial level as the horizon of all perception that can never be reached—Cataldi opts for the second interpretation.

19. Eugène Minkowski, *Lived Time: Phenomenological and Psychopathological Studies*, trans. Nancy Metzel (Evanston, IL: Northwestern University Press, 1970), 52.

20. Merleau-Ponty, *The Phenomenology of Perception*, 330–31.

21. Merleau-Ponty, 331 (my emphasis).

22. Merleau-Ponty, 254.

23. Jean-Paul Sartre, *Nausea*, trans. Lloyd Alexander (New York: New Directions, 1964), 4.

24. Sartre, 10.

25. Merleau-Ponty, *The Phenomenology of Perception*, 339.

26. Cathryn Vasseleu, *Textures of Light: Vision and Touch in Irigaray, Levinas, and Merleau-Ponty* (New York: Routledge, 1998), 60.

27. Maurice Merleau-Ponty, *The Visible and the Invisible*, trans. Alphonso Lingis (Chicago: Northwestern University Press, 1969), 148.

28. Cataldi offers a thought experiment that might clarify what, exactly, Merleau-Ponty is talking about in his discussion of folds. "Try to see the rest of your body as 'belonging'—'out there,' to visibility—in the field of sensibility, as a 'thing among things.' This is one mode of what I call 'opening up onto from out of perceptibility.' If you persist with this exercise, you can begin to experience the percipient or seeing 'side' of your body as a caved-in effacement of a (good) part of your (sensible) face, as a cavity filled with your vision. Now think of your face as a recessed surface, 'folded over on itself,' and notice how difficult it is to say where, precisely, your seeing starts. The seeing side seems to underlie even the region where you 'know' your eyes to be." Cataldi, *Emotion, Depth, and Flesh*, 66.

29. For work on flesh in Merleau-Ponty within continental philosophy of religion, see Richard Kearney, "Merleau-Ponty and the Sacramentality of the Flesh," in Kascha Semnovitch and Neal DeRoo, eds., *Merleau-Ponty at the Limits of Art, Religion, and Perception* (New York: Continuum, 2010), 147–66.

30. Améry, *At the Mind's Limits*, 86; Améry, *Jenseits von Schuld und Sühne*, 2:154.

31. Four out of his five Auschwitz essays even mention a place within the first line. "At the Mind's Limits" starts by recounting a conversation about Auschwitz; "Resentments" opens with a journey through Germany;

"How Much Home Does a Person Need" depicts Améry's illegal border crossing into Belgium; and "Torture" concerns the Belgian fortress
Breendonk. The only essay *not* to begin with immediate reference to a
place is the final one, "On the Necessity and Impossibility of Being a
Jew." In its own way, though, that essay is the most overtly concerned
with place of them all, given its reflections on Jerusalem.

32. Améry, *At the Mind's Limits*, 83; Améry, *Jenseits von Schuld und Sühne*, 2:150.
33. Améry, 85; 2:153.
34. Améry, 83.
35. Améry, 57; 2:111.
36. For a very similar worry about the loss of place, see Robert Harrison's *Forests: The Shadow of Civilization* (Chicago: University of Chicago Press, 2002).
37. See, in particular, Martin Heidegger, "Building, Dwelling, Thinking," in *Poetry, Language, Thought*, trans. Albert Hofstadter (New York: Harper Perennial, 2013), 141–60.
38. Marc Augé, *Non-Places: An Introduction to an Anthropology of Supermodernity*, trans. John Howe (New York: Verso, 1995).
39. Robert Pogue Harrison, *The Dominion of the Dead* (Chicago: University of Chicago Press, 2003), 18.
40. Harrison, 18.
41. Harrison, 19.
42. Giambattista Vico, *The First New Science*, trans. Leon Pompa (New York: Cambridge University Press, 2002), 90.
43. Harrison, *The Dominion of the Dead*, 38.
44. Harrison, 39.
45. Améry, *At the Mind's Limits*, 57.
46. Améry, *At the Mind's Limits*, 57; Améry, *Jenseits von Schuld und Sühne*, 2:111.
47. See Anthony Vidler, *The Architectural Uncanny: Essays in the Modern Unhomely* (Cambridge, MA: MIT Press, 1994), 24.
48. I want to be clear on what I mean. Améry clearly understands that a culture or a birthplace or nation can become violent and brim with hidden tensions. But the confrontation with that brutality comes with the *loss* of home. So long as a place is home, it plays a role of security.

49. Améry, *At the Mind's Limits*, 46; *Jenseits von Schuld und Sühne*, 2:94.

50. Améry, 47; 2:96.

51. Améry, 47; 2:96.

52. Améry, 85; 2:153.

53. For a more complete discussion, see Claudia Benthien, *Haut: Literaturgeschichte, Körperbilder, Grenzdiskurse* (Reinbek: Rowohlt, 1999), chapter 2.

54. There is also another way of understanding the skin's connection to place, namely, as a vessel that surrounds and contains place. I am thinking here of Edward Casey's discussion in *The Fate of Place* of Aristotle's earliest understanding of place as similar to "being in a vessel." What Aristotle meant by the analogy, as Casey explains, was, "As a vessel, such as a glass or a jug, surrounds it content—say air or water—so place surrounds the body or group of bodies within it." Place, while surrounding the object it contains, remains distinct from it. Yet the analogy is imperfect because, unlike an actual vessel, places cannot move. Consequently, Aristotle expanded his definition to "the first unchangeable limit (*peras*) of that which surrounds," or, alternately, "the inner surface of the innermost unmoved container of a body." Place, then, creates boundaries and limits, not by the imposition of human order as something receptive, passively waiting to be filled with an object, but, rather, as something actively circumambient. Edward Casey, *The Fate of Place: A Philosophical History* (Berkeley: University of California Press, 1997), 54–56. This understanding of place as containing and surrounding bodies would fit well with moments when Améry's language positions skin more as a border or protector, rather than identical with the self. For example, when he says, "My skin surface shields me against the external world." Améry, *At the Mind's Limits*, 28.

55. Ashley Montagu, *Touching: The Human Significance of Skin* (New York: Harper and Row, 1986), 60–65.

56. Améry, *At the Mind's Limits*, 28; Améry, *Jenseits von Schuld und Sühne*, 2:67.

57. Améry, 28; 2:67.

58. Améry, 28; 2:67.

59. Améry, 28; 2:67.

60. Améry, 90–91; 2:162.

61. Améry, 28; 2:66.

62. Améry, 27; 2:65.

63. Améry, 35; 2:77.

64. The more obvious source to look for an analysis of torture would have been Jean-Paul Sartre's account in *Being and Nothingness*. Améry knew Sartre's work and particularly admired his piece on antisemitism. He even wrote a letter to Sartre, though Sartre never responded. Yet he looked to Bataille for an analysis of torture. Why? I take Améry to be making a deliberate reference to, and rejection of, Hegel here. Sartre's understanding of sadism follows the general outline of Hegel's master-slave dialectic. For Sartre, the sadist wants to master the freedom of his victim, to force him to negate himself entirely in pain. Yet the sadist can never fully succeed in doing so, because the victim always has the freedom to decide *when* he capitulates to pain. Even if he is overwhelmed and feels his defenses collapse, he still has the ability, Sartre thinks, to decide to capitulate at *this* moment, not the next or the previous one. Thus, much like in Hegel's account, the master is dependent on the slave for his gratification and for his recognition as master, making the relationship ultimately impossible for satiating the master's need for total domination. Améry's German echoes Hegel's particular language of "lord" (*Herr*) and "bondsman" (*Knecht*), as he names the tortured *Folterknecht*.

65. Améry, *At the Mind's Limits*, 35; Améry, *Jenseits von Schuld und Sühne*, 2:77.

66. Améry 35; 2:77.

67. Améry, 36.

68. Elaine Scarry, *The Body in Pain: The Making and Unmaking of the World* (New York: Oxford University Press, 1985), 4.

69. Trauma, of course, has a massive body of literature surrounding it that would be outside the scope of my argument to address. For the classic work on the subject, see Shoshana Felman and Dori Laub, *Testimony: Crises of Witnessing in Literature, Psychoanalysis, and History* (New York: Routledge, 1992).

70. Améry, *At the Mind's Limits*, xiii.

71. W. G. Sebald, *The Natural History of Destruction*, trans. Anthea Bell (New York: Modern Library, 2006), 150.

72. Améry, *At the Mind's Limits*, 32; Améry, *Jenseits von Schuld und Sühne*, 2:73.

73. Améry, 26; 2:63.

74. Walter Benjamin, "Theses on the Philosophy of History," in *Illuminations*, ed. Hannah Arendt, trans. Harry Zohn (New York: Schocken, 1969), 255.

75. Améry, *At the Mind's Limits*, 12–13.

76. Jean-Paul Sartre, *Being and Nothingness*, trans. Hazel E. Barnes (New York: Washington Square Press, 1993), 525. All these distinctions have been made in recent years by thinkers skeptical of the turn toward the body, like the theologian Sharon Betcher. For such thinkers, Améry's invocation of flesh at his moment of total vulnerability would need no explanation. Of course he would reject the body's intimation of wholeness and boundedness at the moment his sovereignty had been wholly violated. Flesh is what remains at the moment of total violation.

77. There is a much broader tradition of flesh that continental philosophy, particularly phenomenology, picks up in the twentieth century from figures like Jean-Luc Marion, Jean-Louis Chrétien, Sartre, and others. I am focusing on more biblical readings of flesh, first because much of the phenomenological work postdates Améry and so he likely would not have had those resonances in mind when invoking the Christian language of "Man made flesh." Second, flesh often is understood in the phenomenological tradition as that which cannot be grasped or instrumentalized, and thus as a site of resistance of sorts. In *Being and Nothingness*, for example, Sartre imagines a scenario where a sadist, who longs to reduce his victim to pure, mindless, suffering flesh, is thwarted by the nature of touch. No matter how the sadist twists and bruises and bites the body of his victim, one of two things always happens. Either the sufferer submits, declaring himself to be pure flesh in a free act of will that defies the power of the sadist to strip away all consciousness, all agency. Alternately, if he does succeed in reducing the victim to a panting body, the sadist no longer understands, "how to utilize this flesh. No goal can be assigned to it because I have effected the appearance of its absolute contingency. It is *there*, and it is there *for nothing*. As such, I cannot get hold of it as flesh; I cannot integrate it into the complex system of instrumentality without its

materiality as flesh, its 'fleshiness' immediately escaping me." Sartre, *Being and Nothingness,* 525. Interesting as this example is, I think Améry would reject it as getting the perspective exactly wrong. Flesh only shows up as mute matter, capable of thwarting the desire for domination—if you believe it is capable of doing so—from the perspective of the grasping, brutalizing hand. Experienced from within, incarnation in flesh is annihilation. I would add that much of continental philosophy suffers from this implicit bias when thinking about touch. Even Derrida and Nancy, when admirably posing the questions "Who touches whom? And how?," miss the more significant question, from my perspective—"Who is touched by whom? And how?" Cited in Jacques Derrida, *On Touching Jean-Luc Nancy,* trans. Christine Irizarry (Stanford: Stanford University Press, 2005), 86. Perhaps the tradition forgets the questions because famous men are not often groped on the subway.

78. Mayra Rivera, *Poetics of the Flesh* (Durham: Duke University Press, 2015), 23.

79. Rivera, 23.

80. Rivera, 30.

81. Cited in Rivera, 36.

82. Rivera, 47.

83. Améry, *At the Mind's Limits,* 39; Améry, *Jenseits von Schuld und Sühne,* 2:84.

84. Améry, *At the Mind's Limits,* 39.

85. Mary-Jane Rubenstein, *Strange Wonder: The Closure of Metaphysics and the Opening of Awe* (New York: Columbia University Press, 2008), 9.

86. Rubenstein, 7.

87. Vladimir Jankélévitch and Ann Hobart, "Should We Pardon Them?," *Critical Inquiry* 22, no. 3 (1996): 572.

88. Améry, *At the Mind's Limits,* 68.

89. Améry, 70.

90. Améry, 72.

91. Vladimir Jankélévitch, *Forgiveness,* trans. Andrew Kelley (Chicago: University of Chicago Press, 2013).

92. In her recent book, *Anger and Forgiveness,* Martha Nussbaum makes a similar point about holding on to resentment. While suspicious, like Jankélévitch, that most of what we call forgiveness is mean-spirited

and transactional, she also argues at length that the cured person ought not cling to resentment because doing so is ultimately futile and self-destructive. Martha Nussbaum, *Anger and Forgiveness: Resentment, Generosity, Justice* (New York: Oxford University Press, 2016).

93. Pamela Hieronymi made a very similar point in her excellent article, "Articulating an Uncompromising Forgiveness." Part of what makes forgiveness so very difficult, she argues, is that "with forgiveness, the offended agrees to bear in her own person the cost of the wrongdoing and to incorporate the injury into her life without further protest and without demand for retribution. (In some cases forgiveness can be uncomfortably intimate: *You must allow me to creatively incorporate the scars that bear your fingerprints into the permanent fabric of my life, and trust that I can do so)*" (my emphasis). Pamela Hieronymi, "Articulating an Uncompromising Forgiveness," *Philosophy and Phenomenological Research* 62, no. 3 (2001): 551. Despite her deep sensitivity to the costs of forgiveness, though, she also holds that we are right to think of the refusal to forgive as blameworthy. The great virtue of Améry is that he echoes Hieronymi's recognition that forgiveness requires accepting, and literally incorporating, the damage caused by another into his body but sheds lingering Christian morality to ask why. Why *should* the tortured man agree to assimilate the lashes of a horsewhip into his body without complaint? Why would anyone consider that an ethical demand to make of a person? Isn't it a sadistic demand to make of the vulnerable?

94. Améry, *At the Mind's Limits*, 65.

95. "I do not, finally, want the mother to embrace the tormentor who let his dogs tear her son to pieces! She dare not forgive him! Let her forgive him for herself, if she wants to, let her forgive him for her own immeasurable maternal suffering; but she has no right to forgive the suffering of her child who was torn to pieces, she dare not forgive the tormentor, even if the child himself were to forgive him!" Fyodor Dostoyevsky, *The Brothers Karamazov*, trans. Richard Pevear and Larissa Volokhonsky (New York: Farrar, Straus and Giroux, 2002), 245.

96. Améry, *At the Mind's Limits*, 70.

97. Améry, 70.

98. Cited in Irène Heidelberger-Leonard, *The Philosopher of Auschwitz: Jean Améry and Living with the Holocaust* (New York: I. B. Tauris, 2010), 183.

4. LOVE

1. G. W. F. Hegel, *Introduction to the Philosophy of History*, trans. Leo Rauch (Indianapolis: Hackett, 1988), 23.

2. Hegel, 24.

3. For a summary of this trend, see Bradley B. Onishi, *The Sacrality of the Secular: Postmodern Philosophy of Religion* (New York: Columbia University Press, 2018).

4. I take Rubenstein to be making a similar point when she argues that Heidegger's Nazism is rooted in his failure to dwell with wonder, not his openness to wonder. Mary-Jane Rubenstein, *Strange Wonder: The Closure of Metaphysics and the Opening of Awe* (New York: Columbia University Press, 2008), 58.

5. Michel Serres, *Conversations on Science, Culture, and Time,* trans. Roxanne Lapidus (Ann Arbor: University of Michigan, 1995), 3.

6. Serres, 2.

7. Michel Serres, *The Five Senses: A Philosophy of Mingled Bodies*, trans. Margaret Sankey and Peter Cowley (London: Continuum International, 2008), 19.

8. Serres, 20.

9. A better example would be to compare the experience of touching both my feet and my face with my hands; introducing an inanimate object obscures the parallel, because obviously scissors are never going to feel themselves to be subjects. The point, as I take Serres, is that nothing will ever happen to my feet that will make me feel as if my soul is at stake, no matter what touches them. I owe this point to Todd Berzon.

10. Serres, *The Five Senses,* 22–23.

11. The other, arguably more famous discussion of subjectivity in Serres comes in his discussion of "the quasi-object," which has been picked up by Massumi in *Parables of the Virtual*. The idea is simple enough. When a player kicks the ball in a soccer game, what is the object and what is the subject? Nominally, the player who kicks the ball is the subject and the ball the object. In reality, though, formulating the situation in such a way mistakes the grammatical subject for the philosophical one. As Massumi summarizes the question, "But if by subject we mean the point of unfolding of a tendential movement, then it is clear that the player is not the subject of the play. The ball is." The

ball organizes the players around it in a way no other single element of the game can. Or, more specifically, the ball is a quasi subject. Brian Massumi, *Parables of the Virtual: Movement, Affect, Sensation* (Durham: Duke University Press, 2002), 73.

12. Serres, *The Five Senses,* 23.

13. Serres, 80.

14. Michel Serres, with Bruno Latour, *Conversations on Science, Culture, and Time,* trans. Roxanne Lapidus (Ann Arbor: University of Michigan Press, 1995), 120.

15. Jean-Paul Sartre, *Being and Nothingness,* trans. Hazel E. Barnes (New York: Washington Square, 1956), 494–533.

16. See Jacques Derrida, *On Touching Jean-Luc Nancy,* trans. Christine Irizarry (Stanford: Stanford University Press, 2005), 66–91.

17. Serres, *The Five Senses,* 27.

18. Steven Connor, *The Book of Skin* (London: Reaktion, 2004), 30.

19. Søren Kierkegaard, *The Sickness Unto Death: A Christian Psychological Exposition for Upbuilding and Awakening,* trans. Howard Hong and Edna Hong (Princeton: Princeton University Press, 1983).

20. Serres, *The Five Senses,* 80.

21. Serres, 80.

22. Connor, *The Book of Skin,* 2.

23. Francis Hutcheson, *An Essay on the Nature and the Conduct of the Passions and Affections with Illustrations on the Moral Sense* (Indianapolis: Liberty Fund, 2003).

24. John Locke, *An Essay Concerning Human Understanding,* ed. P. H. Nidditch (Oxford: Oxford University Press, 1975), II.i.iv.

25. Serres, *Conversations on Science, Culture, and Time,* 7.

26. Timothy Mitchell, *The Rule of Experts: Egypt, Techno-Politics, Modernity* (Berkeley: University of California Press, 2002), 87–89.

27. For an overview of the orientalist history of theorizing the senses, see David Howes, *The Empire of the Senses: The Sensual Culture Reader* (London: Bloomsbury Academic, 2005).

28. Étienne Bonnot, Abbé de Condillac, *Condillac's Treatise on the Sensations,* trans. Geraldine Carr (London: Favil, 1930), xxx.

29. Condillac, 89.

30. Condillac, 93.

31. Condillac, 130–31.
32. See Thomas A. Carlson, *The Indiscrete Image: Infinitude and the Creation of the Human* (Chicago: University of Chicago Press, 2008); Jeffrey L. Kosky, *Arts of Wonder: Enchanting Secularity—Walter De Maria, Diller+ Scofidio, James Turrell, Andy Goldsworth* (Chicago: University of Chicago Press, 2012); Bernard Stiegler, *Technics and Time I: The Fall of Epimetheus,* trans. Richard Beardsworth and George Collins (Stanford: Stanford University Press, 1998).
33. Martin Heidegger, *Being and Time,* trans. John MacQuarrie and Edward Robinson (New York: Harper Collins, 1962), 91–149.
34. These possibilities might have remained mere abstractions, if the adoption of upright posture had not simultaneously involved transformations within the skull. The bone structure no longer had to support the "stresses of cranial suspension," that is, the weight of the skull hanging downward, or the "traction stresses" tearing into food. Instead, the jaws and teeth shrank as the face became disengaged from the back of the skull, creating different possibilities of movement for the tongue, as well as new spatial arrangements for the brain. That meant we no longer had to carry food in our mouths and could develop speech as well as tools, which in turn created a feedback loop in the brain. Speech and the creation of increasingly sophisticated tools led to new paths and possibilities within the brain, which, in turn, allowed for the development of even more complex linguistic, technological, and social systems or tools. André Leroi-Gourhan, *Gesture and Speech,* trans. Anna Bostock Berger (Cambridge, MA: MIT Press, 1993).
35. Which is not to say writing about the hand as the site of connection to the world *necessarily* reduces humans to a friendlier *homo faber,* but emphasis on the hand at the expense of the rest of the body does run the risk of doing so.
36. Connor, *The Book of Skin,* 27.
37. Serres, *The Five Senses,* 34.
38. Michel Serres, *Angels: A Modern Myth* (Paris: Flammarion, 1995), 9.
39. Of course, given that this rumor comes solely from the Catholic patriarch Jerome, it has very little credibility among contemporary scholars.
40. For more on the reception of Lucretius, see Stephen Greenblatt, *The Swerve: How the World Became Modern* (New York: Norton, 2011).

41. Lucretius, *On the Nature of Things,* trans. Martin Ferguson Smith (Indianapolis: Hackett, 2001), 40–41.

42. Cited in Jeffrey S. Purinton, "Epicurus on 'Free Volition' and the Atomic Swerve," *Phronesis* 44, no. 4 (1999): 253.

43. Lucretius, *The Nature of Things,* 44.

44. Lucretius, 46.

45. Lucretius, 46.

46. Lucretius, 41.

47. Lucretius, 42.

48. For an older review of how the relationship has been historically understood, see M. Van Straaten, "Two Studies in Greek Atomists by D. J. Furley," in *Mnemosyne,* 4th ser., 27 (1974): 315–18. For more recent work, see Purinton, "Epicurus on 'Free Volition,'" 253.

49. Michel Serres, *The Birth of Physics,* trans. Jack Hawkes (Manchester: Clinamen, 2000), 82.

50. Serres, 10–11.

51. Serres, 6.

52. Jean-Jacques Rousseau, *Discourse Concerning the Origin and Foundation of Inequality Among Men,* in *Rousseau: "The Discourses" and Other Early Political Writings,* trans. Victor Gourevitch (New York: Cambridge University Press, 1999), 132.

53. Michel Serres, *The Natural Contract,* trans. Elizabeth MacArthur and William Paulson (Ann Arbor: University of Michigan Press, 1995), 47.

54. Serres, 47.

55. Serres, 47.

56. Serres, 47.

57. Serres, 47.

58. Serres, 48.

59. Serres, *The Five Senses,* 246.

60. Serres, 89.

61. Serres, 246.

62. George Orwell, "Politics and the English Language," in *George Orwell: A Collection of Essays* (New York: Harcourt, 1981), 156.

63. Orwell, 88.

64. Orwell, 102.

65. Serres, *The Natural Contract,* 1.

66. Serres, 3.
67. Maurice Blanchot, "The Apocalypse Is Disappointing," in *Friendship*, trans. Elizabeth Rottenberg (Stanford: Stanford University Press, 1971), 104.
68. Stephen Connor, "Introduction," in Serres, *The Five Senses*, 15.
69. Serres, *The Five Senses*, 236–37.
70. Serres, 238.
71. Serres, 138.
72. Serres, 141.
73. Serres, 102.

CONCLUSION

1. Rita Felski, *The Limits of Critique* (Chicago: University of Chicago Press, 2015), 67.
2. Felski, 80.
3. Felski, 160.
4. Talal Asad et al., *Is Critique Secular?: Blasphemy, Injury, and Free Speech* (New York: Fordham University Press, 2013).
5. Eve Kosofsky Sedgwick, *Touching Feeling: Affect, Pedagogy, Performativity* (Durham: Duke University Press, 2006), 123–53.
6. Sara Ahmed, "Happy Objects," in Melissa Gregg and Gregory J. Seigworth, eds., *The Affect Theory Reader* (Durham: Duke University Press, 2010), 31.
7. Donovan O. Schaefer, *Religious Affects: Animality, Evolution, and Power* (Durham: Duke University Press, 2015), 16.
8. Kathleen Stewart, *Ordinary Affects* (Durham: Duke University Press, 2007), 129.
9. Teresa Brennan, *The Transmission of Affect* (Ithaca, NY: Cornell University Press, 2004), 1.
10. Abby Kluchin, "At the Limits of Feeling: Religion, Psychoanalysis, and the Affective Subject," in John Corrigan, ed., *Feeling Religion* (Durham: Duke University Press, 2018), 251.
11. Kluchin, 251.

BIBLIOGRAPHY

Adorno, Theodor W., and Max Horkheimer. *Dialectic of Enlightenment: Philosophical Fragments*. Trans. Gunzelin Schmid Noerr. Stanford: Stanford University Press, 2009.

Ahmed, Sara. "Happy Objects." In Melissa Gregg and Gregory J. Seigworth, eds., *The Affect Theory Reader,* 29–51. Durham: Duke University Press, 2010.

——. *Thinking Through the Skin*. New York: Routledge, 2001.

Alexievich, Svetlana. *Secondhand Time: The Last of the Soviets*. Trans. Bela Shayevich. New York: Random House, 2016.

Améry, Jean. *At the Mind's Limits: Contemplations by a Survivor on Auschwitz and Its Realities*. Trans. Sidney Rosenfeld and Stella P. Rosenfeld. Bloomington: Indiana University Press, 1980.

——. *Hand an Sich Legen: Diskurs über den Freitod*. Stuttgart: Ernst Klett, 1976.

——. *Jenseits von Schuld und Sühne: Bewältigungsversuche eines* Überwältigten. In *Jean Améry: Werke,* 2:7–178. Ed. Irene Heidelberger-Leonard. Stuttgart: Klett-Cotta, 2002.

Anidjar, Gil. "Secularism." *Critical Inquiry* 33, no. 1 (2006): 52–77.Anselm. "Proslogion." In *Basic Writings,* 75–98. Trans. Thomas Williams. Indianapolis: Hackett, 2007.

Applebaum, Anne. *Gulag: A History*. New York: Anchor, 2004.

Arendt, Hannah. *The Human Condition*. Chicago: University of Chicago Press, 1958.

Asad, Talal. *Genealogies of Religion: Discipline and Reasons of Power in Christianity and Islam*. Baltimore: John Hopkins University Press, 1993.

Asad, Talal, Wendy Brown, Judith Butler, and Saba Mahmood. *Is Critique Secular?: Blasphemy, Injury, and Free Speech*. New York: Fordham University Press, 2013.

Augé, Marc. *Non-Places: Introduction to an Anthropology of Supermodernity*. Trans. John Howe. New York: Verso, 1995.

Augustine. *Concerning the City of God Against the Pagans*. Trans. Henry Bettenson. London: Penguin, 2003.

———. *Confessions*. Trans. Henry Chadwick. New York: Oxford University Press, 1991.

Bataille, Georges. *Theory of Religion*. Trans. Robert Hurley. New York: Zone, 1992.

Beiser, Frederick. *The Fate of Reason: German Philosophy from Kant to Fichte*. Cambridge, MA: Harvard University Press, 1994.

———. *German Idealism: The Struggle Against Subjectivism*. Cambridge, MA: Harvard University Press, 2008.

———. *The Romantic Imperative: The Concept of Early German Romanticism*. Cambridge, MA: Harvard University Press, 2006.

Benjamin, Walter. "Theses on the Philosophy of History." In *Illuminations*, 253–64. Ed. Hannah Arendt. Trans. Harry Zohn. New York: Schocken, 1969.

Benthien, Claudia. *Haut: Literaturgeschichte, Körperbilder, Grenzdiskurse*. Reinbek: Rowohlt, 1999.

Blanchot, Maurice. "The Apocalypse Is Disappointing." In *Friendship*, 101–8. Trans. Elizabeth Rottenberg. Stanford: Stanford University Press, 1971.

Bowie, Andrew. *Schelling and Modern European Philosophy: An Introduction*. New York: Routledge, 1993.

Boyarin, Daniel. *Unheroic Conduct: The Rise of Heterosexuality and the Invention of the Jewish Man*. Berkeley: University of California Press, 1997.

Breckman, Warren. *Marx, the Young Hegelians, and the Origins of Radical Social Theory*. New York: Cambridge University Press, 1999.

Brennan, Teresa. *The Transmission of Affect*. Ithaca, NY: Cornell University Press, 2004.

Butler, Judith. *Gender Trouble: Feminism and the Subversion of Identity*. New York: Routledge, 1990.

——. *Subjects of Desire: Hegelian Reflections in Twentieth-Century France.* New York: Columbia University Press, 1987.

Carel, Havi. *Illness: The Cry of the Flesh.* London: Routledge, 2014.

Carlson, Liane F. "Critical for Whom? Genealogy and the Limits of History." *Method and Theory in the Study of Religion: Journal of the North American Association for the Study of Religion,* forthcoming.

—— "Loneliness and the Limits of Theodicy." *Journal of Religion* 98, no. 4 (2018): 339–465.

Carlson, Thomas A. *The Indiscrete Image: Infinitude and the Creation of the Human.* Chicago: University of Chicago Press, 2008.

Casey, Edward S. *The Fate of Place: A Philosophical History.* Berkeley: University of California Press, 1997.

Cataldi, Sue L. *Emotion, Depth, and Flesh: A Study of Sensitive Space: Reflections on Merleau-Ponty's Philosophy of Embodiment.* Albany: State University of New York Press, 1993.

Centre Hospitalier Sainte-Anne. "Centre Hospitalier Sainte-Anne: Historique." http://www.ch-sainte-anne.fr/Etablissment/Historique (accessed January 27, 2015).

Cölestin Just, August. "Friedrich von Hardenberg, Assessor of Salt Mines in Saxony and Designated Department Director in Thuringia, 1805." In *The Birth of Novalis: Friedrich von Hardenberg's Journal of 1797 with Selected Letters and Documents,* 110–25. Trans. Bruce Donehower. Albany: State University of New York Press, 2007.

Condillac, Abbé de. *Condillac's Treatise on the Sensations.* Trans. Geraldine Carr. London: Favil, 1930.

Connor, Steven. *The Book of Skin.* Ithaca, NY: Cornell University Press, 2003.

"Contingent, adj. and n.". OED Online. Oxford University Press, July 2018. http://www.oed.com.proxy.library.nyu.edu/view/Entry/40248 (accessed September 28, 2018).

Derrida, Jacques. *On Touching Jean-Luc Nancy.* Trans. Christine Irizarry. Stanford: Stanford University Press, 2005.

Dostoyevsky, Fyodor. *The Brothers Karamazov.* Trans. Richard Pevear and Larissa Volokhonsky. New York: Farrar, Straus and Giroux, 2002.

Drosdowski, Günther, and Paul Grebe, eds. *Duden Etymologie: Herkunftswörterbuch der deutschen Sprache.* Mannheim: Duden, 1963.

Felman, Shoshana, and Dori Laub, *Testimony: Crises of Witnessing in Literature, Psychoanalysis, and History.* New York: Routledge, 1992.

Felski, Rita. *The Limits of Critique.* Chicago: University of Chicago Press, 2015.

Foucault, Michel. "Nietzsche, History, Genealogy." In *The Foucault Reader.* Trans. Paul Rabinow. New York: Pantheon, 1984. Originally published in *Hommage à Jean Hyppolite,* 145–72. Paris: Presses Universitaires de France, 1971.

—— *The Order of Things: An Archaeology of the Human Sciences.* New York: Vintage, 1994.

Frank, Manfred. *The Philosophical Foundations of Early German Romanticism.* Trans. Elizabeth Millàn-Zaibert. Albany: State University of New York Press, 2004.

Gabriel, Markus. "The Contingency of Necessity." In Markus Gabriel and Slavoj Žižek, eds., *Mythology, Madness, and Laughter: Subjectivity in German Idealism,* 81–94. New York: Continuum International, 2009.

Geuss, Raymond. "Genealogy as Critique." *European Journal of Philosophy* 10, no. 2 (2002): 209–15.

Goethe, Johann Wolfgang von, and Johann Peter Eckermann. *Conversations of Goethe and Johann Peter Eckermann.* Trans. John Oxenford. Cambridge, MA: Da Capo, 1998.

Greenberg, Irving. "Cloud of Smoke, Pillar of Fire: Judaism, Christianity and Modernity After the Holocaust." In Eva Fleischner, eds., *Auschwitz: Beginning of a New Era? Reflections on the Holocaust.* New York: KTAV, 1977.

Greenblatt, Stephen. *The Swerve: How the World Became Modern.* New York: Norton, 2011.

Guenther, Lisa. *Solitary Confinement: Social Death and Its Afterlives.* Minneapolis: University of Minnesota Press, 2013.

Haller, Albrecht von. "A Dissertation on the Sensible and Irritable Parts of Animals." *Bulletin of the Institute of the History of Medicine* 4 (1936): 658–59.

Hamann, Johann Georg. "Socratic Memorabilia." In *Writings on Philosophy and Language.* Ed. and trans. Kenneth Hayes. New York: Cambridge University Press, 2007.

Harrison, Robert Pogue. *The Dominion of the Dead.* Chicago: University of Chicago Press, 2003.

——. *Forests: The Shadow of Civilization*. Chicago: University of Chicago Press, 2002.

Haushofer, Albrecht. "Beethoven." In *Moabit Sonnets*, 41–42. Trans. M. D. Herter Norton. New York: Norton, 1978.

Hegel, G. W. F. *Introduction to the Philosophy of History*. Trans. Leo Rauch. Indianapolis: Hackett, 1988.

—— *Phänomenologie des Geistes*. In *Georg Wilhelm Friedrich Hegel: Gesammelte Werke*, vol. 9. Ed. Wolfgang Bonsiepen and Reinhard Heede. Hamburg: Felix Meiner, 1980.

——. *Phenomenology of Spirit*. Trans. A. V. Miller. New York: Oxford University Press, 1977.

Heidegger, Martin. *Being and Time*. Trans. John Macquarrie and Edward Robinson. San Francisco: Harper Collins, 1962.

——. "Building, Dwelling, Thinking." In *Poetry, Language, Thought*, 141–60. Trans. Albert Hofstadter. New York: Harper Perennial, 2013.

——. *The Question Concerning Technology and Other Essays*. Trans. William Lovitt. New York: Harper, 1982.

Heidelberger-Leonard, Irène. *The Philosopher of Auschwitz: Jean Améry and Living with the Holocaust*. New York: I. B. Tauris, 2010.

Herder, Johann Gottfried. "On the Change of Taste: On the Diversity of Taste and of Manners of Thought Among Human Beings." In *Johann Gottfried von Herder: Philosophical Writings*, 247–56. Ed. and trans. Michael Forster. Chicago: University of Chicago Press, 2004.

——. "On the Cognition and Sensation of the Human Soul (1778). In *Johann Gottfried von Herder: Philosophical Writings*, 187–246. Ed. and trans. Michael Forster. Chicago: University of Chicago Press, 2004.

Hick, John. "Soul-making and Suffering." In Marilyn McCord Adams and Robert Merrihew Adams, eds., *The Problem of Evil*, 168–88. Oxford: Oxford University Press, 1996.

Hieronymi, Pamela. "Articulating an Uncompromising Forgiveness." *Philosophy and Phenomenological Research*. 62, no. 3 (2001): 529–55. doi 10.2307 /2653535.

Hirschkind, Charles. *The Ethical Soundscape: Cassette Sermons and Islamic Counterpublics*. New York: Columbia University Press, 2006.

Hollywood, Amy. *Sensible Ecstasy: Mysticism, Sexual Difference, and the Demands of History*. Chicago: University of Chicago Press, 2001.

Horkheimer, Max, and Theodor W. Adorno. *The Dialectic of Enlightenment: Philosophical Fragments.* Ed. Gunzelin Schmid Noerr. Trans. Edmund Jephcott. Stanford: Stanford University Press, 1987.

Howes, David. *The Empire of the Senses: The Sensual Culture Reader.* London: Bloomsbury Academic, 2005.

Hume, David. *Principal Writings on Religion Including Dialogues Concerning Natural Religion; and, The Natural History of Religion.* Ed. J. C. A. Gaskin. Oxford: Oxford University Press, 2008.

Hutcheson, Francis. *An Essay on the Nature and the Conduct of the Passions and Affections with Illustrations on the Moral Sense.* Indianapolis: Liberty Fund, 2003.

Jablonksi, Nina G. *Skin: A Natural History.* Berkeley: University of California Press, 2006.

James, Susan. *Passion and Action: The Emotion in Seventeenth-Century Philosophy.* New York: Oxford University Press, 2000.

Jankélévitch, Vladimir, and Ann Hobart. *Forgiveness.* Trans. Andrew Kelley. Chicago: University of Chicago Press, 2013.

——. "Should We Pardon Them?" *Critical Inquiry* 22, no. 3 (1996): 552–72. doi 10.1086/448807.

Jay, Martin. *Downcast Eyes: The Denigration of Vision in Twentieth-Century French Thought.* Berkeley: University of California Press, 1993.

Kahn, Paul W. *Political Theology: Four New Chapters on the Concept of Sovereignty.* New York: Columbia University Press, 2013.

Kant, Immanuel. "Idea for a Universal History with a Cosmopolitan Purpose." In *Kant: Political Writings,* 41–53. Trans. H. B. Nisbet. New York: Cambridge University Press, 2003.

——. "On a Supposed Right to Lie from Philanthropy." In Mary J. Gregor, ed., *Practical Philosophy,* 611–15. Cambridge: Cambridge University Press, 2008.

Kantorowicz, Ernest. *The King's Two Bodies: A Study in Mediaeval Political Theology.* Princeton: Princeton University Press, 1957.

Kearney, Richard. "Merleau-Ponty and the Sacramentality of the Flesh." In Kascha Semnovitch and Neal DeRoo, eds., *Merleau-Ponty at the Limits of Art, Religion, and Perception,* 147–66. New York: Continuum International, 2010.

Kierkegaard, Søren. *Fear and Trembling/Repetition.* Trans. Howard V. Hong and Edna H. Hong. Princeton: Princeton University Press, 2003.

——. *Philosophical Fragments/Johannes Climacus: Kierkegaard's Writings*, vol. 7. Trans. Howard V. Hong and Edna H. Hong. Princeton: Princeton University Press, 1985.

——. *The Sickness Unto Death: A Christian Psychological Exposition for Upbuilding and Awakening*. Trans. Howard Hong and Edna Hong. Princeton: Princeton University Press, 1983.

Kleinberg, Ethan. *Generation Existential: Heidegger's Philosophy in France, 1927–1961*. Ithaca, NY: Cornell University Press, 2005.

Kluchin, Abby. "At the Limits of Feeling: Religion, Psychoanalysis, and the Affective Subject." In John Corrigan, ed., *Feeling Religion*, 242–60. Durham: Duke University Press, 2018.

Kojève, Alexandre. *Introduction to the Reading of Hegel: Lectures on the Phenomenology of Spirit*. Ed. Allan Bloom. Trans. Raymond Queneau. Ithaca, NY: Cornell University Press, 1993.

Koopman, Colin. *Genealogy as Critique: Foucault and the Problems of Modernity*. Bloomington: Indiana University Press, 2013.

Kosch, Michelle. *Freedom and Reason in Kant, Schelling, and Kierkegaard*. New York: Oxford University Press, 2010.

Kosky, Jeffrey L. *Arts of Wonder: Enchanting Secularity-Walter De Maria, Diller + Scofidio, James Turrell, Andy Goldsworthy*. Chicago: University of Chicago Press, 2012.

Kosofsky Sedgwick, Eve. *Touching Feeling: Affect, Pedagogy, Performativity*. Durham: Duke University Press, 2006.

Latour, Bruno. "Why Has Critique Run Out of Steam? From Matters of Fact to Matters of Concern." *Critical Inquiry* 30, no. 2 (Winter 2004): 225–48.

Leibniz, Gottfried Wilhelm. *Philosophical Essays*. Trans. Roger Ariew and Daniel Garber. Indianapolis: Hackett, 1989.

Leroi-Gourhan, André. *Gesture and Speech*. Trans. Anna Bostock Berger. Cambridge, MA: MIT Press, 1993.

Lessing, Gotthold Ephraim. "The Education of the Human Race." In *Gotthold Ephraim Lessing: Philosophical and Theological Writings*, 217–40. Trans. H. B. Nisbet. New York: Cambridge University Press.

Levi, Primo. *If This Is a Man and The Truce*. Trans. S. J. Woolf. London: Abacus, 2003.

Levinas, Emmanuel. "La souffrance inutile." In *Entre Nous: Essais sur le penser-à-l'autre*, 107–19. Paris: Bernard Grasset, 1991.

———. "Useless Suffering." In *Entre Nous: Thinking-of-the-Other,* 91–101. Trans. Michael B. Smith and Barbara Harshav. New York: Columbia University Press, 1998.

Lewis, Thomas A. *Why Philosophy Matters for the Study of Religion and Vice Versa.* Oxford: Oxford University Press, 2015.

Locke, John. *An Essay Concerning Human Understanding.* Ed. P. H. Nidditch. Oxford: Oxford University Press, 1975.

Lucretius. *On the Nature of Things.* Trans. Martin Ferguson Smith. Indianapolis: Hackett, 2001.

MacIntyre, Alasdair. *After Virtue: A Study in Moral Theory,* 3d ed. Notre Dame, IN: University of Notre Dame Press, 2007.

———. *Three Rival Versions of Moral Inquiry: Encyclopaedia, Genealogy, Tradition.* Notre Dame, IN: University of Notre Dame Press, 1991.

Mahon, Michael. *Foucault's Nietzschean Genealogy: Truth, Power, and the Subject.* Albany: State University of New York Press, 1992.

Massumi, Brian. *Parables of the Virtual: Movement, Affect, Sensation.* Durham: Duke University Press, 2002.

Masuzawa, Tomoko. *The Invention of World Religions, or, How European Universalism Was Preserved in the Language of Pluralism.* Chicago: University of Chicago Press, 2005.

Matthews, Bruce. "The New Mythology: Romanticism Between Religion and Humanism." In *The Relevance of Romanticism: Essays on German Romantic Philosophy.* New York: Oxford University Press, 2014.

———. *Schelling's Organic Form of Philosophy: Life as the Schema of Freedom.* Albany: State University of New York Press, 2011.

———. "Translator's Introduction." In Friedrich Wilhelm Joseph von Schelling, *The Grounding of Positive Philosophy: The Berlin Lectures.* Albany: State University of New York Press, 2007.

Maugham, W. Somerset. *The Summing Up.* London: Penguin, 1992.

Mazis, Glen A. "Touch and Vision: Rethinking with Merleau-Ponty Sartre on the Caress." In Jon Stewart, ed., *The Debate Between Sartre and Merleau-Ponty,* 144–53. Evanston, IL: Northwestern University Press, 1998.

Merleau-Ponty, Maurice. *The Phenomenology of Perception.* Trans. Colin Smith. New York: Routledge, 2002.

———. *The Visible and the Invisible: Followed by Working Notes.* Ed. Claude Lefort. Trans. Alphonso Lingis. Evanston, IL: Northwestern University Press, 1968.

Minkowski, Eugène. *Lived Time: Phenomenological and Psychopathological Studies*. Trans. Nancy Metzel. Evanston, IL: Northwestern University Press, 1970.

Mitchell, Timothy. *Rule of Experts: Egypt, Techno-Politics, Modernity*. Berkeley: University of California Press, 2002.

Molesky, Mark. *This Gulf of Fire: The Great Lisbon Earthquake and Its Aftermath*. New York: Knopf, 2015.

Mondin, Battista. *The Principle of Analogy in Protestant and Catholic Thought*. The Hague: Martinus Nijhoff, 1963.

Montagu, Ashley. *Touching: The Human Significance of Skin*. New York: Harper and Row, 1986.

Nadler, Steven. *Introduction to Spinoza's Ethics*. New York: Cambridge University Press, 2006.

Nagel, Thomas. "Moral Luck." In *Mortal Questions*. Cambridge: Cambridge University Press, 2015.

Nassar, Dalia. *The Romantic Absolute: Being and Knowing in Early German Romantic Philosophy, 1795–1804*. Chicago: University of Chicago Press, 2014.

Neiman, Susan. *Evil in Modern Thought: An Alternative History of Philosophy*. Princeton: Princeton University Press, 2004.

Neruda, Pablo. "Sonnet XVII." In *100 Love Sonnets*. Trans. Stephen Tapscott. Austin: University of Texas, 1986.

Neubauer, John. "Dr. John Brown (1735–88) and Early German Romanticism." *Journal of the History of Ideas* 28, no. 3 (1967): 367–82.

Neuhouser, Frederick. *Rousseau's Theodicy of Self-Love: Evil, Rationality, and the Drive for Recognition*. New York: Oxford University Press, 2008.

Nietzsche, Friedrich. *On the Genealogy of Morals and Ecce Homo*. Trans. Walter Kaufmann. New York: Vintage, 1989.

Novalis [Friedrich von Hardenberg]. *Das Allgemeine Brouillon*. In *Gesammelte Werke*, vols. 3 and 4. Herrliberg: Bühl, 1945–46.

——. "Logological Fragments I." In *Novalis: Philosophical Writings*. Trans. Margaret Mahony Stoljar. Albany: State University of New York Press, 1997.

——. "Miscellaneous Observations." In *Novalis: Philosophical Writings*. Trans. Margaret Mahony Stoljar. Albany: State University of New York Press, 1997.

——. *Notes for a Romantic Encyclopedia: Das Allgemeine Brouillon.* Trans. David Wood. Albany: State University of New York Press, 2007.

——. *Schriften. Die Werke Friedrich von Hardenbergs.* Ed. Richard Samuel, Hans-Joachim-Mähl, and Gerhard Schulz. 6 vols. Stuttgart: Kohlhammer, 1983.

Nussbaum, Martha. *Anger and Forgiveness: Resentment, Generosity, Justice.* New York: Oxford University Press, 2016.

Olender, Maurice. *Languages of Paradise: Race, Religion and Philology in the Nineteenth Century.* Trans. Arthur Goldhammer. Cambridge, MA: Harvard University Press, 2009.

Onishi, Bradley B. *The Sacrality of the Secular: Postmodern Philosophy of Religion.* New York: Columbia University Press, 2018.

Orwell, George. "Politics and the English Language." In *George Orwell: A Collection of Essays.* New York: Harcourt, 1981.

Peiry, Lucienne. *The Origins of Outsider Art.* Trans. James Frank. Paris: Flammarion, 2001.

Pfefferkorn, Kristin. *Novalis: A Romantic's Theory of Language and Poetry.* New Haven: Yale University Press, 1988.

Pinkard, Terry. *German Philosophy, 1760–1860: The Legacy of Idealism.* New York: Cambridge University Press, 2002.

——. *Hegel: A Biography.* Cambridge: Cambridge University Press, 2010.

Plantinga, Alvin. *God, Freedom, and Evil.* Grand Rapids, MI: Eerdmans, 2008.

Proudfoot, Wayne. *Religious Experience.* Berkeley: University of California Press, 1987.

Purinton, Jeffrey S. "Epicurus on 'Free Volition' and the Atomic Swerve." *Phronesis* 44, no. 4 (1999): 253–99.

Rivera, Mayra. *Poetics of the Flesh.* Durham: Duke University Press, 2015.

Rorty, Richard. *Contingency, Irony, and Solidarity.* New York: Cambridge University Press, 1989.

Rousseau, Jean-Jacques. *Discourse Concerning the Origin and Foundation of Inequality Among Men.* In *Rousseau: "The Discourses" and Other Early Political Writings.* Trans. Victor Gourevitch. New York: Cambridge University Press, 1999.

——. *Emile, or On Education.* Trans. Allan Bloom. New York: Basic Books, 1979.

———. "Letter to Voltaire." In *Rousseau: "The Discourses" and Other Early Political Writings*. Trans. Victor Gourevitch. New York: Cambridge University Press, 1999.

Rubenstein, Mary-Jane. *Strange Wonder: The Closure of Metaphysics and the Opening of Awe*. New York: Columbia University Press, 2008.

Sartre, Jean-Paul. *Being and Nothingness*. Trans. Hazel E. Barnes. New York: Washington Square Press, 1956.

———. *La Nausée*. Barcelona: Gallimard, 2008.

———. *Nausea*. Trans. Lloyd Alexander. New York: New Directions, 1964.

Scarry, Elaine. *The Body in Pain: The Making and Unmaking of the World*. New York: Oxford University Press, 1985.

Schaefer, Donovan O. *Religious Affects: Animality, Evolution, and Power*. Durham: Duke University Press, 2015.

Schelling, Friedrich Wilhelm Joseph. *The Ages of The World (1813)*. Trans. Judith Normal. In Slavoj Žižek and F. W. J. Schelling, *The Abyss of Freedom/Ages of the World*. Ann Arbor: University of Michigan Press, 1997.

———. *The Ages of the World: (Fragment) from the Handwritten Remains of Third Version (c. 1815)*. Trans. Jason Wirth. Albany: State University of New York Press, 2000.

———. *Die Weltalter Bruchstück: Aus dem Handschriftlichen Nachlaß*. In *Schellings Werke*, vol. 4. Ed. Manfred Schröter, 571–721. Munich: Beck and Oldenbourg, 1958.

———. *Die Weltalter Fragmente: In den Urfassungen von 1811 und 1813*. Ed. Manfred Schröter. Munich: Bilderstein/Leibniz, 1946.

———. *Philosophische Untersuchungen über das Wesen der menschlichen Freiheit und die damit zusammenhängenden Gegenstände (1809)*. In *Schellings Werke*, vol. 4. Ed. Manfred Schröter. Munich: Beck and Oldenbourg, 1958.

———. *Philosophy and Religion (1804)*. Trans. Klaus Ottman. Putnam: Spring, 2010.

———. *Stuttgarter Privatvorlesungen: Version inédite, accompagnée du texte des oeuvres*. Ed. Miklos Vetö. Turin: Bottega D'Easmo, 1973.

———. *System of Transcendental Idealism*. Trans. Peter Heath. Charlottesville: University of Virginia Press, 1978.

Schillbrack, Kevin. *Philosophy and the Study of Religions: A Manifesto*. Hoboken, NJ: Wiley Blackwell, 2014.

Schleiermacher, Friedrich. *On Religion: Speeches to its Cultured Despisers.* Ed. Richard Crouter. New York: Cambridge University Press, 1994.

Schmitt, Carl. *Political Theology: Four Chapters on the Concept of Sovereignty.* Chicago: University of Chicago Press, 2008.

Scott, Joan W. "The Evidence of Experience." *Critical Inquiry* 17, no. 4 (1991): 773–97.

Sebald, W. G. *On the Natural History of Destruction.* Trans. Anthea Bell. New York: Modern Library, 2006.

Serres, Michel. *Angels: A Modern Myth.* Paris: Flammarion, 1995.

——. *The Birth of Physics.* Trans. Jack Hawke. London: Clinamen, 2001.

——. *Le Cinq sens.* Paris: Grasset et Fasquelle, 1985.

——. *Le Contrat naturel.* Paris: François Bourin, 1990.

——. *The Five Senses: A Philosophy of Mingled Bodies (I).* Trans. Margaret Sankey and Peter Cowley. New York: Continuum International, 2008.

——. *The Natural Contract.* Trans. Elizabeth MacArthur and William Paulson. Ann Arbor: University of Michigan Press, 1995.

Serres, Michel, with Bruno Latour. *Conversations on Science, Culture, and Time.* Trans. Roxanne Lapidus. Ann Arbor: University of Michigan Press, 1995.

Shalamov, Varlam. *Kolyma Tales.* Trans. John Glad. London: Penguin, 1994.

Shorter, Edward. *A History of Psychiatry from the Era of the Asylum to the Age of Prozac.* Edison, NJ: Wiley, 1997.

Spiegelberg, Herbert. *Phenomenology in Psychology and Psychiatry: A Historical Introduction.* Evanston, IL: Northwestern University Press, 1972.

Spinoza, Baruch. *The Essential Spinoza: Ethics and Related Writings.* Trans. Samuel Shirley. Indianapolis: Hackett, 2006.

Steinkamp, Fiona. Introduction to *Clara, or, On Nature's Connection to the Spirit World.* Trans. Fiona Steinkamp. Albany: State University of New York Press, 2002.

Stevens, Jacqueline. "On the Morals of Genealogy." *Political Theory* 31 (August 2003): 558–69.

Stewart, Kathleen. *Ordinary Affects.* Durham: Duke University Press, 2007.

Stiegler, Bernard. *Technics and Time 1: The Fault of Epimetheus.* Trans. Richard Beardsworth and George Collins. Stanford: Stanford University Press, 1998.

Surin, Kenneth. *Theology and the Problem of Evil.* Eugene: Wipf and Stock, 2004.

Taves, Anne. *Fits, Trances, and Visions: Experiencing Religion and Explaining Experience from Wesley to James.* Princeton: Princeton University Press, 1999.

Taylor, Charles. *A Secular Age.* Cambridge, MA: Belknap Press of Harvard University Press, 2007.

Taylor, Mark C. *Hiding.* Chicago: University of Chicago Press, 1998.

Tieck, Ludwig. "Ludwig Tieck Biography of Novalis 1815." In *The Birth of Novalis: Friedrich von Hardenberg's Journal of 1797 with Selected Letters.* Trans. Bruce Donehower, 126–36. Albany: State University of New York Press, 2007.

Tilliette, Xavier. *Schelling: Biographie.* Paris: Calmann-Lévy, 1999.

Van Straaten, M. "Two Studies in Greek Atomists by D. J. Furley." *Mnemosyne,* 4th ser., 27 (1974): 315–18.

Vasseleu, Cathryn. *Textures of Light: Vision and Touch in Irigaray, Levinas, and Merleau-Ponty.* New York: Routledge, 1998.

Vico, Giambattista. *The First New Science.* Trans. Leon Pompa. New York: Cambridge University Press, 2002.

Vidler, Anthony. *The Architectural Uncanny: Essays in the Modern Unhomely.* Cambridge, MA: MIT Press, 1994.

Visker, Rudy. *Michel Foucault: Genealogy as Critique.* London: Verso, 1995.

Voltaire, François-Marie. *The Works of Voltaire,* vol. 36. Trans. William F. Fleming. New York: E. R. Dumont, 1901.

Weber, Max. *The Protestant Ethic and the Spirit of Capitalism.* Trans. by Peter Baehr and Gordon C. Wells. New York: Penguin, 2002.

Wellmon, Chad. "Lyrical Feeling: Novalis' Anthropology of the Senses." *Studies in Romanticism* 47, no. 4 (2008): 453–77.

——. "Touching Books: Diderot, Novalis, and the Encyclopedia of the Future." *Representations* 114, no. 1 (Spring 2011): 65–102.

Wirth, Jason. *The Conspiracy of Life: Meditations on Schelling and His Time.* Albany: State University of New York Press, 2003.

——. *Schelling's Practice of the Wild: Time, Art, Imagination.* Albany: State University of New York Press, 2015.

——. "Translator's Introduction." In Friedrich Wilhelm Joseph Schelling, *The Ages of the World. (Fragment) from the Handwritten Remains: Third Version (c. 1815)*. Albany: State University of New York Press, 2000.

Wood, David W. "Translator's Introduction." In Novalis, *Notes for a Romantic Encyclopedia: Das Allgemeine Brouillon*. Albany: State University of New York Press, 2007.

Žižek, Slavoj. *The Indivisible Remainder: An Essay on Schelling and Related Matters*. New York: Verso, 1996.

INDEX